Life in the Air

Surviving the New Culture of Air Travel

Mark Gottdiener

ROWMAN & LITTLEFIELD PUBLISHERS, INC.
Lanham • Boulder • New York • Oxford

ROWMAN & LITTLEFIELD PUBLISHERS, INC.

Published in the United States of America
by Rowman & Littlefield Publishers, Inc.
4720 Boston Way, Lanham, Maryland 20706
http://www.rowmanlittlefield.com

12 Hid's Copse Road
Cumnor Hill, Oxford OX2 9JJ, England

British Library Cataloguing in Publication Information Available

Library of Congress Cataloging-in-Publication Data

Gottdiener, Mark.
  Life in the air : surviving the new culture of air travel / Mark Gottdiener.
    p.   cm.
  Includes bibliographical references and index.
  ISBN 0-7425-0028-4 (cloth : alk. paper)—ISBN 0-7425-0029-2 (pbk. : alk. paper)
    1. Air travel—United States.   2. Aeronautics, Commercial—United States—
Passenger traffic.   3. Airports—United States.   I. Title.

  HE9787.5.U6 G68 2000
  387.7′0973—dc21   00-057586

Printed in the United States of America

♾™ The paper used in this publication meets the minimum requirements of
American National Standard for Information Sciences—Permanence of
Paper for Printed Library Materials, ANSI/NISO Z39.48-1992.

Contents

1

Introduction: Air Travel as a Simple Fact of Life

And Icarus flew too high, the wax holding his feathers melted and he fell to earth . . .

Flying in an airplane was once a special event that happened either to the lucky few who braved a barnstorming demonstration or the reluctant airmen caught up in war. During the early days of propeller-driven commercial flights, passengers dressed up for trips in hats and suits, and women wore gloves In-flight cocktails were served. "Out of consideration for child-free travelers, babies were deemed too young to fly" (Marin 1999). Only the affluent could afford seats on an airplane; others took the train or bus. Now there are few people in this country who have not flown at all. According to Congressman Bud Shuster (R-Pa.), over 660 million passenger trips were taken in 1998—almost twice as many trips as there are people in the United States. Hundreds of thousands of us took more than one flight. Most travelers are frequent fliers, using air transport the way people in the past used automobiles and trains for regular business trips, even commuting.

In the United States there are more than two million air travelers daily on over 20,000 flights (Wald 2000). Most impressive, our domestic system of air travel is the finest in the world. Millions of trips are carried out with astounding safety. Not a single person died in a commercial U.S. plane mishap operated by a major

1

carrier during 1998, although the record in 1999 was worse and included several celebrity crashes. While many of us still suffer from a fear of flying, it has always been safer than routine trips by car and never more so than in recent years. Fatal accidents occur one hundred times more frequently by car, and there are new reports that airlines are improving their safety record in daily operations (Goetz 1999).

Air travel is also increasingly inconvenient. More and more people complain about it, despite the sterling safety record of our domestic carriers. Crews and equipment are locked into such tight usage, as carriers strain to meet the ever-increasing demand, that flights are often delayed or canceled. The uproar from consumers finally reached Congress after the summer of 1999 proved the worst in history for delays. Yet, one year later, writing in July 2000, the situation seems to be deteriorating further. According to one report (Zuckerman 2000), "Delays in June [2000] rose 16.5 percent from June 1999 . . . and with air traffic continuing to expand at a time when few new airports or runways are on the drawing board, delays may be a fact of life for years to come, airline executives and government officials say."

Meals, overcrowding, abusive passengers, cramped seating, poor cabin service, and the sheer boredom of being stranded in air terminals for inhumanely long waits are also on the growing list of laments from consumers. So far, both airlines and public officials have demonstrated few concrete responses to these problems. Since the 1970s, the increasing frequency of air travel for business and personal use, such as tourism, has made flying a common experience for people around the globe. All countries have created an infrastructure to service airplanes and their passengers. More and more frequently, humanity literally *lives* in the air. We have populated the atmosphere above our world with a swelling density. Flying, along with facing its inconveniences and risks, has become a necessity for many of us. Complex, multidimensional contemporary life is increasingly knit together by plane trips. This book is about the new air realm where people now live. Air space is a space of flows inhabited temporarily by single individuals but on an aggregate scale by a mass of humanity. Las Vegas, for example, is home to slightly over 1 million permanent residents, impressive for a desert location, yet it hosts over 30 million tourists a year in that same space. More than two-thirds of its tourists visit via airplane. They cycle in and out at regular intervals through McCarran International Airport, representing a major *human vortex* on our planet. Airports like O'Hare and Dallas/Fort Worth, the first and second busiest airfields in the world, act as other human vortex points. They also function as mini-cities, not simply passenger terminals.

Once the domain of plucky pilots who took off in all kinds of weather to deliver the mail, air travel is now a multibillion-dollar industrial sector. Its business is not simply about passengers. Commercial aviation increasingly relies on airfreight to get products and information from one point to another. Both FedEx and United Parcel Service have their own fleets of planes. Airports are not only passenger terminals, they are centers for warehousing, shipping, light manufacturing, and increasingly, retailing. The newest air terminals are also constructed as *growth poles* to attract business of all kinds. Developmental strategies for many regions around the country, such as western Connecticut, the Denver area, and South Carolina, have showcased new airports as part of their schemes.

At the same time, the air transport industry has always been the scene of ruthless capitalism and bitter labor disputes. Its history is not pretty. People have been destroyed and driven to suicide. Entire companies built up from scratch with blood and sweat have been plunged into ruin, sometimes overnight. Union disputes have been contentious, if not violent. An entire profession, the air traffic controllers, was manhandled and restructured by national politics. To this day, the industry is plagued by the failure of either free enterprise or strict governmental intervention to address the needs deriving from its essential nature as a much-depended-upon public good.

Many people who fly seem unaware of the recent history of the airline industry and its current status as a deregulated sector of the economy. Left to strict competition among its privately owned companies during the last two decades, air transportation has been molded and altered completely by the victors in a ruthless battle for control of assets and routes. The complex structure of the industry following deregulation means that a few large companies now dominate the skies with a growing number of "bargain carriers" filling in the spaces. Ticket prices are reasonable for popular long-haul routes, although they have now been increasing, but exorbitant for travel between less popular, marginalized locations. A confusing array of restrictions and time limits on fares afflicts consumers. Travel times have increased and delays or cancellations of flights are increasingly common.

Crowded skies—planes lined up taxiing to take off

With so many people flying, complaints about the present system are heard more frequently. Horror stories abound. In one case, passengers were abandoned on board a jet in a snowstorm for over eight hours, unable to deplane to the terminal. In other cases, flights have been delayed or canceled without notice and without explanation, thereby inconveniencing businesses, vacation travelers, and everyday passengers, if not actually ruining their plans completely. Once upon a time, friendly stewardesses provided in-flight service that made passengers feel warm and fuzzy; flying is now a scene in which progressively more people express outrage at overcrowding, frequent delays, bumping, poor service, and lousy meals.

The clamor has been so great that in 1999 members of both the House and the Senate introduced bills to address the growing number of passenger complaints. There is an "Airline Passengers Bill of Rights" afoot in the nation. As one newspaper account summarized,

> Being an executive in the airline business was no fun last week. At a congressional hearing in Washington and later on live television, the mother of a 6-year-old boy tearfully recalled how her son was molested for hours by a 15-year-old boy while both were in the custody of [an airline]. Such stories, and a host of less disturbing but still annoying complaints about the way airlines treat their customers, are striking a raw nerve with millions of people who travel. The deteriorating quality of airline service has the full attention of some of the nation's most frequent travelers: members of Congress. . . . It isn't clear whether Congress can really take meaningful steps to help change the fundamental problem most air travelers face: There are so few big airlines available in most cities that there is virtually no competition. But there is no question that Congress is on the verge of attacking the problem. (Belden 1999)

Regulating air travel again after decades of deregulation will not be easy. Despite the growing tension produced by a groundswell of customer complaints, others in the country and in government remain reluctant to tinker with a system that largely works on this immense scale. Air travel is now recognized as a necessity of life. Larger planes have been proposed that will carry even more passengers in the future. Construction and renovation of new terminal facilities are projected at tens of billions of dollars within the next few years. Air transport has become one of our nation's biggest industries. Flying could not be more popular and more relied on. Despite serious complaints about service, few people decide to stop flying. On the contrary, new passengers are on board each day.

This book is not just about air travel. It is about the emergent *social world* of flying. It concerns air space and behavior in the air the way someone else might look at cities and street behavior. Economic, political, and cultural aspects are all considered. Air space is complex. It involves a growing infrastructure attuned to the needs of flying. Air terminals, their surrounding regions, and their associated industries have become increasingly important to our economy. Airports have become specific places in their own right that, in a certain sense, now rival central city areas. In fact, airports today are very much like cities.

Frequent flying has also produced its own culture. Rules of behavior are subscribed to in the air. Unique behaviors at terminals and in the passenger cabin have emerged that contrast with life on the ground. This book explores traveling etiquette, eroticism, and the horrors of environmental threats. Air travel has its own cognitive dimension as well. Mental states as much as the physical ordeal of flying enter into the discussion. Emotional breakdowns at terminals are not uncommon. Jetlag is as much a problem of bad thoughts as the corporeal crossing of time zones.

Flying has its surprises. Some are strictly cultural, such as the unique experience of bi-coastalism, a human activity that is only possible because of our present society's evolution. Others concern the growing need of businesses to knit the world together through frequent personal contact. Only now have we begun to appreciate our emergent global culture. The world is shrinking just as opportunities for travel expand.

In short, this book is about air travel—about surviving air travel—in *all* its aspects and dimensions. In part 1, I consider the infrastructure on the ground, followed in part 2 by the new significance of the airport space. Next, part 3 covers life in the air, especially the very personal nature of air travel, and ways to deal with its many concerns. This is the self-help segment of the book. Part 4 discusses the significance of air travel and its increasing use due to the *space/time compression* of daily life on our planet. Part 5 addresses the business aspects of the industry, especially the record of the last 20 years after deregulation. Ruthless capitalism and labor conflict are examined, and the effects of deregulation that have led to growing consumer concerns are discussed. In a final segment, I return to the wonder of flight and the need for us to think about our future that is so clearly aimed at the heavens.

Part 1

The Airport

2

The Terminal as Transition Space and Gateway

The airport generates business, it attracts industry, and it creates jobs. But its significance goes beyond its contribution to the balance of payments. . . . It creates a sense of . . . being at the heart of things, in both a symbolic and a practical way.

Deyan Sudjic, 1992

THE AIRPORT AS TRANSITION SPACE

It has become common for architectural critics and analysts of the current urban scene to speak about *liminal* spaces as increasingly characteristic of the new, franchised-built environment. Commercial enterprises strive to provide a unique experience for their customers that segues one milieu into another. The space of intersection between the street and the interior, the outside and the inside of a building, is a liminal space, a *threshold* to a distinctive way of eating or shopping. Boundary connections are extremely important in the design of city shops catering to upscale consumers. Tiffany's on Fifth Avenue in Manhattan is simply not a "drop-in" department store. Just a few blocks further north, the spectacular toy store F. A. O. Schwarz is. The former is constructed as a fortress, while the latter has the feel of a glassed-in, open-air market. Situated on the plaza, across from Central Park, the toy store is a threshold space, as is the plaza itself.

Airports might be considered liminal spaces *par excellence* because of their function as thresholds. Yet I prefer a different word. When standing at the portal of a themed restaurant or park, especially one that offers some totalizing fantasy

The terminal as gateway—passengers funnel in and out of its entrance.
(AP photo/Bill Sikes)

environment, such as Disney World or the Rainforest Cafe, you are poised at a spot that functions as a space of *transition*. It is precisely this alteration in the way you experience space that is distinctive of these new environments. Entering the space triggers new feelings of self, new identities that are set off by stimulators engineered within the new consumer fantasy domains. Hence, the term "transition space" is used to describe the new forms of architectural commercialism because they connect with the altered ways that people experience themselves. In this sense, the airport is the definitive transition space. Trips are nothing if they are not existential.

The new spaces are not produced simply to provide people with a novel way of experiencing the self. Themed parks, restaurants, and malls possess an instrumental purpose: They are spaces for consumption that stimulate the spending of money (Gottdiener 1997). They are not merely environments that offer a threshold to a new or different experience, in a liminal sense. Rather, they have a business purpose. As spaces, they effect a transition in the status of the individual from a generalized participant in daily life, perhaps as either a pedestrian or auto commuter, to the particular status of consumer. Within these environments, people still have the ability to experience the self in different ways as well as spend their money. This is especially true of malls or other quasi-public spaces that allow people to engage in the communion of others, and these places create and exploit that communion. Nevertheless, the new spaces also operate instrumentally to alter the status of individuals and manipulate the acceptance of their role as consumers, as happy spenders of money, in addition to stimulating new media-fed fantasy modes of self-identity.

THE AIRPORT AS GATEWAY

Airports operate as transition spaces in more ways than malls or theme parks. They incorporate all the elements of engineered fantasy environments, but also serve as transition spaces for travelers. It is precisely this multiplicity of effects that makes them gateways. Literally acting as the conduit from one physical location on the planet to another, they facilitate the shrinkage of the globe and transcend both space and time. They also effect a change in existential status from people being immersed in the complex roles of everyday life to that of being a traveler, of someone escaping not only the bonds of earth but of daily existence as well. Trips by air are exciting because they promise a change. We experience locational difference as cultural, linguistic, culinary, interactive, and physical differences. This altered subjectivity is best captured by the role of the traveler or tourist. Even people journeying by air on business can indulge in the fantasy of tourism. Travel is always an adventure, always an encounter with the "new."

Airports are the gateway to the "other," i.e., another staging area of action outside the ordinary bonds of existence. A trip, any trip, provides us with the freedom to escape our daily routine. Even if the purpose of travel is business, the trip is a kind of vacation. According to Cohen and Taylor (1992), the holiday trip

is a setting in which constraints can be relaxed if not rejected, identities slip if not disappear, a place where lives are rejuvenated if not changed. The holiday is the archetypal free area, the institutionalized setting for temporary excursions away from the domain of paramount reality. More than any other everyday escape, the holiday is a small-scale replica of the great escape messages of our culture. Reverberating right through religion, folklore, artistic expression and mass culture are powerful symbolic and allegorical messages around the theme of a move to a new land. Pilgrims and seekers after spiritual enlightenment must move to new landscapes: somewhere outside the walls of the prison is the Holy Grail, El Dorado, Shangri-La.

Because they represent the transcendence of space and time, airports function as gateways and as transition spaces; they personify the "great escape." Precisely for this reason, air transportation possesses the aura of romance and exoticism, of possibility, difference, and a new chance for daily living. Early in its history, this romantic element of escape to some fantasy location was the strongest aspect of commercial aviation's appeal. The existential element of air travel, expressed as the possibilities provided by the airport, is captured in a short story by Edward Handy entitled "Landing." A traveling salesman is so bored with air travel and his life on the road that he lapses into a moment of transition in an airport bar while waiting for his change of planes. Instead of boarding when the flight is called, he remains seated at the bar watching *The Wizard of Oz* on television, a film that he never had the chance to see all the way through as a child because it ran past his bedtime. Now he decides that it is much better to miss his flight than miss this chance to watch Dorothy's big adventure come to its conclusion. Life, he realizes, is a constant series of choices and alternative paths chosen. Air travel, and especially this particular moment in the airport, provides him with the possibilities of a new life that is there for the taking. Only his constant routine had locked him in and had prevented him from arriving at this understanding before that epiphany in the airport bar.

> I glance at the gate and try imagining landing in Syracuse. But I can't. . . . I catch my reflection in the mirror behind the bar. There must be better routes. When I glance back at the gate, something is wrong with the lights. People are lining up in the dark. And as I watch, the whole idea of walking over there and on through the cold jetway ramp begins to seem like only one possible future, and not the inevitable one I'd imagined minutes ago. I can feel myself latching onto this, onto the thought of innumerable futures and lesser selves, ones that I can always turn away from. How if I simply sit here, the pressurized door will close down on all of that. Another life, one that did not become. (Handy 1998)

Certainly it is an emotional mechanism very much like this that also lies behind an extreme version of such behavior. In recent years, airport authorities have discovered that some fraction of people found wandering around terminals live there permanently and never leave. They constitute a special class of the homeless who have become so not through circumstances elsewhere, but precisely and exactly by *missing their flights*. They became homeless upon arriving and entering the airport.

> Twenty years ago, two researchers reported on 49 patients who had been picked up at the airport and admitted to the psychiatric ward of San Francisco General Hospital over a seven-year period. None of this group was actually homeless, *although some were in transit*. Roughly half were diagnosed as schizophrenic but, unlike some other reports in the literature, their psychiatric troubles were found to be unrelated to the stresses of flight. Rather, air travel was instrumental to some grander, often ill-formulated scheme. Half of them either had no travel plans or *were just beginning their journeys*. (Hopper 1991, 155, emphasis added)

Research on this phenomenon of airport aimlessness reports two ways people wound up in this state. Some of the homeless had been in transit. Instead of changing planes, they never left the airport and suffered a breakdown, much like in the "Landing" account above. Others were just beginning their journeys, arriving at the airport fully packed and prepared with a ticket, but never getting on their planes.

According to an early report, "Clinicians identified a distinctive 'syndrome' in these 'peregrinating paranoids' who sought to use commercial airlines to maintain interpersonal distance, . . . to vary the environment, and to act out a delusional system on a grand scale" (Miller and Zarcone 1968, 364).

In a major study of this population,

> the airport was found to figure prominently in their delusional system, chiefly as a symbolic representation of connection with the family. . . . Strikingly none of these persons had taken up residence in the airport as a survival alternative to emergency shelter elsewhere. The choice of the airport, it seems, was made on *symbolic rather than utilitarian grounds*, the act not of a will determined to preserve its independence but of an imagination lost in the throes of disorder. The airport had apparently come to represent concretely the focus from which time and space would somehow be bridged and the safety, security, and reassurance of reattachment to loved ones might be established. (Shapiro 1982, 455, emphasis added)

The airport as "gateway," so potent a symbol that it triggers delusionary episodes, is little appreciated by the millions of passengers who travel by air each day. Early in the history of commercial passenger aviation, airport designers had yet to arrive at this understanding of its important social function. They extrapolated their design from train stations. Large halls were built that condensed areas for ticketing and waiting in modified versions of Grand Central Station. Symbols from the surrounding region were stressed in a manner that made them less gateways to some exotic destination miles away than embarkation points for the local area. To an extent, this regional system of symbols can still be found as a motif in airports today. McCarran International Airport in Las Vegas is an extreme example. The décor focuses the attention of all passengers, those who are leaving as well as those arriving, on the expected behavior of the locale—legalized gambling. Slot machines of all kinds saturate this airport space, as do the sounds and signs of the mega-casinos just down the road.

The old Denver airport, Stapleton, like the brand new terminal of the Buffalo-Niagara International Airport, provides a less obvious example. A stroll through Stapleton's shops, when it was in operation, provided a display of regional, local signifiers, mainly exploiting the Wild West theme. Businesses selling cowboy and western attire, Wild West accessories and souvenirs, as well as the Frontier coffee shop, anchored the airport mall. At the new Buffalo-Niagara International Airport, the mall contains a motif representing Niagara Falls along with ample water displays outside, thereby connecting it to the region that has been developed for tourism immediately adjacent to the city.

More recently, the function of air transportation at Denver changed when the old Stapleton terminal was abandoned in an effort to make the location a hub for the transfer of flights to and from the coasts of the country. Local authorities exploited this property by building a new airport 20 miles away from the city.

Entrance to gate areas always involves a security check in U.S. terminals.

The multibillion-dollar Jeppesen terminal has an interior that emphasizes the hub function while retaining certain symbolic elements signifying the local region. Hub sign systems transform an airport by minimizing its connection to the local region. Instead, the hub symbols at Jeppesen terminal, like those that also characterize Chicago's O'Hare, now carry the suggestion that the terminal is a *gateway to the world*, while the Wild West theme of the old Stapleton facility has been buried in the plethora of mall shops occupying the new three-story terminal miles away. In this sense, we can observe that regional airports possess sign systems that signify the local area, while the décor of hubs and the larger air terminals are comprised of more cosmopolitan signs signifying global travel.

3

The Airport as Shopping Mall

[The Schiphol International Airport Mall] consists of three, almost identical shopping centres. . .

Amsterdam Airport Web Page

Beginning in the 1970s a major change affected all airports. Wide-bodied jets—the massive Boeing 747, Lockheed's L-1011, and McDonnell Douglas' DC-10—were introduced and required more taxiing space on airport runways and greater distances between gates. Airports throughout the country were renovated. Perhaps the single most significant transformation was the way old railroad-style terminal clusters were deconstructed and stretched out to accommodate the needed configuration. As a consequence, a new breed of terminal designers resorted to the use of the pedestrian concourse to connect gates, passengers, and personnel with the functional nodes of the terminal such as baggage claim, transfer flights, and ground transportation. By stretching out terminal space, however, an opportunity was created to increase the retailing function of the airport. Since that time, the merger of the mall with the terminal has become the principal innovation in airport design.

Airports have always had shopping, especially duty-free shopping in international terminals. In Europe, for example, Frankfurt International Airport is well known as a shopper's paradise and also boasts a bowling alley; see their website at www.frankfurt-airport.de. Its extensive mall facilities encourage airlines to use the location as a hub for flight changes. The same is true for the Schiphol Amsterdam Airport. According to its Internet site:

> The award-winning Amsterdam Airport Shopping Centre consists of three, almost identical shopping centres, in the various parts of the departure lounge. In total there are 47 shops with an assortment of more than 120,000 articles. Every shop has bimonthly special offers and every article has a worldwide guaranty. . . . The shops are open all day from first to last departure of the aircraft. . . . Forty outlets, bars and restaurants offer a varied and friendly atmosphere. (<www.schipol.nl>)

Schiphol is not just a mall—it also offers casino gambling, making it a miniversion of Las Vegas. Duty-free shopping at Schiphol includes audio and video equipment, cameras, confections, a delicatessen, diamonds, household electrical goods, films, flowers and plants, jewelry and watches, clothing, leather, liquor and tobacco, perfumes, shoes, souvenirs, sunglasses, and toys. These objects are all instantly recognized as desirable commodities through years of conditioning by global, mass-media advertising. They are the normative gifts of our emergent world culture, just as they are the material anchor points for the new modes of desire created by the simulated media/advertising environment. The fully developed international airport mall functions as a mall like any other.

Developers of domestic terminals have also married the airport with the mall. Owners hope to take advantage of the propensity to consume among travelers in transit as well as local residents who are attracted there. The air terminal in Las

Airport shopping progressed from travel items, seen sold in the photo, to a wide variety of goods as the terminal merged with the mall.

Vegas relies on gambling to exploit the same condition of travelers who are waiting for flights. The best example of melding air travel with mall shopping is the operations of the United Kingdom's British Airports Authority (BAA). It runs Airmalls at Heathrow, Gatwick, Stansted, Edinburgh, Glasgow, Aberdeen, and Southhampton. In the 1990s, it was contracted to develop and operate an Airmall at the Pittsburgh International Airport. The key marketing concept of the Airmall is the "No Rip-Off Guarantee." According to the company's statement, "If you find a product that you bought at Airmall cheaper in a comparable location, call us on it, at 1-800-ITS-FAIR. And we'll refund the difference. And that's guaranteed."

In short, while most travelers have experienced shopping at airports with prices considerably higher than in the local area, Airmall guarantees that the prices in its shops are competitive with those in the surrounding region. The Pittsburgh airport, in other words, is also a mall and a destination for local residents to shop as well as servicing passengers in transit. "Whether you're traveling to Pittsburgh as a destination or changing planes, you will be greeted by warm smiles, friendly faces and 100 shops and restaurants for you to browse through, shop, relax and dine. Besides providing free shipping of your purchases, and no sales tax on clothing, we guarantee that all our prices are exactly like regular mall prices." (airmall.com 2000)

Stores at the Pittsburgh airport include Bally Shoes, The Nature Company, The Athlete's Foot, The Body Shop, PGA Tour Shop, The Gap, London Fog, Clinique, and Jockey. Other stores sell leather, sunglasses, candy, watches and jewelry, music, electronics, and books, and there is even a pet store. Just like any other mall, the Pittsburgh airport has many places to eat, including shops that sell pizza, pretzels, deli fare, yogurt, baked goods, Chinese food, hamburgers, and sandwiches, along with a restaurant featuring steak, several bars that serve food, and a juice and salad bar. Its Internet site listed 42 stores seeking new employees on November 7, 1998.

The selection of stores typically found in malls seems to have been replicated in airport facilities almost everywhere. Even those terminals that have undergone renovation and added mall shopping have offerings that are familiar to any frequent mall shopper. In Philadelphia, a recent renovation of the terminal added food offerings that included the standards—pretzels, yogurt, candy, coffee, hamburgers, and pizza—and shops selling books, jewelry, chocolates and candies, Bath and Body Works, The Gap, PGA Tour Shop, Sunglass Hut, Wilson's Leather, and electronics stores. The same can be said of new terminals, such as the Denver International Airport, which was built from the beginning with mall shopping in mind. The over $4 billion Jeppesen terminal consists of three concourses, each with its own shopping areas. The expansive building contains hundreds of stores selling food, specialty items, and the typical array of mall-franchised commodities.

Mall shopping at the airport can be a very lucrative business. Retailers, for example, noted that they experienced a boom in sales after increased security measures were put in place following the explosion of TWA flight 800 on July 17, 1996. According to a newspaper account:

> The tougher security measures have been an unexpected boon for airport retailers. . . . "People are buying more books, gifts, and magazines," confirms Steve Johnson of Westfield Corp., which runs the retail operations for Washington's National and Dulles airports. Johnson says revenue in July and August is up 15 to 18% over last year. (*USA Today* 1996, 10-B)

Terminals themselves differ with regard to their ability to turn a profit. Publicly run airports, like those operated by the Port of New York and New Jersey Authority, such as Kennedy International, "have notoriously low rates of profit on their cash services, like food and drink" (Wald 1995). As airports have integrated their functions with the mall form, they have had to pay more careful attention to competition from shopping facilities elsewhere in the region. Like local malls, airports compete for customers. For this reason, the BAA company that operates the Airmall at Pittsburgh has received attention for its marketing innovations. It was once the British Airports Authority, a civic enterprise that was privatized by the Thatcher government in the 1980s. Its commercial success has led other privately owned companies to enter the world of airport management. According to one report:

> An American company, Lockheed Air Terminal, Inc., manages many airports like the ones in Burbank and Albany. When the Canadian Federal Government needed a new terminal at Pearson International [outside Toronto], it turned to private companies because they had the investment capital. Lockheed spent $550 million (Canadian) to build Terminal 3, now home to United, American and other carriers. (Wald 1995)

As a consequence, many more airports will probably be privatized in the future to take advantage of mall shopping possibilities.

One outcome of the push for more profits is the further expansion of the "airport as destination" concept. If the terminal building can be a mall that attracts shoppers as well as travelers, it can also function as an entertainment space that attracts people out for a good time, in competition with urban downtowns. According to one report (Okun 1996), several airports have incorporated trendy, upscale dining as part of their offerings for the general public:

> The colorful Wolfgang Puck Express in the LA airport, for instance, features some of the dishes the well-known chef is famous for—his thin sourdough crusted pizzas and elaborate salads. There's also Rhino Chasers, a microbrewery based restaurant with an adjacent Daily Grill. . . . In Tucson, the airport features an outpost

of the El Charro Cafe; El Charro is said to be the oldest Mexican restaurant in Arizona and has been ranked as one of the top ethnic restaurants in the country. In the Denver International Airport, [there is] the Northern Trail Bar and Grill, a neighborhood pub [that serves Denver-style steaks]. (Okun 1996)

Discovering the mall at the airport should not be as surprising to people as it might be. After all, mall shopping has penetrated a variety of environments. One of the most successful malls, in terms of profit per square foot, is called the Forum Shops and is located at the Las Vegas gambling casino Caesars Palace (Gottdiener 1997). Although it seems that terminal designers may have turned to shopping as a way to fill up the enlarged spaces after introduction of wide-bodied jets, the combination of relatively affluent passengers with time on their hands and no place else to go means that mall shopping is an inevitable outcome of the new designs. Merchandising penetrates all forms where there is a ready market. Even restaurants, such as the themed franchise Hard Rock Cafe, earn a significant proportion of their profits through commodity sales.

The issue is not whether we should commercialize the spaces in between the gates at the terminal, because this is inevitable in our economic system, but what the ultimate design of new terminals will look like and how these new terminals will be perceived by passengers. Traveler-friendly places, like Denver's new Jeppesen terminal, and the duty-free shopping of places like Frankfurt and Amsterdam in Europe are attractions in their own right. It is the appearance of these new, multifunctional and innovative spaces, such as Kansai Airport in Osaka, Japan, that makes terminal construction so promising, especially in our society where cities continue to be plagued by problems.

4

The Airport as City and Community

Airports are now like small cities, mind-numbing ground stations for the booming subculture of the business homeless.

Richard Rayner, 1998

APRIL 5, 1993

I am sitting in the food court at O'Hare Airport outside of Chicago. This particular food court is the best of its kind in the country. What can I compare it to? Consider other places. Placed within the pedestrian tunnels are snack bars serving those horribly fat Polish sausages which turn around and around in a glass-enclosed rotisserie. You can have them with optional melted cheese topping on a bun. Or why not order that other staple of airport food—the ready-made, microwaveable sandwich? This meal comes complete with a side-order of potato chips and beverage, all for only $12.95.

The food court at O'Hare is different. It's not a snack bar, it's a multicultural restaurant. They actually prepare food. The front is a series of ethnic shops each offering *la specialité du maison*—pizza, hamburgers, Chinese food, and the like. After you purchase your meal, you can proceed further into the food court, which opens into a large cafeteria fronted by a plate glass window wall for viewing planes taking off and landing. The court has ample seating at little Formica tables.

I am sitting at a small table having a plate of Mongolian beef and rice sautéed by the friendly Chinese girl at the oriental food stand inside. I have a wait of one hour and forty-five minutes before my connecting flight. It's better to eat moderately healthy Chinese food, I have decided, than to wait for the airline meal of high-sodium, high-fat designer food. Of course, if I had planned ahead, I could have ordered a vegetarian meal, or some such alternative. But traveling through O'Hare, the availability of the food court makes that unnecessary—if you have the time between planes, that is. Halfway through my meal, a very attractive, young blonde woman walks over to my table and sits down. She looks at me and says, "Would you like a date?"

I think to myself that I didn't hear her correctly, but I'm also sure that I have. The spicy rice and beef turns dry in my throat. I try to talk but can't, and so I take a quick gulp of my soda. She says it again, while I pause. I *did* hear her correctly the first time.

"You mean here? Now? What do you mean?"

She looks at me and then turns slightly away so as not to threaten me. "If you will follow me, I'll show you." She pauses. "OK?"

"You mean a blow job?" I try to visualize what this is all about.

She doesn't say anything, just waits and looks out the window. She wants me to respond, but I can't. Finally, my meter runs out. She walks away without looking at me.

I'm stunned but then I become curious. I watch her walk away. She goes to the opposite end of the food court. There's another man sitting alone. He's a fat, overworked businessmen in a polyester-blend suit, a bread-and-butter customer of the airlines. She approaches ever so slowly, like she's out for a Sunday stroll. She sits down at his table. They talk. In a few minutes the girl gets up and walks out. The man hurriedly picks up his belongings, gulps his last sip of coffee, and then follows her. I watch her walk briskly away as she enters the massive glass-enclosed gangway of airport tunnel B. The man is close behind but struggles to keep pace. They disappear outside in the pedestrian traffic of the corridor.

I spent my allotted airport time that day waiting for my connecting flight by watching the people in and around the food court. Several times I saw her walk by, sometimes with men.

THE AIRPORT AS CITY

The contemporary air terminal is like a city. As it became a multifunctional site, it also developed an urban culture. The implosive articulation of a many-purposed pedestrian crowd creates a critical mass of social density, much like the busy downtown district of a large central city. With enough interacting people, the scene itself emerges as a distinct feature of place, more than the sum of individuals. The terminal abandons its significance as a backdrop and assumes the power of independent character in the public melodrama. This reversal of foreground and background reduces the individual to a part of the mass and has been a characteristic of cities since the nineteenth century. To be sure, the airport still has scenes of immense drama, such as the reuniting of a family after a flight, but now the terminal space, as a *mise-en-scène*, dominates aspects of interaction despite the comings and goings of individuals. Terminal space in our biggest airports has transcended the human performances it contains.

Some literary critics have remarked that this reversal of foreground and background is a principal characteristic of new, postmodern culture. Postmodern literature attempts to capture the reality of contemporary culture where individuals and individual personalities have been absorbed by the supersaturating mediascapes that now dominate interaction. According to Young and Caveney, this new sensibility is expressed in the fiction of Brett Ellis:

> The aggressive territoriality of Ellis' books suggests that geography and place, once a fictional hinterland for critics to interpret as they might, have gradually come to dictate the themes and structure of the novel, leaving emotional issues to become amorphous, to function as background. . . . In *Less Than Zero*, it is ultimately the city that owns and spawns the people and against whose implacable background all attempts at understanding can be no more than frail rags blown on the Santa Ana winds. (Young and Caveney, 1992, 23)

For most of us, this postmodern characteristic of the airport is perceived by intention. Travelers are always only part of the general scene. Through years of media conditioning, we no longer marvel or even pause at emotional scenes like reunions or separations that punctuate the more mundane reality of waiting for flights. An encounter with terminal space is only a temporary stopping-off time between planes and locations. Who among us ever intended a trip to the airport to be anything more substantial? We do not live in airports nor do we make spending time there an important part of our social life, despite efforts by developers to marry the terminal with the mall form in order to attract general-purpose crowds. Time spent in terminals is dead time, a blank period during which we already find ourselves forgetting the experience while it is still happening. Terminal time, for most of us, is only an inconvenience while we wait for planes.

Yet if we abandon the subjective perspective of our individual dramas and look at the airport with more objective eyes, another dimension pops out, much like an optical illusion that once went unnoticed. Foreground and background reverse themselves in a postmodern sense. The terminal is a temporary container of the human drama, but by itself it assumes a reality and world of its own as the different functions it offers to the public become more developed in scale and scope by airport designers. Shopping has become more elaborate in many airports; so too are the dining facilities. Major airports now have hotels attached to them and there are fitness centers adjacent to terminals. For $8, a traveler with time on his or her hands can work out at Miami International's airport hotel. Los Angeles International (LAX) advertises a $10 rate at its 24-hour fitness center contained within the Airport Hilton. In short, the visit to a terminal, like a trip to the city by reluctant suburbanites, is the one thing that matters for *everyone's* air travel aspirations and for a significant number of people who stop by to shop and even to eat or exercise.

The airport is like a city, a busy metropolis containing thousands of people at any given time. Las Vegas's McCarran services over 20 million tourists a year. People pass in and out of cities, only they tend to do so using a longer scale of time. Airports speed up this process of temporarily dwelling in place, but they may host millions in their own fashion each year. Like a city, an airport's concourses are its grand boulevards. Potted trees and plants often line the walkways, as do shops of increasing diversity. People live, love, and sometimes even die in airports. Babies are born there; children are abused or abandoned. High drama reunites loved ones and bears witness to final departures. But, like the city, the terminal space merely houses this temporary drama, and only its physicality endures. Everyone else is there for the briefest possible moment in their lives.

The contemporary airport is like a city because of the scale of operations and the fact that it possesses its very own economy. Chicago's O'Hare, for example, serves 185,000 passengers a day. It is the busiest airport in the world and is the hub for two major airlines, United and American. Running O'Hare requires a city-sized labor force—it employs 50,000 people. The entire complex comprises almost 8,000 acres. "To walk from one end of United's 'C' concourse to the other end of American's 'L' concourse, the longest journey you can take in the airport, takes a minimum of 15 minutes. People frequently get lost. At 6 P.M. in the main terminal it's rush hour" (Rayner 1998, 41). Airports not only have an urban-scale

Forlorn passengers search for lost luggage among bags removed from busy carousels. (AP photo Denis Paquin)

employment base, they have their own economy. Food, clothing, and even different kinds of shelter can be purchased; a class system regulates the latter. For the hoi polloi there are molded plastic chairs, some with soft cushions—hardly a place to spend time in comfort and yet many people sleep on such accommodations. For the wealthy, airlines operate exclusive, members-only clubs that offer luxurious amenities tucked away in special sections of terminals. American Airlines situates its Admiral's Club unobtrusively along the intersecting corridor between the H and K concourses at O'Hare. United's Red Carpet Club has two locations at the same airport, one near gate B-6 and the other on the C concourse after gate 16. Inside, members can relax in comfort, even sleep, or if they prefer to work, can plug in their laptops and help themselves to complimentary beverages. An observer at one of the clubs noted that business people dominate this exclusive enclave hidden within the terminal. "The first thing that most of them do, before opening their laptops or helping themselves to coffee, sometimes even before taking off their coats and dumping their packs, is to reach for a phone and punch in a calling card number. Only then do they settle down. . . . It's a check in, not with the airline or even the office, but with themselves" (Rayner 1998, 42).

Airports are big business. Revenues from parking, shopping, and food services run into the millions of dollars. McCarran Airport in Las Vegas makes over $22 million a year on gambling alone. Often the airport even helps to revitalize the urban area within which it is located. John Wayne Airport in Orange County, California, was originally planned as a small facility meant as a suburban adjunct to the mega-airport of LAX located across the county border. It was designed to handle a maximum of 400,000 suburbanites a year. So convenient was it for the burgeoning Orange County population that John Wayne now handles more than three million passengers each year. The entire region has benefited from new businesses and industries choosing to locate near the facility. This successful airport, like many others, has become a county *growth pole* for new business. In Tennessee, a $59 million makeover of the Nashville airport in the 1980s resulted in an additional $500 million pumped into the local economy annually and the creation of more than 5,600 airport-related jobs with a payroll of approximately $170 million (Anderberg 1988).

At least one economist has attempted to quantify the multiplier effect of airports on the local economy (Lichfield 1977). Employment generated by the airport itself is only one component of economic benefit. A second sector of industries linked to the facility includes warehousing, marketing, and trucking. Finally, a third sector is comprised of services that enable the airport and linked businesses to function properly. Estimating the economic effects generated by the airport becomes difficult for sectors two and three because of leakage to the surrounding environment that may also play a role in money-making activity. Nevertheless, Nathanial Lichfield estimates a large multiplier effect of 2.2 to 1 in sector three; i.e., in service employment that is generated by the airport and adjacent industry. That is, for every worker hired in sectors one and two, 2.2 are eventually hired by the businesses servicing those sectors. From the information mentioned earlier regarding the labor force at O'Hare, for example, we can see that its direct employment of 50,000 workers results in the additional support of 110,000 service workers in the surrounding area, according to Lichfield's multiplier. This figure alone is along the same scale as the employment base of a medium-sized city.

One of the fastest-growing economic aspects of airports is their function in warehousing and the importation of commodities as airfreight. This cargo business aspect is often a hidden dimension of airports because of our conscious emphasis on the terminal as a traveler's gateway. According to one estimate, however, airfreight accounts for as much as 20 percent of a carrier's revenue. And "it improves passengers' options because the more cargo an airline ships, the greater the variety of flights at an airport" (Fehr 1995). Air cargo business has made a considerable impact on the economy of Dulles International, for example.

> Guests at the wedding reception Saturday night . . . will not soon forget the flowers. Each of the 25 tables at the Four Seasons Hotel in Georgetown was adorned with a five-foot-high centerpiece of pastel-colored roses, white hydrangeas, and ivy atop a stone cherub.
>
> What the 235 guests could not know was how the 1,500 roses got there. Those varieties are not grown locally this time of year, so they were shipped from Holland on a KLM Royal Dutch jetliner that arrived Wednesday night at Dulles International Airport. The delivery is part of a cargo industry at Dulles that ships about $10 billion worth of products a year, ranking Dulles 25th among U.S. airports and moving up. (Fehr 1995)

In short, airports process people and commodities for profit. So do cities. As with cities, airports generate income and add value to the goods that pass through their space on the way to other locations. The above example illustrates the growing role that international businesses play in the airport economy. The level of this activity rivals in importance that of the central city due to the power of the global economy. Some observers even suggest that the contemporary reality of global goods and services uniquely positions the airport as a focus of economic activity that will one day overshadow the large central city. Regions around air transport facilities may be the new growth poles of our society. According to one observer:

> With international transactions, production flexibility, and speed characterizing the new economy, air cargo will play an increasingly important role. No other means of transportation better satisfies global just-in-time logistics—logistics requiring that producers receive and ship smaller quantities more frequently, more quickly, over longer distances. Already airfreight accounts for more than one-third of the value of U.S. products exported, a share that will surely rise in the years ahead. Interna-

tional air cargo shipments are projected to grow at least 7 percent annually during the 1990s, with the booming Pacific Rim routes generating double-digit annual growth rates throughout the decade. (Kasarda 1991, 16)

In many places, such as the Alliance Airport near Fort Worth, Texas, or Mississaugua, Ontario, adjacent to the Pearson International Airport of Toronto, regional development is already a product of the rapid growth of business connected to air transport facilities.

The airport is like a city because it has become a general-purpose public space that enables all kinds of behaviors. Prostitutes and thieves find this place as attractive as the seedier streets of downtown. High crimes, shocking crimes, have long been associated with airports because terrorists have chosen to attack on airport grounds—hence the elaborate airport security measures in place today. But ordinary thieves operate in the unsecured parts of an airport every day. Heathrow Airport in England was commonly known as "Thiefrow" because of the amount of theft from passengers' baggage. Kennedy Airport in New York was a Mafia playground where cargo was routinely pilfered. The film *GoodFellas* presents the Hollywood version of a spectacular multimillion-dollar Lufthansa payroll heist that took place at Kennedy International. Even the lesser thieves, like pickpockets and purse-snatchers, ply their trade in airports, adding to the complexity of their urban aspects.

Airports are also a space for the sex trade, demonstrated by my experience at O'Hare, and this raises many questions. Where did the woman service her customers? Are airport authorities aware of what goes on under their roof? Information from other airports might provide a clue. At Charles de Gaulle airport, in Roissy, France, the terminal for the non-French airlines is constructed with the parking levels directly below the passenger terminal. Local prostitutes plying their trade have used this parking space for their activities. The practice was discovered when an unfortunate young Englishwoman was killed several years ago in the parking area after becoming disoriented in the lower levels of the structure. She was mistaken for a prostitute, physically assaulted, and killed.

In fact, murder is not an unknown occurrence at airports. Killings at air terminals are usually reported only in the local papers. If you are traveling, you normally would not hear about such things. At Denver's old Stapleton Airport, authorities reported the activities of a serial killer who stalked businessmen and killed them in toilet stalls. He or she—security could not determine the gender of the killer and left open the possibility that the men were in the toilet for sex—worked infrequently. Between 1989 and 1993 a total of five bodies had been found—all murdered in the same way, with their throats slit. Now that Stapleton has closed, the new airport seems to have avoided a recurrence of these incidents, yet the killer remains at large. As in the city, theft, murder, and the sex trade interweave their occurrence with the more mundane activities of ordinary routines and daily life.

Many airports are not only like cities, they take on a classic urban form. Roland Barthes, the French critic, claimed that the classic city emerged during the European Middle Ages. More than just a collection of comparatively high-density residential living and shops that serviced its population, a city concentrated in one space all the essential functions of civilized society. Airports have transformed over the years to fully functional urban spaces. Barthes's classic city contained within its center a building of the municipal authority, a court, a market, an open forum for pedestrians, and usually dominating, a religious temple or sacred site. The contemporary airport married to the mall form, like Denver's new Jeppesen terminal, can be considered a huge market. It also contains a chapel or multidenominational sacred space, security offices for its own police, emergency medical facilities, communication facilities, command and control centers, and although most users are rushing to and fro, immense spaces for pedestrian communion. At Rome's international airport, the emphasis on the sacred function expanded when the Vatican announced in February 2000 that indulgences would be sold to sinners in the terminal chapel. No doubt the heavy volume of traffic in and out of Rome was too much a temptation for the Holy Father to resist.

Cities are different from airports because the former possesses residents, that is, people who stay within the space for an extended period of time. But some airports are like cities in this regard because people live in them too. In the late 1980s, for example, one estimate claimed that there were several hundred homeless people living in the three airports of the New York City area (Holloway 1995). The most extreme case is that of Merhan Karimi "Alfred" Nasseri, an exiled Iranian, who had been stranded inside France's Charles de Gaulle airport since 1988. Writing in 1997, a reporter observed:

> When Alfred Nasseri arrived at Charles de Gaulle airport in 1988, he paused in the lounge to jot a few words in his diary while waiting for the authorities to sort out a small immigration matter. Nasseri is still there, more than nine years and 6,000 diary pages later, unable to enter France and unable to leave. He is a man without a country in a Europe that, technically at least, is without borders. . . . [His] long sojourn in Terminal One of the airport near Paris is the curious result of misfortune and government bureaucracy. . . . At night he falls asleep in the brightly lit lounge, waking up before 6 A.M. to wash up in an airport restroom. Nasseri speaks no French and depends on the kindness of flight attendants who keep him supplied with shaving kits, toothbrushes, and toothpaste from stocks reserved for passengers. They also give him their meal tickets, which he can use in the terminal restaurants. (Kraft 1997)

A happy event occurred almost two years later, in September 1999, when Nasseri was granted a refugee document from Belgium, and his papers were finally accepted by France. The 54-year-old Nasseri was then free to leave the airport after 11 years. Yet this "scandalous and unbelievable saga of bureaucratic misbehaving" is not over. Nasseri refused to leave because his airport life was the only one he had known since leaving Iran. According to one account, "The airport's chief medical officer said that in September Nasseri was finally given the necessary papers to leave the airport, but so far hasn't used them. 'He has been badly affected by all this. . . . Now we have to try and get him out of here'" (Moseley 1999).

As recently as January 2000, there were no reports that Nasseri had yet left the terminal facility. In a bizarre statement, the airport doctor revealed that—aside from a minor toe infection—he had not treated "Alfred" for any medical problems during his entire 11-year entrapment. "This is the living proof," he said, "that man can survive in an airport" (Moseley 1999).

There are other kinds of people who live at airports. The case of schizophrenics who break down within these "hyper-spaces" has already been discussed. Most of the people who call their local terminal "home," however, are simply homeless. According to one report, "Many homeless prefer conditions at the climate-controlled, relatively crime-free airports to those in the street" (Holloway 1995). Once compared in this way, the local air terminal seems to be a very rational choice. Street people are often victimized by criminals and certainly subjected to the vagaries of weather. A stay at the airport not only offers escape from the harsh conditions of the inner city, but many homeless simply blend in because it is quite common to see people with lots of baggage nodding off and lounging around in the terminal areas.

> It takes some ingenuity for a homeless person to end up at an airport; if it didn't, the terminals would be littered with people. . . . Those who find their way to Kennedy are drawn by its creature comforts. Even the garbage is of higher quality for those who like to rummage. . . . And the safety, the warmth, and the supply of bathrooms and restaurants are unparalleled. It is like living in a 24-hour mall. (Holloway 1995)

Authorities who monitor this situation often find it frustrating because many of the homeless blend in so well with the general traveling population. Estimates of the total number of people living in terminals across the country are therefore not reliable. Some places have identified permanent residents as a problem. "In Chicago, the city opened an 80-bed shelter four years ago to draw the homeless from O'Hare Airport after things went too far: some people brought in plants to decorate their corners" (Holloway 1995).

The homeless are not the only ones using airports as overnight accommodations. Sleeping in terminals is a common experience of travelers who journey on a standby budget, students who come and go on cheap flights while on vacation, passengers stranded by inclement weather, and others who are inconvenienced by various incidents that require them to spend considerable time in airports waiting for the next flight. The practice is so common that there is even a website entirely devoted to rating terminals for sleeping called "The Budget Traveller's Guide to Sleeping in Airports" at <www3.sympatico.cadonna.mcsherry/

airports.htm>. Arranged alphabetically, the online guide prints reviews by fellow voyagers detailing the pros and cons of sleeping in individual terminals. Many reviewers tell you exactly where the best sleeping arrangements can be found in the sprawling mega-airports like Dallas/Fort Worth. In one account of the Atlanta facility, a reviewer voted thumbs down:

> A few years ago I had to sleep in the Atlanta airport. It was miserable because there were lots of men who were wandering around the airport late at night and they were continually hitting on me. . . . They kept offering to bring me home. And would not leave me alone until I got up and walked away from them. I had to keep moving. ("Budget Traveller's Guide" 2000)

Because this website strives to make its information most useful, it prints multiple reviews that often inform prospective voyagers just how to negotiate space for the best night's sleep. A second review of Atlanta says:

> I've read postings that the Atlanta airport is hell to sleep in, but if you know where to go it is wonderful. The new international terminal recently constructed for the Olympics has soft squshy *[sic]* leather couches with adjacent tables with telephones. I felt like I was at home in bed with a nightstand! No one bothered me there, (they did in the regular terminal). ("Budget Traveller's Guide" 2000)

Chicago's O'Hare got mixed reviews. One person said it would be easier to sleep inside a plane engine; others also complained about the high level of noise. Some reviewers liked the friendly security staff that avoided hassling travelers. Dallas/Fort Worth failed because reviewers complained about the "noise, noise, noise, constant TRAMM action, as well as hundreds of people tromping all over wherever you're trying to sleep." But another reviewer recommended, "Just as you walk in the terminal, the carpeted area next to the windows is a good spot to crash."

One reviewer, who liked the new Denver International Airport (DIA), described a typical experience of being stranded that was made more pleasurable by the terminal's plush accommodations:

> My entire youth group was forced by an airline . . . to spend over 24 hours in the airport as they put two or three of us on different planes throughout the next day. DIA has many comfortable couches and benches, grouped in a circular pattern to ensure togetherness. The places in which most people sleep, in the main concourse, is *[sic]* semi private because of the trees that are dispersed within the couch area. The Burger King is open pretty late. No noise except the PA droning on about un-attended baggage. . . . Overall, DIA is possibly the best sleeping airport in the US. ("Budget Traveller's Guide" 2000)

Predictably, reviewers found Las Vegas' McCarran inhospitable because of both the incessant noise from its many slot machines and the obvious fact that, as a

24-hour town, the terminal was busy every minute with its seating spaces constantly occupied. Los Angeles was rated low except for the Bradley International Arrivals building, which was considered a find for the weary traveler searching for a quiet place to crash. New York airports were equally busy, but Kennedy had many possibilities because of its separate terminal arrangements and the fact that there were fewer international flights at night.

THE AIRPORT AS CITY: TEMPORARY COMMUNITY AND THE TERMINAL

On May 10, 1992, I experienced being stranded at an airport. I was flying a red-eye bargain trip out of Newark to Los Angeles using one of the minor airline carriers. When I arrived at the check-in at about 11:00 P.M., I was informed that the flight had been canceled. The next one left at 7:00 the following morning. For several hours after that, I alternated between yelling at the airline personnel behind the counter and aimlessly wandering the halls of the terminal. Exhausted, I finally returned to the airplane gate designated for the morning flight in order to sleep. I discovered over twenty people had been caught in the same predicament and were now lounging around the gate area. By 3:00 A.M. we had all pretty much introduced ourselves to each other and had created a *temporary community,* united most directly by our profound, mutual hatred of our bargain carrier and its poor service. Submerged in conversation and occasionally nodding off while lying on the floor with my head propped on my carry-on bag, the remaining hours went by swiftly.

This incident at the airport made me think of something else, the nature of community in Southern California. When I first moved out there in the 1970s and booked a real estate agent to find a home, I was told to take a cold-hearted approach to housing. I had assumed we all have attachments to the physical building where we live. These feelings tend to increase in fondness and intensity the longer we reside in any one particular location. Many years can pass but the sight of our original home is purely evocative and stimulates strong feelings. My Southern California real estate agent warned me not to be emotional about housing. The market was so good, with prices inflating almost every month, that home ownership was one of the best ways to acquire wealth. I was told that I should purchase a home that was "a good investment value" rather than a comfortable place to live where I might be enticed to put down roots. I was told to consider living in the house for just about three years and then to move up to a more costly one after cashing in on my accrued equity. "That's what everyone does," said the real estate agent.

I had problems looking at a home that way. For me, it was a matter of developing an emotional attachment to a physical location, to the house, to the street where I lived, to the people, and to the community. But the longer I stayed in

Southern California, the more I realized that moving up was not just a real estate agent's slogan to sell more houses, it was a way of life. My entire neighborhood was filled with quasi-transients, people who stayed in one house for only a few years. Under those circumstances, it was impossible to construct the kind of neighborly relations that I had come to expect from years of living back east. My best friends were people I met at work or through our religious affiliation, or most often, they were the parents of our children's friends, at least the ones that we liked and chose to get to know. Everyone else—neighbors, neighborhoods, schools, local merchants, mail carriers, the lawn service, the pizza delivery boy, Saturday's Jehovah's Witnesses, and the police—was interchangeable and often faceless. Every neighborhood of every new home had the same kinds of people.

The modern airport is an awesome space that speeds up this contemporary process of *transient* social interaction. It is a place where the average stay is only about an hour. The air travel regimen pushes people along through one end of the terminal and out the other—planing and deplaning on an immense scale of thousands and tens of thousands each day. People in the terminal usually keep to themselves. They deploy brilliant mechanisms to maintain their shell of social reserve. Your neighbor seated with you waiting at the gate, the friendly flight attendant who smiles and greets you, the ticket agents who say "Have a nice flight," the snack bar employee and newspaper vendor, all come and go with the same regularity and absence of emotion in your life. They fade in and out of consciousness with a swiftness that defies memory. The airport is a place where we have passed through but never really *been*.

Occasionally, however, and, perhaps much too often to suit most travelers, this highly forgettable dead time turns into a memorable experience. When we get stuck in terminals for unexpected waits, we are forced to deal with our surroundings. Suddenly through these circumstances, things that once went unnoticed when we used the terminal at our convenience, now begin to loom large in our consciousness. The bathrooms may bother us because we now notice they are not clean. People waiting like us begin to get on our nerves. Little children, once adorable when we only needed to give them a quick glance, become horrible dwarf monsters that irritate us immeasurably as we spend unexpected, long hours in transit.

One of the most debilitating aspects of tedious, unscheduled terminal waits is precisely the fact that these spaces are not our homes. They are not comfortable. We miss our favorite chair or even our bed. The people that we are stuck with in the airport are also strangers. They are not our friends. Trapped in the terminal, we miss home, hearth, family, and community. At times, however, the temporary situation of unattached strangeness turns into a temporary community. Travelers beseiged by the same inconvenient delay become friends. Human interaction, under these circumstances, has an awesome power. It can turn a traveler's nightmare into a tolerable and even unforgettable experience.

DE-TERRITORIALIZATION AND THE AIRPORT

New social relations based on air travel are challenging our concepts of home and community. They are summed up by the concept of de-territorialization, or a general de-emphasis of the importance of significant places, like home and community, in contemporary daily life. According to one observer, "Today's executives live everywhere at once, inhabiting a growing community of the air that is responsible to no nation or governing body but only to the imperatives of commerce" (Iyer 1998, 37).

Current changes caused by frequent air travel and de-territorialization are quite profound. Until quite recently in human history, space and time were considered absolutes. The here and now were graphically and fundamentally distinguished from both the past and the future. Dreams of time travel were inspired precisely by this unconquerable barrier of absolute time that hemmed in our lives by birth at one end and death at the other. The very same was true for absolute space, which constituted a barrier of its own. For thousands of years, the concept of travel meant something done with arduous labor that involved considerable time and energy. Travel was the ultimate and most distinct form of displacement.

In an opposite sense, our domicile or domestic location represented a formidable anchoring point. The home, in particular, was a place with a specific ambiance, surroundings, and personalized touches that represented the accumulation of our daily life over many years.

Now transportation, information, and communication technologies have erased the once insurmountable barriers of space and time that hemmed in our daily lives. By disentangling the idea of the home as a personalized place from any reference to a given space, and by allowing us instantaneous access to places across the globe, transport, information, and communication technologies are deeply reshaping the experience of both home place and travel. According to Salvino Salvaggio:

> For several million people a telephone number, a house, a local bank, a post office, and a local newspaper, have already been replaced by an entirely deterritorialized cellular phone and answering service, an e-mail address, a set of credit cards, as well as media of world communication. (Salvaggio 1999)

For many business travelers, the home as a unique place condensing family relations across the generations has been de-emphasized in favor of the serial use of temporary locations, such as hotels, that advertise themselves as "a home away from home." Many jobs are less dependent now on any one location than the use of many locations woven together as spaces for work using the laptop, the cellular phone, the Internet, or the fax. This mode of de-territorialization involves a progressively greater population and results in a redefinition of home, place, space, and local community.

THE AIRPORT AND DE-TERRITORIALIZATION:
THE CREATION OF A NEW CHARACTER

Decades ago, the academic field of urban sociology argued that a person's character was produced by the particular place where he or she lived. City people, for example, were said to be distinctively, qualitatively different from country people. The cause of such difference was claimed by these early researchers to be based on the separate molding patterns of the urban and rural material realms. The nature of space, in turn, affected social interaction. Different environments produced different realities which, it was believed, produced different kinds of character, different personality types.

We still believe in these stereotypes and differences today, although we may not attribute their generative cause to the quality of the environment alone. Character is more rightly believed to be produced by countless causes, especially the cultural modes of behavior we inherit from our families and intimate social contacts. Today we know that people are not the products of cities or suburbs, they are simply passing through and dancing to the tune of other, more powerful social forces. Most Americans move more than once in their lifetimes, mainly for employment purposes. Less and less can we say that some single individual is a product of a particular place but—and this is the point—more and more people are products of transient lives and transient spaces.

The airport is the ultimate symbol of the new American reality since we are all just passing through from one location to another. Our friends are more for the moment than for a lifetime; the places we stay and the people we interact with come to us because of situations. We are less the stalwarts of stable communities than temporary residents in a transitory social communion of fellow travelers. Whenever we are forced to spend long periods of time at an airport, we may become part of a larger community, the communion of fellow stranded travelers. We share some laughs, some strong negative opinions about air travel, some personal confidences, and sometimes even a night in the terminal lounge, but when the boarding announcement for our flight finally comes, we walk onto the plane without so much as a goodbye to our new friends, never to see them again.

Transitory social communion and the foregrounding of the airport as a character in personal drama was depicted in the recent film *In the Company of Men*. Two young men who work for a generic company as executives are seen in an equally generic airport as the movie opens. According to the Blockbuster cover, "Two executives on assignment at a branch of the anonymous company they work for decide to get back at all the women they believe have hurt them professionally and personally." They hatch a bizarre plot of aggression aimed at a generalized object—all women—while lounging in the placelessness of the aiport terminal on the way to their out-of-town assignment. This opening sequence recalls another classic film by Alfred Hitchcock, *Strangers on a Train*. Here the premise is derived from the anonymity and class segregation of train travel in the 1940s. Two upper middle-class young men meet each other in the lounge car of a transnational train and hatch a murder plot that one of them does not take seriously until it is much too late.

Against the backdrop of the airport, the two protagonists in the newer film conspire but with a similar difference in motives. Yet they are not murderers. The damage they intend to commit is purely emotional. They decide to find a "plain Jane" who has obviously not been dating and to shower her with affection so that, for the first time, she has not only one suitor but two. Their object is to make her fall in love with at least one of them and then to expose their ruse, thereby destroying her with the realization of false love and the open manipulation of her emotions for sport. As in the earlier classic, however, there is a catch: only one of these men is playing and he is actually manipulating the other toward his doom.

In the Company of Men brings out in sharp relief the inhumanity of lives spent in transition, of men without community, without serious attachment to others, who wander the nation by air on company business and who have so little left of true character that they derive entertainment from creating and feeding off of human misery.

Could the airport, as a distinct milieu that is increasingly dwelled in as we adjust to lives spent in air travel, be helping to create or amplify a new social character—the uncaring, detached, self-contained individual armed with laptop, Walkman, credit cards, cellular phone, Palm Pilot, and business agenda? Observers of first-class travel, for example, note that passengers in that privileged section are too busy doing work while traveling to communicate with each other. In fact, being able to do work while having almost every other comfort catered to is the very premise of first class. The same observations have been made about the premier membership clubs in the terminal. They are set up with first-class business services—fax, copy machines, comfortable chairs, and tables for laptops. Hours and hours of watching ordinary people waiting for planes confirms that they rarely talk to each other. Walkmen with personal earphones are ubiquitous. Sitting with novel or newspaper in hand is most common. Airport lounges have their own TV broadcasts courtesy of the airport satellite channel, a division of the old Turner network. Departure lounges are not commonly a place for social communion.

At the turn of the century, Georg Simmel, a brilliant urban sociologist living in Berlin, observed a version of this social isolation and considered it a defining characteristic of the city. The "urban" is precisely that place where we encounter each other as *strangers*. Urban life, Simmel argued, consists of the most focused instrumental relations with others. We interact with people who sell us things for the purpose of buying, who process things for us in bureaucracies, and who share the same space but do not seek to be our friends. Simmel demonstrated that this characteristic urban life contrasted greatly with rural life. The latter involved people who knew each other intimately, who may have relied on each other for services but often did not demand cash payment, and who had a more multidimensional connection with each other through long-term family and community friendships. For many people in the city, especially newcomers, the relative coldness of urban life was difficult to take.

The airport has taken on the characteristics of Simmel's city to an extreme. It has all the trappings of a thoroughly instrumental space with even less of a need for people to interact. In fact, the airport norm is one of *non-interaction*. People are *expected* to keep to themselves in airports. We celebrate the anticipated transition to the social status of traveler by collapsing into our shell with the typical props of magazine, laptop, or blasé gaze that means for us all, "I'm just killing time." We do not bother others and they are not expected to bother us. When they do, the situation thus created becomes quite uncomfortable. One of the pet peeves of frequent fliers is the encounter with a chatty neighbor.

Simmel, however, also mentioned that urban life has a positive side. Freed from the bounds of traditional society that dictates how we engaged in life, the city enables us to invent a new one. In the role of stranger, we are no longer bound by the social attributions of others. Simply put, in the large, urban environment, I not only can be anyone I want, I can also find the services and social infrastructure to pursue my personal goal of becoming who I want to be. For a person fleeing the farm to pursue a career in the theater many years ago, for example, there was no other place to go but the large city. Generations upon generations of city people have discovered and invented new modes of living by exploiting the freedom of anonymity that urban life offered over the course of history. The city for Simmel was nothing less than the veritable site of civilization. As the airport takes on more of the complex shadings of the city as well as its multifunctional public space, we may pause to wonder if these increasingly visited terminals are not the new generators of our future civilization.

THE AIRPORT AS CITY: URBAN ANONYMITY—INVENTING THE SELF

In March of 1996, I was invited to an urban planning conference in Brazil. The meeting was held at a medium-sized city, São José dos Campos, about a two-hour drive from São Paulo. Knowing one of the hosts, a famous Brazilian urbanist, by sight kept me from having the usual case of jitters accompanying a flight to a foreign country. He told me that he would meet me at the airport just outside the Brazilian Customs office. The São Paulo terminal is always crowded; after clearing Customs, I searched in vain for my host among the throng in the central area. My friend was nowhere to be seen.

I noticed a well-dressed man holding a clipboard in the middle of the crowd. He was surrounded by several professional-looking men holding travel bags and staring into space, waiting. Seeking some connection out of there, I walked over to him, thinking that perhaps my friend could not make it and that this man was one of the organizers.

"Are you with the conference?" I asked.

"Why, yes, I am," he said in perfect English.

"I mean the one in São José dos Campos?" I asked again so that I could be reassured, since Brazil is such a large country.

His face lit up with a big smile. "Exactly!" he exclaimed. The other men waiting with him also agreed. "And what is your name?" he asked.

When I told him, he positioned his clipboard and looked down the list of names. He did this twice and then said, "How do you spell it, again?"

I told him and he went through his ritual one more time. "But, you're not on the list," he said sadly.

I had that sinking feeling. "Maybe there was some mix-up. I'm definitely supposed to be at the conference. In fact, I'm expected to give one of the key speeches."

That seemed to reassure him and he said, "OK. Just wait here with these gentlemen and we will all be leaving soon. I have one more flight to meet." I stood to the side in silence, perplexed but also relieved that I belonged to someone.

Several minutes passed. We all waited, bored out of our minds. Then, in the distance, I saw my Brazilian friend chatting happily and walking with a well-dressed woman, seemingly oblivious to my needs at the time. They were coming down a flight of stairs leading into the central space of the terminal and it was impossible to miss them from my vantage point. I excused myself and walked quickly over to them. After we went over their excuses why they weren't at the Customs exit to meet me and why they were wandering around late, I told them that I had found another group going to the conference and a man who was one of the organizers.

The woman with my friend protested in disbelief. "That's impossible!" she said. "I'm the organizer of the conference."

Now I was confused. I was happy to be united with my true hosts, but I was also curious. Who was the man with the clipboard, we all wondered? What was *their* conference about? We walked back over to the group. My friend spoke to him in Portuguese, then he started to laugh hysterically. So did the man with the clipboard. To my complete surprise, I learned that this same city has a secret military base and they were holding a conference of some kind at the very same time that included military experts from the United States. My hosts could not stop laughing because they pictured me going along with this group as one of the key speakers. I certainly would have been allowed to do so, since I had been accepted by the man with the clipboard who seemed relieved at finding another American expert to join his group, even if my name wasn't on the list.

That day in the São Paulo airport, I assumed a new identity without any effort and quite by accident. Had my friends not appeared, I would have been whisked off with the "other" military experts by the nice man with the clipboard to some high-level military conference. Who knows, I might even have been able to contribute something to the proceedings and thereby embarked on a new career. Certainly it was the quality of transition and anonymity at the airport that gave me this chance at a new life.

Extrapolating from Simmel, airport life—air travel as a mass and commonly experienced part of daily life—may be the enabling milieu for a further extension of urban creativity and innovation, both personal and professional. The new air space in which we increasingly live may just be where the new ideas driving our economy and culture are conceived, where the insightful breakthroughs are first thought, or where the reorienting flashes of brilliance for entire industries or enterprises first spark. The airport is not just an extension of the city, it is a new kind of milieu that is *like* the city. It amplifies the creative energies of society by fostering an extreme form of urban isolation and anonymity as a hiatus from the intensively linked corporate social life on the ground. Within air space, we are free to conduct our lives or to create new ones, to encounter new ideas, or seek out new experiences. Air space is as rich a staging milieu for modern life as is the city. In many respects, it may be replacing the latter as more and more people become frequent fliers. Someone once noted that at any given time, the thickest concentration of brain power in our country is located at O'Hare. What would happen if all these professionals and geniuses linked up together for an hour, instead of killing time while waiting for their respective planes?

5

Eroticism and the Airport

The eroticism of the city is the lesson we can draw from the infinitely meta-phorical nature of the urban discourse. I am using the word in its broadest sense. . . . I would understand the word 'eroticism' as a substitute for the word 'sociality.'

Roland Barthes, 1973

The anonymity of the airport milieu is supercharged with eroticism, with sexual innuendo, and with promise. Every type of person parades before us. We watch the crowd and are stimulated by sexual fantasies. Gazing at strangers in a crowded terminal is an erotic activity. Here too the terminal shares its ambiance with the large city. French semiotician Roland Barthes has written how our gaze in public places entices us through the encounter with others. "The city, essentially and semantically, is the place of our meeting with the *other*, and it is for this reason that the center is the gathering place in every city" (Gottdiener and Lagopoulos 1986, 96). If this observation is true of the city, it is even more so of the large air terminal, which manufactures centrality through its collection spaces for people on the move. This encounter with the crowd transports us to the *imaginary* dimension of sociality, the erotic dimension of our fantasy life.

Traveling alone strips both men and women of their family and work status and frees up identity so that it is pliable and chameleon-like. At the airport, chance encounters take on a logic of their own that resonates with the mode of transition space. We are who we say we are and we have the perfect freedom to speak with anyone who wishes to reciprocate. We can invent a new personal history

38

on the spot. Short-lived, like x-rays or fireworks, these identities need only serve us for as long as we lounge before the boarding call is broadcast.

Everyone has heard the stories of "bathroom sex" in planes. Such scenes have already been depicted in several Hollywood movies. Love with the perfect stranger in flight is known as the "Mile High Club." Because this activity is now a part of our everyday folklore, it must happen frequently enough, yet it remains suspect. More like a symbol of the freedom of air travel and its anonymity, more like a wish for the realization of that very freedom that air travel provides than a common practise, it nevertheless stimulates the imagination. Airplane bathrooms are tight, cramped spaces. Chevy Chase and Beverly D'Angelo had their difficulties in the film *Las Vegas Vacation* negotiating this space in their attempt to live the fantasy. In the throes of passion, Chase steps into the airplane toilet and stains his leg blue, getting soaked in the process. The lore (and lure) of airplane sex reflects a deeper reality of the desire for sexual relations in public with a stranger that is stimulated by the encounter with the crowd—the *other,* in the Barthes sense—on a grand, non-threatening scale.

March 6, 1994. I was on my way to small town in Sweden and was changing planes at the Copenhagen airport. I had a three-hour wait, having just come in on an international flight from the States. Walking through the terminal just to kill time I noticed a gorgeous young woman seated on a bench facing the large plate glass windows overlooking the runway. She must have been about 19 and was tall, blonde, and beautiful. I walked by her seat, getting a closer look, while passing the time waiting for planes. She was absorbed in reading a book and I noticed that it was by Faulkner.

"Here's an opening," I thought. I kept going and walked further down the corridor, but then turned back. When I came up to her bench again, I sat down at the opposite end. She paused from her reading and looked up at me. I smiled. Then I said, "What an intense way to wait for a plane, reading Faulkner."

She laughed and we started a conversation. She was a Swedish college student in America on her way home to Malmö. Our discussion kept going. In fact, she was eager to talk and we became friends.

Because we were both between planes but enjoyed each other's company, our relationship progressed at an accelerated pace. It was almost like watching a filmed romance from beginning to end at fast speed. We met first on the bench. Then we had our first date at the coffee shop. Still liking each other we eventually moved to the cafeteria for food—a second date? A romantic interlude followed. Commitment. Finally, we had to leave on our separate ways. Separation. The whole affair took two hours.

Airport spaces are a free zone for sex. Hookers work the terminal. Happily married businessmen can catch an affair on the road and no one at home is any the wiser; women in business can do the same. It is easy to find topless dance clubs next to airports and the nearby motels do a great business in short-term room rentals. A recent report is typical:

A short distance from the John F. Kennedy airport is a hotel that one regular says is a good place to have an affair. It's a place where flight attendants stay. According to the bartender, at 10:00 attendants from United arrive, at 10:30 Delta, then between 12 and 12:30, the Costa Rican airline, "that's the hot chicks from South America." (Konigsberg 1998)

Is this reporter saying that even some men who are not traveling may actually hang out at the hotel bar and troll for liaisons with attendants? Maybe so. More significant were a commuting businessman's comments about sex while traveling. "I allowed myself to do some twisted stuff, things my wife would definitely not want to know about. Just imagine what it's like to be somewhere where nobody knows you. It's like a parallel universe. And when you're done, you come home as your old self" (Konigsberg 1998).

Airport anonymity can be exploited in the pursuit of successful but very temporary sexual encounters. Air space is a "free area," a place where women and men who like sex with strangers, both male and female, find each other. More importantly, airport sex is an indicator of the freedom from daily life and everyday identity that is characteristic of travel. But even this exploitation of minimal interaction involves a risk. Once we taste such freedom from our everyday constraints, it might be difficult to return to "ordinary" life. According to Cohen and Taylor (1992):

> The "taste of freedom" provided by a prisoner's release on license can very much change how he sees his prison. Visiting a free area, then, involves some risks. There is a slight gamble in these temporary absences from everyday life, even though the return route is clearly mapped out and the excursion is at the most only to the edges of an alternative reality.

The freedom of air travel, then, cuts several ways. Frequent flying can bring bad dreams. The man at the airport bar lamenting the "twisted things" he did while traveling can't really go back home again to the mental state he once had as a family man. That's why he's at the hotel looking for his next liaison. For most people, however, one joy of air travel is the *imagined* dalliance with the "perfect stranger." We feed off the eroticism of the crowd, our voyeur's thirst quenched from hours waiting for the next flight out.

Perhaps the most explicit domain in which the erotic aspects of air travel remains evident is in the air. Early in the history of commercial aviation, women were employed to monitor the cabin passengers. Stewardesses originally were professional nurses, because many fliers got airsickness from the experience. Later, companies converted these airborne angels of mercy to attractive, desirable servers. For decades, stewardesses were forced to remain single in order to keep their jobs. The emphasis was on youth; when they turned thirty years old, their days in the air were numbered. As Petzinger (1995) points out, although they were all dressed professionally, the corporate air carriers hoped to convey a subtle message: by common knowledge of their status as single women, any male on board could try to get lucky.

Eventually, during the heated days of competition in the 1970s and just before the advent of deregulation, the innuendo associated with the status of stewardess burst forth in its full sexuality. Carriers broadcast ads that deliberately exploited the theme of sex. The now defunct National Airlines ran television ads in the 1970s that featured a beautiful woman as a stewardess saying, "Hi! I'm Debbie. Fly me." Other airlines featured a modified striptease as attendants who started flights fully dressed would systematically shed their jackets, scarves, and other apparel until they were down to bare basics that were still legal—a blouse and skirt. Some airlines even went further by dressing their attendants in mini-skirts (Petzinger 1995). To this day, the sexual elements of the flight attendant/ air passenger relation remain despite the stress of overcrowded flights and declining service quality that characterizes air travel at the beginning of the twenty-first century.

6

Boredom, Delays, Cancellations

Air travelers find that killing time can be a terminal challenge.

Brenda Alesii, 1995

A LONG STAY IN DENVER

March 9, 1994

My plane was 15 minutes late coming in from Chicago. It was to do a turnaround at the Los Angeles airport (LAX), where I would board it, and then scoot back out to Denver where I was to get a connecting flight to the East Coast. My itinerary gave me 45 minutes to meet the connecting flight at the old Stapleton Airport in Denver, 15 more minutes than the standard half-hour allocated for connections by travel agents. Making the switch, of course, depended on departing LAX on schedule. Now my lead time was cut to a bare half-hour as I waited in the terminal.

Finally, we were allowed to board the plane in Los Angeles. Precious seconds and minutes ticked by as the flight crew secured the passengers. Although we were ready to leave, we didn't move. We sat there for 15 more minutes while I agonized over the distinct possibility that I was going to miss my connecting flight in Denver. Apparently, there is a sensor on the outside of the plane that indicates when stormy (humid) weather is ahead. It's a small dome with a hole in it that

42

must be covered by tape to work properly. After an eternity of waiting, the pilot announced that the tape over the weather sensor was missing and they had to have a mechanic replace it. Ordinary tape and an ordinary, simple job, but regulations required that a certified mechanic make the repair. We sat there on the runway for over an hour before a certified mechanic could be found who would repair the sensor. Doing nothing on the plane, mixed together with the knowledge that I would now miss my flight in Denver, was agonizing. Already strapped on the plane, I had nowhere to go but to reflect on my own tragic flight schedule.

So now I sit in transit in the Denver airport, having missed my flight and with a long wait to my next connection. Neither at home, nor at my destination; in between and nowhere. I'm hungry and pissed off. The super-expensive, extra-fatty airport food means self-destruction. The bad feelings have to go somewhere, so I take them out on myself and order a self-destructive meal—a hamburger with French fries—but have enough sense to decline the offer of cheese.

As I sit eating my meal with three more hours to kill before the next available flight, a sense of things having gone wrong overwhelms me. I had been told that the airline would book me on the next plane out, but even so that meant an inter-minable wait of over four hours in the Denver airport. I know that this delay is but a temporary inconvenience and that soon I shall be where I want to go, left with only a vague memory of frustration and anger to mark the event. But still, I cannot seem to shake the negative emotions in my current limbo state, sitting in the greasy, fatty, smoky, and overpriced Frontier food shop.

When you use an airport just to change planes, you don't care where the transfer is done, provided it goes as planned. I tried to avoid traveling through Chicago because O'Hare is almost always hit by bad weather in the winter. But who wanted to be stuck in Denver?

The number of delayed and/or canceled flights has reached excessive levels, especially during the busy summer months of 1999 and 2000. (AP photo/Nick Ut)

I wrote the above lines while sitting in the restaurant one hour into a four-hour wait at the Denver airport. At the time, I had no idea what would happen next. I simply assumed that taking out my pad and pen and expressing my feelings would be a healthy way to spend the time. I did not know just how bizarre a turn events could take.

I finished eating and decided to walk around the airport just to get some exercise. I was still plenty pissed off. About a half-hour after eating I noticed that my stomach was on fire. I had tried to avoid all coffee and alcoholic beverages during the long day in order not to get stressed out, but I made the error of buying a bottle of lemonade to go with my food. Bad enough that I ate an airport hamburger when I never eat hamburgers or steaks at home. The combination of red, fatty meat and hyperacidic lemonade was wreaking havoc on my suddenly tender stomach. I went over to a snack bar and thought that perhaps if I drank some milk, it would calm things down. I still had two and a half hours to go before my flight left.

When I sat down to drink the milk, I noticed that my heart was beating unusually fast. It was pounding in my chest. I couldn't help but notice it, so I took my pulse. It was a steady 120 beats a minute, about the same pace as when I did mild exercise, except that I was sitting down. I drank the milk but my pulse rate remained constant at 120. *This is odd*, I thought.

My stomach felt about the same. A little less fire after the milk, perhaps, but I still had a bloated, upset sensation. I decided to walk over to my gate. Two hours left to go. I sat down near the entrance. I noticed several people from my California flight. I took my pulse again. It was 120. No change. A half hour later, while I had been sitting down all the time, my pulse was still 120. I felt like gasping for air, yet I was not quite out of breath. It was a strange sensation. My pulse had been racing now for over an hour and I attributed the rapid heartbeat to the stress of my layover since I hadn't had coffee all day.

Eventually, the hours went by and my plane was being boarded. My pulse remained at a steady 120 beats a minute. I hadn't begun to feel any worse than I had several hours earlier. When my row was called, I got on the plane. After a while, the stream of passengers stopped parading by and the flight attendant had secured us all in seats. I could feel my heart beating rapidly. We were ready to go. The flight was crowded and there were two people sitting in my row, all of us cramped and uncomfortable. Everything would sort itself out, I thought, once we took off and my long ordeal would begin to near its end. Then the pilot made an announcement: due to delays with other aircraft because of the weather, there were several people who were assigned to take this flight but who had not yet arrived. The pilot told us that he was instructed to delay takeoff in order to accommodate the missing passengers. A loud, collective groan could be heard up and down the cabin. I began to become very ill and I dreaded thinking about my pulse rate, which had surely increased.

Oh, no! I thought in horror, *not another delay!* I felt angry again. It was too stuffy in that seat and the air conditioning was hardly working. I felt nauseous and my heart was beating faster and louder. The last passengers finally arrived and the flight attendant closed the door. The plane lurched backward as it left the gate and I felt worse. I got up and rushed to the front where a flight attendant was standing in the galley. I told her that I was having a very rapid heartbeat.

She looked alarmed and banged on the pilot's cabin door. The door opened and she told the flight officer that she had a passenger with chest pains.

I immediately told her that I was not having any chest pains. "I feel nauseous," I said. She told me to sit down right there on her jump seat.

The pilot said, "Oh, shit!" and returned the jet to the gangway.

Another flight attendant came by. She also asked me if I was having chest pains. I said no.

She asked me if I had carry-on belongings.

I said yes and described them to her. A few seconds later, she came back with them. The plane stopped and they opened the door. I walked out, dizzy and weak, assisted by one of the flight crew.

The woman who met the plane took me to the service desk at the airport gate, where I sat down. After she called for a paramedic, she asked to see my baggage claim check and radioed to have the bag removed from the plane. She looked very concerned and she asked me if I had any chest pains.

I said no.

The paramedic arrived. He asked me if I had any chest pains.

At this point, I was getting rather tired of being asked about chest pains. I said, "No." I told him I was having a rapid pulse and that my stomach was upset. He took my pulse and it was still 120—no surprise to me! My stomach felt awful and I wanted to vomit because I felt bloated and on fire, but not nauseous any longer. The paramedic said that he would take me to a quiet lounge area where he would hook up a cardiogram monitor. I got on his scooter and we went a few feet into the Red Carpet lounge area reserved for United members.

I sat down and he placed an oxygen tube under my nose. I felt better almost immediately. He hooked me up to his portable cardiac monitoring unit; my pulse was still 120 and my blood pressure was 140 over 90. *That's about what it is when I exercise*, I thought.

An airline employee showed up with my bag. She started asking me routine questions and I answered them as best I could. I told her all about how I missed my flight because my plane got in late and how I had to wait over four hours in this stinking, awful airport. She seemed very concerned. I asked the paramedic if I could get unhooked so that I could go to the bathroom and try to vomit. I told him that I had the kind of feeling that you have when you feel awful and, if you could only vomit out your stomach contents, you would instantly feel better. He let me go to the bathroom. I stood over the toilet bowl and stuck my fingers down my throat, but try as I might, nothing happened. My pulse was still racing.

I returned to my seat and the paramedic hooked me up again. He said that I should go to the hospital and get checked out. I told him that I didn't have any chest pains. He said that I had been sitting down for a long time but my pulse rate was not normal. He made this observation in a way that was calculated not to alarm. Because I didn't have any chest pains, I wasn't worried; however, I certainly didn't feel well. The problem seemed to be my stomach, not my heart, and I told him so. I asked him if he thought that the rapid pulse was dangerous or cause for going to the hospital. I did not want to go to the hospital, I wanted to get on another flight to my destination. The paramedic persisted in choosing his words very carefully. He repeated that my pulse rate was not normal so I shouldn't fly and, instead, I should be checked out at the hospital. I remembered thinking that breathing the oxygen was certainly clearing my head. Slowly, I thought, I would get better but I wondered why my pulse rate remained elevated.

The airline representative came over again. She gave me the very bad news that there were no flights that evening to my destination, but she added that I could catch the first flight out the following morning. She said this to me hopefully, with a smile. The paramedic said that, in that case, I should definitely go to the emergency room and be checked out. He seemed worried, or rather, he was worried but tried to hide his concern.

The airline representative said, "You might as well do what he recommends—you have to stay overnight anyway." She went back to her desk to make arrangements for me.

I explained to the paramedic that I thought I would be all right and that I didn't know why my pulse was so high. The United Airlines representative came back. She said that she had made a reservation for me on the first flight out the following morning. She also said that she was giving me a voucher for one night at a motel near the airport and another voucher for one cab ride from the hospital. She reminded me that I should call her after the hospital, if they let me go, so she would know how things went and whether they would keep me overnight. I was overwhelmed by her concern and grateful to the airline for taking care of me, despite the chaos of my trip.

I turned to the paramedic and said, "OK, I'll go to the hospital." He was very relieved when he took out his walkie-talkie and asked for an ambulance. A little while later, a porter showed up with a wheelchair accompanied by an airport security guard. I felt silly as they wheeled me past the crowds and across the terminal, down an elevator, and outside where the ambulance was waiting.

At the hospital I was wheeled into the emergency room. The place looked hi-tech, modern. The room had several beds, each separated by a curtain that could be pulled closed. I laid down on the bed and two hospital technicians hooked me up to the cardiac monitoring machine and oxygen. Later, an orderly came by to take some blood. I asked if that was necessary and he looked at me like I was crazy.

The orderly left and it was quiet in the room. A woman from the admissions office came by to ask whether or not I had health insurance. When she was reassured that I did and that I was employed, she looked relieved. She asked me a lot of questions again about what happened. As I told my story intently, filling in all the details, she gave that knowing kind of smile that accompanies *full understanding*. I had gotten up to the part in the narrative where I was taken off the plane and sequestered in United's Red Carpet lounge, when she couldn't contain herself any longer.

"Oh, it's the altitude!" she blurted out. "That kind of thing happens all the time at the airport." Then she added, "Don't worry."

I dropped out of my reverie and stopped the retelling of my saga. I said, "What happens all the time?" I asked. I was both confused and astounded.

"Oh, people are always getting dizzy and nauseous at the airport. It's because of the altitude. You came from sea level and had a four-hour wait. Some people can't adjust to the altitude. Usually everyone passing through here to change planes waits for too short a time to notice the effects." As an afterthought, she added, "Don't worry. It's just the long wait."

I was astounded. *This horrible ordeal was all because of the altitude*, I thought. *Why didn't anyone at the Denver airport say anything? Why did they keep acting like it was a heart attack? Why didn't they just give me the oxygen sooner? No wonder I felt better once they gave me oxygen.* The paramedic was just acting cautiously in order to protect my life. But were they also covering up if they had seen that kind of thing before, as the girl suggested? Was this the dirty little secret of the Denver Stapleton airport? No oxygen?

After well over an hour, a young doctor appeared. He identified himself as a resident and started to examine me. My pulse rate was now reduced and, with the steady supply of oxygen, I was feeling much, much better. He said that I was probably all right, but that he had to make sure. My cardiac output from the machine had been examined by the cardiologist and I was OK.

I told this doctor that the receptionist had said my problem was the altitude, because I was stuck at the airport for four hours. I told him that my problem was probably a combination of bad food, stress, and the altitude, and that I wanted to get out of the hospital fast, because I was now feeling fine. He said that the altitude could very well have been a factor in the high pulse rate. He said that people who live regularly at higher elevations have bodies that adjust to the altitude by having more red blood cells. Without them, the heart has to work harder to supply the body with oxygen. When you travel quickly from sea level to a high altitude, your body adjusts by having a more rapid heart rate. For just about everyone at the airport, it is a temporary situation. Then the doctor discharged me into the Denver night.

BOREDOM

Boredom is the bane of air travel. When mixed with stress—indeed it is a part of the stress of flying—it makes for a deadly combination. The closest many people come to hell on earth is when their plane is poised on the runway waiting to become airborne, and the pilot announces a control tower delay on the runway—stress and boredom in their most deadly forms. Boredom is perhaps the main reason that passengers put up with awful airline food. At the terminal we surround ourselves with diversions. People bring laptops, Walkmen, Palm Pilots, cell phones, and other toys to play with while seated in departure lounges. They fill their arms with magazines and newspapers. We see bored fliers at the terminal, lost in the daze of killing time, blank-stare-eating pizza slices or donuts or frozen custard. Watching others waiting makes us bored as well.

Air terminals reek with the tedium of killing time. There may be lucky occasions when passengers break the mold and make noise, exhibit some emotion, or act in some other demonstrative way that provides us with a human spectacle, countering that stultifying atmosphere of just waiting for something to happen. According to one newspaper account (Alesii 1996), seasoned travelers consciously attack *time busting*. They organize their work so that they can do it at the terminal. "People-watching" is also rated highly as a time-killer. Most of us, however, are merely victims. We watch and wait.

Having to deal with killing time, with being bored, is one of the most stressful aspects of modern life. Caught in a seemingly interminable traffic jam is very much like being delayed at the airport waiting for hours to connect with a flight, and commuters often sit in traffic jams everyday. Something about the boredom of the air travel experience, however, makes it more stressful. My experience in Denver illustrates one of the major differences. When traveling by air, we are often blindsided by the *unexpected*. Sticking to schedule is the very essence of com-

Passengers dutifully waiting for their flight kill time as best they can.
(AP photo/Daniel Hulshizer)

mercial aviation, because companies need to cycle their fixed number of planes and crews in and out of airports on a routine basis. No doubt, unforeseen disruptions of that minute-by-minute schedule are as traumatic for the airlines as for the passengers.

Normal flight experiences require people to cope with boredom; ordinarily the stressful nature of killing time is kept manageable by toys like cell phones and diversions. When boring situations arise unexpectedly, however, they are most stressful. We arrive for a trip at an airport understanding that we will have a certain wait at a distant terminal, if we are connecting to another flight. Unexpected cancellations or delays that wreck this anticipated reality play havoc with our ability to cope precisely because they surprise us. At these times, the ordinary mechanisms we use to combat boredom, such as reading a magazine or listening to music on a cassette player, don't work because they require a certain degree of calmness. How can we remain serene when we are made angry by some airline event that disrupts our schedule?

The present-day structure of air travel makes maximum use of hubs and spokes. For the average traveler, this means that we must change planes en route at least once before we reach our final destination. When flights are canceled or delayed, travel itineraries are wrecked and we are left stranded or inconvenienced by alternative flight arrangements. Yet all passengers should be aware that any trip schedule is open to the unexpected, unanticipated probability that something might monkey-wrench the timing of takeoffs or the linking to connecting flights. As one observer notes:

> Airlines do not guarantee their schedules. They try to adhere to published schedules because it is less trouble than retooling frustrated passengers. But weather, air traffic, mechanical difficulties, rules governing crew hours and hundreds of other causes, including human error, can upset schedules. The government exercises only a few regulations over passenger service . . . and there are no federal requirements on how passengers on canceled flights are to be treated. (Wade 2000, 4)

With the pressures produced by an increasingly taxed system, airlines have adopted the practice of canceling flights rather than delaying them. In this way, equipment can be shuttled to more expedient needs and, if a decision is made in a timely manner, passengers can be notified at home that other flight arrangements have been made. Betsy Wade (2000, 4) recommends the following to air travelers who seek to minimize the ill effects of unforeseen cancellations. It is best to confirm a flight just before driving to the airport. Passengers flying to events that are very important, such as weddings or job interviews, should consider traveling a day earlier, especially when flying during seasons of possible weather delays. Finally, she also recommends that passengers travel light and with carry-on luggage so that they can take advantage of alternative arrangements quickly.

Another reporter, Bob Tedeschi, makes a critical observation that tempers Wade's advice. If you call an airline, it is not always possible to get through. "All too often, though, the phone call devolves into a ten-minute holding pattern of its own, accompanied by music that wouldn't otherwise find its way near your eardrums" (Tedeschi 2000, 24). He suggests that, in these circumstances, the Internet and its airline websites may prove a more reliable alternative for getting up-to-the-minute information on flights. In short, before leaving the house, log on.

Finally, I can also recommend, based on experiences such as the one in Denver, that it is worthwhile learning how to cope with stress, anger, and boredom before becoming an airline passenger. Meditation and various other mechanisms for coping with the unexpected are essential skills when flying today.

Even the most heroic efforts dealing with delayed flights and boredom pale to insignificance next to the trauma of an extended, unexpected layover when trying to make an airline connection. Consider the following ordeal:

SNOWSTORM IN DETROIT

On January 2, 1999, a thick snowstorm suddenly struck the Detroit area. The blizzard dumped almost a foot of snow in a few minutes. Halfway into a busy day, the airport had to be shut down. We often hear news of airports being closed or flights canceled due to winter weather, but only rarely do we get to understand what those kinds of unforeseen delays really mean. They have to be experienced firsthand. One of the outcomes of that particular storm was that people who had landed and had to change planes in Detroit were now stranded in Detroit when the airport closed. The comparatively lucky ones, those who had already disembarked from their planes, were stuck in a snowstorm limbo at the terminal. The ones consigned to a greater hell were those whose planes had arrived just before the shutdown. Their planes could not get access to unloading gates because the jets that had already landed couldn't leave the terminal. Consequently, the last planes to arrive before the shutdown were stranded on the runway or in the taxiing areas. Those passengers had to face eight to ten hours on their jets without relief. Their agony seems unimaginable.

A friend of mine was caught in this horror show. He spent about 30 hours in the Detroit terminal and I was curious to know how he managed. He was flying with his two boys on a ski vacation from Buffalo to Aspen. They had to change planes at Detroit since it was a Northwest Airlines hub. Leaving Buffalo that Saturday morning, the sky was overcast but no snow was in sight. On the way, they flew into the storm that was now ravaging the entire Midwest, drawing up moisture from the Gulf of Mexico. Arriving in Detroit just before noon, they flew into the snow and the driving winds. It took them over one hour just to taxi in safely to the gate where they disembarked. He was lucky that there was an open gate for the jet. By the time he got off the plane, he had already missed the connecting flight to Aspen. At the time, my friend was pissed off because the airline didn't hold the flight for the late-arriving passengers. He knew that carriers couldn't keep delaying takeoffs to accommodate all passengers, because they would never get off the ground; what he didn't know at the time was that his connecting flight had never taken off. Instead, it had gone to the de-icing area but then had to remain there because traffic across the middle section of the country was shutting down due to the storm. My friend was one of the lucky ones, so to speak.

I asked my friend to tell me the saga of spending all those boring hours inside the terminal. He said that at the beginning he and his sons were upbeat. It was 1:00 P.M. when they got off their plane, and the airline booked him on a flight at 7:00 later that day. He headed over to a sitting area because he noticed that the airport TV channel was broadcasting a Buffalo Bills playoff game. For the next few hours, he enjoyed watching along with his sons and other stranded Buffalonians, even though their team lost. Around 3:00 other flights began to be canceled. Then full paralysis set in as a major national hub, O'Hare, was shut down. Other airports, such as St. Louis and Minneapolis, Northwest's main hub, closed too.

They were still slated to depart at 7:00 that evening. But, curiously, no announcements for boarding calls were being made at the gates. By 5:00 huge lines were forming as more and more people became stranded when places like O'Hare closed. When a major hub shuts down, it backs up the entire national system. When Chicago closes due to a storm, that's really bad news for all travelers. My friend remained optimistic. Around 5:00 he took his boys to dinner. There still wasn't a mad rush for food and they were able to find seats in the terminal cafeteria.

While they ate they watched the chaos forming around them. More and more people were packed into the airport. No announcements about the status of the flights were being made. This worried my friend, who got up several times to check with airline personnel. Every time he spoke to someone, he got a different answer. Such varied responses were particularly disconcerting at the time.

Crowds of passengers milled about the terminal by 7:00 that evening and my friend's flight had not yet been announced. There were now huge lines of horribly frustrated travelers clustered around the check-in counters. "There were thousands of people simply trying to get answers about their flights and hundreds of airline personnel trying to give answers that they obviously didn't have," he later told me. Just after 7:00 P.M., when my friend and his two sons had expected to be flying out, they announced that the airport had officially closed for the night. Airline personnel quickly disappeared and the frantic question-and-answer sessions were now over.

My friend's first thought was to get out of the terminal to lodging near the airport. He made his way to ground transportation only to find that there was none. Because the roads had closed, there was no public transportation to or from the airport. He couldn't go anywhere. The disappointed family returned to the crush of humanity in the terminal. My friend estimates that there must have been upwards of 10,000 travelers stuck inside.

By that evening the bathrooms became overtaxed. Maintenance crews were not working. Barely enough floor space was available to accommodate all the hapless "guests." Some airline personnel were still manning the ticket counters, so most people spent the next few hours rebooking flights for the following day. My friend spent his time trying to get information after he made his rebooking. "You could go to the check-in counter or back out to the main terminal. Depending on where you went and who you talked to, you got different answers." The best he could do was to get a flight for 7:00 P.M. the following evening, and because it was a confirmed reservation, he took it. Aside from meaning that he would have to spend the entire next day at the terminal, he would lose another day of his vacation in transit.

At about this time, he noticed that the airline personnel had boarded all the jets that were parked at the terminal and emptied them of their blankets and pillows. These were now stacked up on the check-in counters along with cans of soda and snacks for anyone who cared to take them. Then my friend noticed the first unpleasant act by authorities. For some reason they turned all the TV sets off. It was barely 8:00 in the evening. People were left to their own devices with literally nothing to do. He noticed lots of people milling around, but wherever he went he could not escape the crowd stuffed inside the terminal.

At around 11:00 P.M., the terminal authorities dimmed the lights, but it was hardly any easier to sleep. There was barely enough room for everyone to stretch out on the floor and there was also the nagging thought that someone would walk too near, if not on top of you. In order to pass the time, my friend settled on a routine at the terminal that consisted of four basic activities—walking, talking, eating, and working on airline reservations in order to get out of there as soon as he could. Most people talked with each other as a pleasant way to pass the time. Surprisingly, the fast-food places did not run out of food, although some items on the menu were no longer available. The same was true of the restaurant. It continued to serve meals, although it also ran out of some items. As the night wore on, fewer and fewer airline personnel could be found. Somehow they all managed to disappear. The bathrooms simply got worse and worse and by the middle of the night, they were unusable by the squeamish.

Too uncomfortable to sleep, my friend talked the night away with his two sons. At around 3:00 A.M., he was too uncomfortable to lie on the floor so he got up and walked the entire length and breadth of the airport just to keep busy. Air carrier monitors flickered in the semi-darkness and kept him company. It was then that he heard the sound of jets leaving the facility. Eventually he was able to form an impression, which he still believes is accurate, that this activity emanated from the commercial side of the airfield. Cargo was flying. Companies like UPS were probably functional once the snowstorm cleared.

He heard several rumors in the early morning hours. People had no real information but one person told him that the airport wasn't going to open until 4:00 P.M. the next day. Someone else, less optimistic, said that the airport was closed for several days. He heard many different times and several different stories during his walk among the thousands crammed in the facility that night. This was a different kind of purgatory.

Early in the morning, when dawn was breaking and the sky outside began to lighten, he noticed that the storm was gone. He went back to his sons anticipating the imminent return of the airline personnel. Soon, he thought, the airport would be revving back into gear. Around 8:00 in the morning he noticed that a new time was posted for his flight out to Aspen. It said departure at noon. Unfortunately, there were no personnel around to confirm the good news. Nevertheless he made his way to the check-in counter at the posted gate to wait. He was not the first one there—two other people were already waiting in line. The minutes and hours went by while they talked and still no airport personnel appeared. The line became longer. About a half hour before their flight was to take off, an airline representative showed up and opened the check-in facility. My friend was able to confirm his booking on the flight, although he was also informed that there was now a departure delay. He and his sons got their things in order and entered what they hoped was the final phase of waiting.

My friend dared not leave the gate area while he waited for the boarding call. They stood there a few hours more, making a total of roughly six hours standing around waiting directly for this particular flight. They were informed that the plane was ready to go except that the airline had no pilot. During the delay, the airline had hoped to make up the necessary personnel and take off. Finally, at 4:00 P.M. on Sunday, they boarded the flight for Aspen and took off. It had been 27 hours since they had landed in Detroit the previous day.

Perhaps surprisingly, my friend was not particularly disturbed by this experience, even though it shortened his vacation. As a seasoned air traveler, he knew that delays due to weather are common in the winter and have to be tolerated. The airport time was spent with his two sons and that helped him to pass the time. Finally, he also mentioned that other people that night had a worse experience— the thousands who were left stranded for many hours *inside* the airplanes at Detroit and who couldn't get out into the terminal. In fact, he saw one woman freak out getting to the gate following a seven-hour wait in her jet. She was being led away in handcuffs because she assaulted a flight attendant in anger. Other confined passengers threatened lawsuits. My friend was thankful that he left the next day. People who managed to leave the airport the previous evening for hotels nearby couldn't get back to the terminal in time during the day and missed the afternoon flights. Then the bad weather hit again, and once more, evening flights were canceled. For some passengers, their ordeal lasted yet another day.

My friend did have some negative remarks. He felt that the terminal facility was ill-prepared for a big storm. The grounds crew and those responsible for clearing the roads did not get back to work early enough, he thought. It was just his impression but he felt that once the storm ended, the airlines could have gone back into operation at least by getting flights already in Detroit on their way. He felt that information was handled poorly. The airlines didn't have any uniform knowledge of flight status. Most of the people spent their time trying to get information about their flights and they had little luck. The chaos characterizing the terminal that night was a result of both dissonant information and a lack of information.

The winter of 1998–99 may well be known in the future as a turning point in air regulation. January's nightmare in Detroit was not the only traumatic event. I was also caught later in the year, on March 7, in a smaller-scale version of the same thing. I had been visiting the Boston area and was returning to my home outside Buffalo. That Saturday, the Boston area was hit by a heavy snowstorm that blew in from the west. Sometime during the night or early morning hours of Sunday the snowfall turned intermittent. I woke up on Sunday, the day of my expected departure, to clear and sunny skies. There was less than a foot of accumulation on the streets and, as the air warmed up, it seemed to me that the city's transportation networks returned to normal. Cars, trolleys, and taxis all whizzed by as I went for a morning walk.

Arriving at Logan International Airport, however, a different story prevailed. I had made my first mistake as an air traveler in winter. I assumed that simply because snowfall was relatively light and the sun had now been shining steadily for hours and hours, whatever adjustments air carriers and terminals made were probably implemented by the afternoon, and that my plane and indeed the entire schedule of the airline would be functioning normally. This was a very stupid assumption, indeed. From that day on I vowed to always *always* check with the airlines when there is bad weather in the winter *prior* to checking out of my hotel. If phone lines are jammed, it is even possible to get information from websites.

I entered the terminal at 3:00 P.M. for a 4:30 P.M. flight, only to be greeted by a scene of chaos. Flights had been canceled and hundreds of people were set free to roam around the airport making whatever arrangements they could. Most of the stranded passengers had formed a line in front of the carrier's check-in counters that snaked around the barriers and out into the main passenger concourse extending off to the horizon. I could not see its end.

At about this time, a second aspect of the "being stranded" experience occurred. As any other passenger stuck in the same situation, I needed information. My flight was canceled, so what should I do? I assumed that all the people who had chosen to wait in line were stuck there because of the cancellation of their flights and that the appropriate thing to do was join them. I would probably get the information I wanted by eventually making my way to the counter and also get a rebooking on the next available flight. Instead, I decided to approach the counter directly just to obtain information. My friend had told me that in Detroit the air carrier's personnel had performed with less than distinction in this matter. Information was hard to come by and employees were not always helpful or forthcoming when quizzed. This time, however, the experience with my carrier at Logan was different. A friendly woman who was walking behind all the computer terminal personnel stopped to help me. When I told her my flight was canceled, she mentioned that my best bet was to ignore the line and instead go directly to the phones, call the airline, and rebook that way.

I followed her advice and she was correct. More importantly, this helpful employee saved me hours of waiting in line in a true mob scene, even if she could do nothing about my stranded status and the eventual long wait for a flight out. So, another tip is the one she gave me, call the airlines to rebook rather than wait in line. In fact, had I made that same phone call from the hotel and checked my flight because of the bad weather, I probably would not only have been told about the delays but would have been rebooked all at once. I could have spent the hours waiting not in the terminal but in the relative comfort of the hotel.

Waiting at airports has its own mental mechanism that may make the time pass somewhat easily. People in airports are filled with the expectation of flight. If they are delayed, they think ahead to their final destination. There is plenty of time to imagine being on the plane and continuing the trip. By this device, people confined to the terminal have some distance from their experience. They can tolerate being there because they are not really there, they are only in transition.

A second means of passing the time derives from the social situation. If you are traveling with others, delays are often quality family time. Even if you are alone, you can participate in the temporary communion of fellow travelers by talking the night away. It can even be fun, at least for a while. The large crowd of fellow sufferers can be comforting. If you are experiencing some hard luck, at least there are plenty of others who share it. How different, then, are these circumstances to, for example, being stuck in a horrible Los Angeles traffic jam, where you sit alone in a car, eating every single atom of stress and having to take it without relief? Different too is terminal waiting when compared to the unfortunate souls who were caught inside their jets on the runway, with literally no place to go for eight hours. Airplane seats and the airplane environment are uncomfortable enough when you are flying. The passengers who suffered the most, almost beyond comprehension, were those who remained out on the tarmac, in their planes, with toilets overflowing and no food or water until a gate opened to receive them. The eight-hour wait that many of them had inside the plane that day in January 1999 was the one outrage that, more than any other, spurred on Congress to consider the "Airline Passengers Bill of Rights."

Personal histories demonstrate the negative aspects of the air travel business. First, carriers are overextended and they operate by maximizing their national service with the bare minimum of equipment. They have neither extra pilots nor planes to spare. When one or more planes in this complex schedule are delayed at some airport in the country, many flights that also depend on that same equipment have to be canceled immediately. The same is true for mechanical problems and/or crew problems, which also cause flight delays and cancellations. Western New York, an area that has been marginalized with poor airline service, is an example of another aspect to the "on-the-edge" way air carriers operate today. When problems do arise, they immediately cancel service to marginalized cities such as Buffalo and use their equipment for their more lucrative routes. In short, whether the snowflakes are falling thick or thin, delays on other routes usually mean that passengers going to Buffalo, Rochester, Syracuse, or Albany are simply screwed. Travel during the winter means putting up with overextended airlines. It means delays and/or cancellations even if the snowfall is not heavy. In fact, one strongly suspects that the snow is merely an excuse to cancel flights due to delays.

A second factor that apparently operates to aggravate a passenger's ordeal is that terminal authorities seem to be incompetent. When snow hits, some of these places, like airports at Detroit or Boston, can't clear the fields so that operations can resume in a timely manner. After experiencing a snowfall of a few inches during the night and early morning, the authorities at Logan Airport in Boston could not return the field to full operation by the following afternoon. At one point, a pilot announced over the intercom that the airport had been using only one runway all day. Planes taking off have to be coordinated with flights coming in. Similar situations, such as that outlined previously in Detroit, had even poorer maintenance. How incompetent can the airport management be in organizing snow removal and runway maintenance? Ultimately, it is this failure to return airfields back to full operation after bad winter weather that paralyzes the entire carrier's system and creates cancellations and the inconvenience of tedious, long terminal waits.

As the list of complaints lengthened from the fallout of that fateful winter of 1998–99, public inquiries were held and bills were introduced in Congress that are still being debated.

Part 2

Nowhere Architecture

7

Place and Placelessness

As airports become cyberized and malled up, the downtown cities they serve become increasingly redundant to the business traveler. Travel will be reduced to an essence of inoffensive white space: the airport, the airplane, the airport, the airplane, the airport again.

Richard Rayner, 1998

The travelers' environment is interpenetrated by global connections and commercial modes of marketing from companies around the world. Among the characteristics of this cultural implosion is the phenomenon of world-scale franchising, which leads to ubiquitous marketing of name brands. Global franchising and mass media marketing now structure what people from every society consider to be a normative purchase to satisfy a particular need. This is especially true for consumer items such as video players, computers, cameras, clothing, packaged vacations, watches, scarves, household appliances, and sports equipment, as well as fast food. These ubiquitous commodities increasingly comprise the content of our emergent global consumer culture.

The air traveler moves through an environment containing this consumer global culture comprised of franchised stores, rental cars, commodities, and services that seem the same just about everywhere. Architect Rem Koolhaas calls this milieu "nowhere architecture." "Anyone can visit Benetton anywhere on Earth; in Slovenia you can rent a Daewoo from Hertz," says Koolhaas. "It's not necessary to buy presents when traveling because the same things are for sale everywhere" (Copeland 1994). In addition, you can buy a McDonald's hamburger in

Orange County, California, or Madrid, Spain, or Tokyo, Japan, and experience the very same kind of built environment in all three places.

Much earlier than the recent spate of writings celebrating our mobile society, the geographer Edward Relph (1984) wrote about the proliferation of new spatial forms, characterizing them in terms of "place and placelessness." By this he meant that, on the one hand, the architectural reworking of commercial spaces has produced a host of environments that are familiar everywhere, like the franchised stores discussed above. These locations are endowed with *placelessness*. On the other hand, everyday life has provided particular locations with distinctive characteristics that are relatively unique. These locations represent the quality of *place*—they possess a sense of place.

Relph's "placelessness" and Koolhaas's "nowhere architecture" are both experienced at airports and through air travel. At the terminal, we recognize brands of food and coffee franchised in our own neighborhoods. Airport mall shops sell merchandise that is all very familiar from countless hours of watching television and exposure to forms of mass media advertising. Flying has become routine. Frequent travel makes the journey 35,000 feet high a blasé experience. We know about safety measures, airline food, entertainment options, and, absent the unexpected, how to pass the time. On arrival, even to an unknown foreign country, we know that we need to negotiate the terminal space and make our way to ground transportation before reaching our hotel. In short, air travel has not only become commonplace through experience, but is now a part of our emerging global culture, structured by mass advertising, franchising, and the Internet. Air travel may be the very symbol of that worldwide culture.

However, Relph was wrong to create a dichotomy between place and placelessness because there are always elements of both in any milieu. Every good building must foster a sense of place even if it is designed to do other things as

That venerable institution, the airport bar, provides people with a sense of place because bars are a familiar part of sociality in daily life.

well. Every location contains within it spatial markers and a cultural style that make it a definitive location, a material realm within which people interact, linger, and live. Airports are a new kind of space that provides portals to the realms of both place *and* placelessness. The best airports are designed, not as minimalist structures or "nowhere architecture," but as distinct spaces that allow people to enjoy, relax, and interact within an environment that captures the imaginative realm of flight.

The airport is a new kind of space, a new kind of experience, and a remodeling of some very old aspects of the built environment. New terminal designs make them so interesting and attractive that they have become places in their own right, even if they are principally meant as transition spaces for the new "vectored" social practices. While terminals, for instance, are exemplars of the new environments housing people on the move, many passengers actually spend more time within airport facilities per trip than they do at the bank or even the supermarket. We just don't think of them that way.

8

Airport Architecture: Creating a Sense of Place

The airport is a hybrid kind of space, one for which there are next to no conceptual frameworks.

Deyan Sudjic, 1992

The white peaks of the Jeppesen Terminal, visible from several miles away, are reminiscent of the Rocky Mountains.

Visitors Guide to Denver International Airport, 1996

The first airports in the United States were constructed in the 1920s and the first terminals in the 1930s (Savona 1992). In the construction of the first-generation terminals, a comparatively simple design without gates was used to allow direct access to planes. Second-generation terminals, which were built in the 1950s, had to accommodate the introduction of gates due to the increasing demand for air travel. By the 1960s and 1970s, further expansion of traffic demand created the third generation of terminals with the introduction of newer, bigger jets. Now the form of the airport, this fourth generation, continues to evolve with new mega-projects in places like the United States, England, and Japan.

Despite obvious, compelling functional needs, air terminal design from the early 1950s to the present incorporated symbolic elements. Architects built airports using symbols that produced a themed environment no matter how minimally these associations were drawn. These symbolic considerations also changed over time, adding a distinctive overlay to the purely functional alterations of the airport terminal. At first, designers stressed the central terminal building and its ticketing facilities in their schemes. Most commonly, they chose a theme that recalled the waiting rooms of the great railroad passenger terminals of the past.

Early airport buildings were conceived as an extension of the 19th-century transportation experience. Terminals were given vaulted waiting areas adjacent to ticket counters much in the same style as the older railroad stations. Over time, however, functional requirements and aesthetic tastes both changed, providing airport terminals with symbolic motifs referencing the associations and romance of flight.

In the 1960s, Kennedy International Airport, which at that time was the principal embarkation point in the United States for foreign travel, stressed its role as the gateway to the world. Each of its major terminals was isolated on a connecting roadway and designed by individual architects. One of the most impressive buildings was the TWA terminal designed by the Finnish architect Eero Saarinen, who later crafted the look of the main terminal building at Dulles International outside of Washington, D.C. Metaphorically, the TWA terminal at Kennedy International embodies the expression of flight. Long arching concourse tunnels made of reinforced concrete swoop down and away through a large central interior space that serves as the ticketing, baggage claim, and restaurant area. From the outside, the use of molded concrete created a sculptural, flowing form with a configuration that suggested a bird in flight. The central space was framed by expansive windows that bathe the interior in natural light and allow views of the runways. Passengers can watch as the giant planes, like 747s, take off and land, while they wait under the signs of foreign air carriers surrounded by posters depicting life in exotic locales. The same overarching symbol of a bird in flight was also used in the recently completed Buffalo-Niagara Falls International Airport, designed by Cannon Associates. This avian metaphor remains one of the most potent symbols of the third and fourth generations of airport architecture.

Saarinen applied the concept of design themes to Dulles International. Unlike Kennedy, however, Dulles was conceived as a regional terminal referencing the

Long check-in counters add to the feeling of placelessness
in airport terminal buildings. (AP photo/Nick Ut)

importance of its Washington, D.C., location. The central terminal building was emphasized in the airport design, constructing an analogy to the 19th-century train station. Saarinen's Dulles terminal carried this to an extreme by centralizing all airline ticketing and baggage functions within the large terminal space. As a result, embarking and disembarking passengers were required to take a second means of transportation, an airport bus or "mobile lounge," to or from their respective planes before they could fly, claim their baggage, or leave the facility. Passengers who have experienced the Dulles terminal are well aware of this inconvenience. People unlucky enough to have to change planes endure an excruciating period of waiting and riding in the airport transports while the clock ticks away toward the time when the gate to their plane shuts. Newer concoursed terminals allow late-arriving passengers making a connection to run to their gate. You can see this mad dash of passengers in the United Airlines facility at O'Hare. The pain of Dulles's terminal comes from the need to wait for the transporter—the fate of catching a connection is in someone else's hands.

Internally, then, Dulles leaves much to be desired. From the outside, however, the terminal makes a dramatic, austere statement. Saarinen designed the exterior as a giant wing poised to take off at any moment. A sloping roof with aerodynamic-like details creates this effect. Consequently, Dulles is a marriage between the old railroad terminal of the first- and second-generation designs and the new romance of flight that characterizes more contemporary buildings.

By the 1980s, the railroad terminal theme had become obsolete. One reason was the technological advance of wide-bodied jets that now dominate air flight. The new planes require more space to maneuver and dock in and out of flight bays. Their introduction 20 years ago necessitated the alteration of almost every

Wide-bodied jets, like the 747 and L-1011 in the photo,
forced airports to be redesigned in the 1980s.

major airport in the country, giving local authorities a chance to renovate with more contemporary styles. Another impetus for the change in image was the realization that, with a greater volume of air traffic, many passengers used airports to transfer from one flight to another rather than to embark or disembark. Consequently, the preferred, developed space was transformed from the terminal/ ticketing area of the regional gateway that recalled the 19th-century railroad days to the broad, expansive concourse areas of the national and international gateway.

Terminal concourses are the arteries that allow the free flow of passengers from plane to plane, ground transportation to flights, or from plane to baggage claim to home. Unlike the older rail-style terminal spaces that centralize people and functions within one area, concourses can range across linear space, spreading out to accommodate wide-bodied jet flight bays and the dizzying mix of travelers scurrying to and from planes. Their principal drawback is the length of time people require going from one plane to a connecting flight using concourses. Walking distances of up to 1,000 feet are now considered acceptable. However, in some terminals, such as United's facilities at O'Hare, the walk between concourses is very much longer; in immense spaces like Dallas/Fort Worth, people movers—such as trams or light rail shuttles—become a necessity, thereby replicating the stressful problem encountered at Dulles. With the new configuration emphasizing pedestrian concourses in place in the 1980s, airport designers rediscovered the role of merchandising. Long corridors filled with waiting travelers created the possibility for the commercialization of the spaces in between airline gates. Incrementally, the large airport began to assume the proportions of a pedestrian shopping mall, as discussed earlier.

After the need to renovate and expand facilities became imperative following the introduction of wide-bodied jets, many airports did not restructure by commissioning entirely new designs. Instead, they simply pecked away at existing terminal buildings and added on by accretion without any integrating plan. The result in some locations, such as Heathrow outside London, was a disappointing mélange of buildings and corridors that subverted the symbolic unity of the terminal facilities. As one analyst observed, "The image of the airport terminal has recently been undermined due to the paste and fit policies of new expansion. This may explain the lack of excitement experienced by most air travelers in airport terminals" (Savona 1992). More devastating than thematic confusion, many of the restructured terminals in the 1970s introduced the element of chaos into the experience of changing flights or, for that matter, embarking and disembarking, making it difficult for people to use the facilities.

Gatwick, outside of London, illustrates the confusion experienced at many airports enlarged by accretion.

In June 1997, I was traveling to Finland. My flight routing required that I change airports as well as planes. Arriving in Gatwick, I had to take a transfer bus to Heathrow for my final flight. Passengers experience a similar inconvenience when they have to move between the airports servicing New York City and I had done this kind of maneuver before in the States but never in England. At Gatwick, I dutifully followed the signs to the Heathrow shuttle. I walked through one small corridor after another, many with boarded up walls because of new construction. I found myself no longer in anything that resembled a terminal. Instead, I was caught in a maze. Pedestrian travelers around me were equally lost. Finally, I arrived at a corridor that promised an exit. Taking it to the end, I found myself completely outside the terminal building facing a no-man's-land of traffic and parking structures. The door closed behind me. Turning, I noticed that it was a secured exit that locked from the inside. There was no way back in! I reluctantly had to work my way around to the main terminal again, carrying my bags while dodging traffic, in order to start my quest all over again.

As bad as Gatwick is, Heathrow is worse. Deyan Sudjic calls it "a permanent building site" (1992, 149) because it seems to have been under construction since its opening in the 1950s. Its character extends to the Internet. An attempt to connect with its website on June 30, 2000, found this message: "Sorry, our web site is under construction." Heathrow is typical of many airports that were built before the wide-bodied jets and the explosion of passenger use occurred in the 1970s. It continues to be altered by "extension, demolition, new construction and adaption" (Sudjic 1992, 153). Airports like Dulles or Heathrow no longer function well and probably need to be torn down and replaced by totally new structures that can both accommodate the largest jets and also handle the high volumes of passengers more conveniently. My personal experience at Gatwick signifies the dissatisfaction many feel about the design inadequacies of reworked airports. Only recently has a greater consciousness evolved that conceives of better designs for the emergent "mega-terminals" of our new global, air culture.

As one architectural critic observed,

From the highly structured bureaucratic maze of Charles de Gaulle, through the organized chaos of Heathrow, to the haphazard nightmare of many American airports (where each airline has its own terminal) air travel—*the* mode of transport of our era—had not until now evolved a humanly satisfying way of moving from land transport to flight. (Davey 1991)

Another problem with accreted airports is that they add to the stress of travel. Waiting is made worse by the condition of the terminal facility itself. Simply put, airports like Logan International in Boston are a mess. Expanded by accretion, they have a dismal quality that is only broken up by a few airy spaces where new construction has occurred. Most of the terminal houses airline functions in low-ceilinged corridors painted gray. Dreary and claustrophobic, this environment becomes oppressive while waiting to catch a rescheduled flight. Compare this to the newer Denver International Airport. Logan has its new parts, too, but what makes the two spaces differ is the lack of peacefulness at Logan. It fails to create a pleasant public space; it has no interior harmony such as that available at the completely new Jeppesen terminal, supplied by the overarching design of the environment.

Beginning with the 1980s, architects began to realize a serious vision of what a newly transformed terminal area might look like—one that reflected the aesthetic of air travel rather than the 19th-century sensibility of the railroad. Several commissions opened up as entirely new airports were constructed from scratch, a rarity for many years prior to that time, along with the opportunity to completely renovate other existing structures. Conceptual change of this kind, realized in the material forms of original or renovated structures, provided architects with a new vocabulary for the airport that would reference both contemporary needs and sensibilities. Perhaps the first noteworthy project was the renovation of the United terminal at O'Hare to accommodate wide-bodied jets in the late 1980s by the architect Helmut Jahn of Murphy/Jahn, Chicago.

American air travel presents a dilemma to designers. On the one hand, the terminal facility must process large numbers of passengers who arrive by car rather than mass transportation. Unlike in Europe, arriving passengers require road space at terminal entrances as well as a large quantity of reserved space for parking facilities. The space demands on the air side of the terminal have also increased remarkably. Travel by wide-bodied jets as the new norm means that airports must also disperse gates and taxiing areas to accommodate the larger aircraft. At the new facility of O'Hare,

> the configuration used at the United terminal had been established in its general lines in the mid-1970s when it became apparent that the existing terminals were not adequate to handle the new wide-body jets. The solution proposed a set of two parallel concourses separated by exactly the distance needed for two 747s to pass. This allowed for easy entry and exit of aircraft and an expansion of the number of gates over the existing terminals, but would not create any major increase in walking distances within the terminals. . . . Once this decision was made, taxiing patterns and sight lines from the control tower dictated other constraints, including the length and height of the concourses. (Bruegmann 1988)

Along with this configuration, the receiving end of the terminal was redesigned to accommodate the crush of arriving cars and people. Jahn's solution included a road built on a curve against the terminal structure that maximized the space for auto access. The principal terminal building was extended, with a minimum distance between the road on the one side and the airplane taxiing space on the other. The latter provided "a thin linear interface between automobiles and airplanes" (Bruegmann 1988) so that arriving passengers could make a direct visible connection with their airplanes and flight, despite the immense scale of the terminal itself. The ticketing pavilion was also centralized and de-emphasized to the benefit of the long, linear concourse areas. Jahn designed these with high, curved, glassed-in ceilings emphasizing natural light, recalling the great arcade spaces of Paris, and a folded truss system of supports creating "one of the grandest spaces ever built for transportation" (Bruegman 1988, 32).

The gate areas of the new space were split between two parallel concourses that were then connected by an underground tunnel. Jahn used this opportunity to create a unique structure, a pedestrian walkway that featured a sound and light show along its length. Although not without controversy, including complaints about the comparatively long walk between planes, this tunnel and its display became a singularly remarkable feature of the facility (Gottdiener 1997).

The most distinguishing characteristic of Jahn's design is the visible connection between the automobile road on the one side of the comparatively thin terminal area and the planes coming and going on the other. Large glass windows and a generous use of linear space were used to create this relationship. So effective was this architectural statement that it seems to have inspired other airports.

Stansted Airport north of London, for example, designed by Sir Norman Foster and completed in 1991, possesses a similar aesthetic. Foster's design is based on two key propositions. "First, the path from land to air should be carefully delineated, agreeable and dignified; and second, the drama of air travel should be celebrated." Stansted, like the United terminal at O'Hare, is made of glass for complete transparency. "All the support elements are in white tubular steel, reducing their apparent size, and refinement is further enhanced by the pinpoints which allow the spars to taper at each end" (Davey 1991, 43).

According to Peter Davey, the new breed of airports, which included Stuttgart (designed by von Gerkan and Marg) and Kansai in Japan (designed by Renzo Piano) are meant to express the new aesthetic "and they will be *places* worth visiting in their own right" (Davey 1991, 34, emphasis added). In short, the new architectural practice aims to overcome the chaos and placelessness of the accreted airport by a holistic conception that emphasizes the allure of air travel while creating an interior that possesses a sense of place and allows for social communion. The intent of designers is not just to create a minimalist experience intended to move people swiftly from land to air or back again, as some observers have suggested, but to capture the special, spectacular aspects of air travel so that the terminal space acquires a strong sense of place in order to attract people in its own right.

Architect Foster designed the interior of Stansted to be functional and to resonate with the overarching theme of the entire structure. He mandated that commercial spaces be enclosed within low-lying walls that did not detract from the natural lighting elements and the visible line to the passenger gate and jet taxiing areas. Unlike the case of American airports, however, Stansted does not have to contend with large numbers of automobiles. The airport instead emphasizes its access to mass rail transport. Consequently, Foster was able to construct a rectangular terminal housing ticketing, commercial, and travel functions without much thought to arriving passenger cars.

The Hong Kong International Airport, also designed by Foster, is a spectacular application of his ideas and is the largest enclosed space ever made. Built on a 3,000-acre island that had been reclaimed from the harbor at a cost of $6.3 billion, it has a single terminal building of 5.57 million square feet that stretches for three-quarters of a mile. Like Stansted, however, Foster aimed for a clear, unobstructed view from one end of the terminal to the other despite the spectacular scale. According to one account, "Instead of intimidating the visitor, it provides a clarity of movement. You know where to go because the architecture points you in the right direction and because the outdoor views let you see where the planes are" (Pearson 1998, 92).

In contrast to the dismal, enclosed spaces of accreted, extended airports that borrow from railroad stations of the past, the new spaces designed by Foster celebrate flight and elevate the traveler's mood. As Foster remarks about his design philosophy for the new Hong Kong megafacility, "It is a quest for calm spaces bathed in filtered natural light—views to the aircraft, the sea, and the mountains, so that you always know where you are—an uplifting experience to bring a sense of occasion to air travel." Pearson also adds, "An essential element in creating a seamless experience for travelers is limiting changes in level. Indeed, arriving

Hong Kong International Airport—the largest single-story structure in the world. The almost mile-long terminal building, shaped as an inverted "Y," can be seen behind the lined-up jets.

passengers can stay on one floor, from getting off the plane to stepping onto a train that will take them to town" (Pearson 1998, 92).

Foster's Hong Kong International is simply spectacular. The terminal space, an engineering marvel, is covered by a 45-acre roof. Built in the shape of a Y, the terminal allows passengers to arrive or leave at the base through easy access to public transportation or automobiles. The facility contains 38 jetways deployed along the twin arms of the Y and is designed to accommodate 35 million passengers each year.

In short, a new aesthetic specific to airline terminals has emerged. It deemphasizes ticketing areas and the elements of the 19th-century railroad terminal in favor of a direct, visible connection between passengers and their jets. High domed structures using natural light create a large scale that helps minimize the intrusive aspects of airport commercialization. Their airy feel, helped along by large plate glass walls, seems an antidote to the kind of oppressive enclosure of the older airports that have grown by adding on. The spectacular structure of the new terminal spaces seems to float in the air or to be poised to take wing.

There are some, of course, who are dissatisfied with the new style. Increased walking times are certainly a sore point at United's O'Hare's facilities, for example. There are also observers who simply misunderstand the significance of the new aesthetic entirely. According to Manuel Castells (1996), the Barcelona Airport built in 1992 and designed by Ricardo Bofill represents an attempt to create a minimalist experience without a lingering sense of place according to the "architecture of nudity." Castells projects his own personal fears about flying in an interpretation of this building. For him, the structure is unique because it does not try to cover up

> the fear and anxiety that people experience in an airport. No carpeting, no cozy rooms, no indirect lighting. In the middle of the cold beauty of this airport passengers have to face their terrible truth: they are alone, in the middle of the space of flows, they may lose their connection, they are suspended in the emptiness of transition . . . and there is no escape. (Castells 1996, 421)

The Bofill design for Barcelona is not exemplary of the best new airports, but the real issue is how Castells mistakes the significance of the terminal space. He cannot conceive of an airport as a distinct place that can create a social life of its own out of positive social communion rather than fear. The new airports are designed to foster a sense of place, exhilaration, and an uplifting transition from earthly living to air flight. As Norman Foster asserts, his air terminal spaces are designed to allow people to relax and linger.

Castells completely misinterprets the airport experience. The new terminal spaces have assumed the dimensions of a city by offering a complex mix of functions and opportunities for social interaction. The best of the new airport spaces foster a contemplative atmosphere that massages fears rather than forcing passengers to confront them. With a strong sense of place and an increasing mixture of malls, hotels, entertainment facilities, workout rooms, chapels, and upscale dining, the best of the new air terminals are places in which people can spend considerable time, despite the ordeals of boredom, layovers, and canceled flights.

Not every new airport, furthermore, is designed *à la* Sir Norman, as a glass house. At the gigantic Denver International Airport, the Jeppesen terminal "is distinguished by a 34-peak tensile fabric roof" meant to symbolize the nearby Rocky Mountains. Encompassing 53 square miles, with five full-service runways and space for 13,000 parked cars, the immense airport opened in 1995 at a cost of over $3 billion. Denver International was built 23 miles northeast of the city in an effort to capitalize on the new significance of airports in global economic development. Incorporating some of the latest technology, the terminal area is wired with fiber optics and 28 miles of underground fuel pipes that service planes. Also installed is a fully automated baggage check-in and retrieval system. An ambitiously constructed underground train moves people to and from gates. In addition, "With more than 4,300 foot separation between runways and high-resolution final approach monitors, as many as three aircraft can land at the same time on parallel runways—even during bad weather" (*Visitor's Guide* 1996, 19).

Unveiled with considerable hoopla, the airport suffered a series of humiliating failures of its infrastructure. The tent roof was judged "gauzy," runways developed cracks shortly after construction, and the multimillion-dollar baggage system chewed up luggage to such an extent that it had to be closed down. New landing fees required airlines to surcharge passengers, making tickets through Denver more expensive than they were at the old Stapleton Airport downtown. Yet, standing on the first level of the grand atrium space, with the tent roofs more than 100 feet above, bathed in natural light, the terminal offers a unique experience for airports that is comparable to the mega-scaled indoor public space of the Mall of America outside Minneapolis, Minnesota. It has become something that all designers of contemporary airports hope for, an attraction as a place in its own right. A recent newspaper report commented on both the success and failure of the facility:

> People go to Disneyland and they may also pay extra or go out of their way to see the concourses that are as long as 11 football fields, atriums decked out as jungled Mayan ruins, neon rainbows and the breathtaking translucent tent roof. Even the subway tunnels are decorated with art such as the 5,280 tiny propellers that whirl with the gust of each passing train (one propeller for each foot of Denver's elevation). But the ultimate success or failure of the mega-airport will depend on the predatory forces of the industry. Stapleton, the faithful old airport that will be retired

the day Denver International opens, might have the ambiance of a high-school cafeteria, but you can step off your plane, retrieve your baggage from a tried-and-true
baggage system, hop in a car and get to downtown in 12 or 15 minutes. (Ring 1995)

This account draws an inappropriate conclusion. Critics ignore the intent of
the airport as something more than a destination. Designed as a hub that will
capture traffic going to and from the West and as a grounding site for globally
situated commerce and industry, the scheme of the planners was to create a growth
pole facility. The area that includes the airport has been developed for warehousing, light industry, and shipping—an idea that is at the cutting edge of new development logic for the turn of the century. At present, unfortunately, this growth
pole dream remains unfulfilled in Denver. Infrastructure problems persist, although the once-reviled baggage retrieval system now works. Several airlines,
such as Continental, have abandoned the new facility as a hub. Others, such as
United, have had to retain ticket surcharges to cover the higher user costs. The
new Denver International continues to play to mixed reviews. What we are left
with, however, is a distinct space that serves the needs of regional developers for
a 21st-century growth pole, and an attraction that fulfills the desire of airport
aficionados for a terminal that people will visit because it is a unique space—
and not only because it serves as a traveler's gateway.

A good example of what the planners for Denver's new facility had in mind is
the Dallas/Fort Worth International (DFW) Airport that was opened in September 1973. Hardly distinctive as architecture, it is nevertheless the second busiest
airport, after O'Hare, in the world with over 2,100 flights daily. Dallas/Fort Worth
was constructed from the beginning as a growth pole, the first of its kind in the
United States, on a total of 17,637 acres approximately 18 miles from the central business district of downtown Dallas. The original investment was $1.6 bil-
lion, a spectacular sum at the time. According to its website, "Remaining the
single most important economic asset in the North Texas region, DFW Airport
has been a significant factor in the relocation and expansion of more than 400
businesses to Dallas/Fort Worth" (Dallas/Fort Worth International Airport 2000).

Now the airport authority estimates that the facility generates "more than $8.4
billion annually to the North Texas economy and generates more than 167,000
jobs." In short, the airport is not simply a minimalist space to be traversed quickly
by pedestrians. It is, however, notorious for its overlong and inconvenient distances between gates for connecting flights.

In addition to its commercial retailing function, DFW is also a growth pole
with a multimillion-dollar air cargo industry that rivals many cities. Its major
drawback when compared to more recently constructed facilities is its total lack
of airport design aesthetics that have been almost forgotten in favor of its economic function.

The core of the regional economic benefits comes from the businesses that are attracted to the airport itself. Best illustrated by the case of cargo distribution, warehousing, and shipping, these activities are central to the DFW airport's economic impact. There are more than 100 freight forwarders in the area. In 1997, almost one million tons of cargo were shipped from the facility. There are 2.1 million square feet of cargo space, U.S. Customs and other federal inspection agencies, livestock quarantine facilities and fumigation services, and direct connections to highway and rail. In addition, "The DFW area serves as the site for two official functions of the North American Free Trade Agreement: the Labor Secretariat, a three-nation panel that handles labor issues, and the NAFTA Customs Center" (DFW Airport website, accessed January 9, 1999).

Dallas/Fort Worth markets itself as being located four hours or less from any city in the United States. Perhaps that is one of Denver's problems; it aspires to be a competitor of the Texas facility. At present, it is difficult to say whether this growth-pole function of airports can be capitalized on by more than one or two regional airports. These kinds of megaprojects are still very much on the minds of regional developers. Placing the obvious economic aspects of major airports aside, while considering them as unique spaces with a stable population by day and night, they have emerged as thoroughly new places which function more like a growth pole than the kind of temporary spaces that we associate with terminals and air travel.

Perhaps the crowning achievement of contemporary airport construction in this century is the spectacular Kansai International Airport built at sea on an artificially constructed island five kilometers off the mainland in Osaka Bay, Japan. Considered "the concrete realization of futurists' dreams" (*Architectural Review*, 1991), it may very well prove to be the best symbol of industrial society's hopes as we enter the new millennium. Its faith in technology is an extreme form of modernism that surpasses efforts at both Hong Kong and Denver International. Conceived as a 24-hour, self-contained but porous environment, it houses within the planned scheme its own urban area called Aerocity—which includes hotels and shopping centers, as well as the magnificent, immense terminal building designed by Renzo Piano Building Workshop, Japan. Among its notable features is a projected ecologically sophisticated "natural" environment that links with and surrounds the terminal building.

> Provided not only with a clean slate—a new island, no less—on which to create the most rational and efficient terminal possible, Piano's clients . . . are also committed to achieving his unique organic structure and spiritually uplifting "natural" environment which includes a forest of specially-adapted, salt-water trees flowing around and into the terminal itself. . . . The passenger will pass through such environments as the tree-filled international arrivals canyon which cuts through all levels carrying vertical circulation, the bustling commercial area on level 3, intentionally

subdivided from the international passenger departure processes on level 4, and arrive at the tapering wings, the glazed wall of which gives a panoramic view of the steel birds flying around and resting on the tarmac, and on to the sky and rolling hills over Osaka. . . . From the provision of means to keep the trees in bloom, and of computerized robotic hawks to keep birds away, to the constant and perfect synchronization of all its systems, Kansai airport represents a total faith in technology and relies for success on the technology's total efficiency. (*Architectural Review* 1991, 86)

9

The Airport Sign System

Another dimension of the rich ambiance created by air terminal design involves the sign systems that function as the information net for passengers. Often neglected in commentaries on airports, terminal sign systems contribute significantly to the creation of a sense of place in otherwise transient spaces. While all interior commercial spaces require sign systems to steer customers through the environment in the most functional fashion, airports differ from themed environments because their interiors must perform this task in an exemplary manner. Passengers arriving at the terminal, disembarking from flights, or requiring a change of planes must be able to negotiate the space of the airport terminal with ease and rapidity. The sign systems of terminals, therefore, are quite explicit in their *denotative* content. They announce, point, direct, guide, and provide up-to-date information on flights and flight statuses. Air terminals use electronics, fast-resolution TV screens, computer-generated graphics, and information displays to provide timely information to passengers. Graphic designers are employed to create large, readable signs that guide passengers to the appropriate gates. Good airline terminals are, above all, easy places to negotiate the tasks of embarking, disembarking, and transfer to connecting flights. Their success in these tasks is due largely to properly functioning sign systems. The airport sign systems are another source of the emergent sense of place because of their denotative power and the skill by which they communicate function and location to passengers.

According to Hart (1985, 139), airport sign programs serve three main purposes:

1. Direction and Orientation—the direction and guidance of the flow of outbound and inbound traffic
2. Identification of locations—such as ticket counters, lobbies, baggage claims, gates, concourses, telephones, restrooms, car rentals, banks, and shops
3. Information on flight arrivals, departures, baggage, special services, and regulations

Some airports have monitors that are easily accessed by pedestrians, others situate them in poorly located places that make them hard to read because of low ceilings or passenger crowds. Accreted airports suffer from poor legibility, making it difficult for passengers to find the functions they need. Furthermore, not every terminal possesses an effective, *legible* sign system. Many facilities fail in this regard, hampering the efficient functioning of the terminal. According to Hart, disorientation can occur due to:

1. The transition in surroundings—entering or leaving planes, buildings, highway, and outside transportation
2. A transition in the mode of transport, such as at Dulles International discussed earlier
3. The complexity of terminal facilities, for example, the case of Gatwick and other airports that are chaotic in plan due to growth by accretion

Corridors seem to stretch out to infinity as signs direct passengers
to their appropriate gates. (AP photo/Ted S. Warren)

Sign systems must still facilitate the quick movement of passengers despite the source of disorientation. For example, a passenger entering the disembarkation area after obtaining a ticket or perhaps after deplaning from elsewhere may pause at concessions and purchase something. Upon resuming the walk to the next plane, the passenger must be able to reorient himself or herself quickly. Despite the chaos of construction and the long walk between gate and the next step in travel plans, passengers may need to be directed clearly to their new destination. Inadequate sign systems result in passenger delays, perhaps missed planes which back passengers up; increased costs of travel; and the need for more personnel to help in a disorienting airport.

Airport sign systems are an important dimension of the visit to a terminal and one element in the creation of an attractive sense of place. This new mode of communication—reading, translating, interpreting, and responding to the principally visual cues of this unique vocabulary—is necessary for a passenger's transit through the airport. A segment of this new language is even regulated by the government. All airports have been designated a special letter code that is uniform across the world. Helvetica Medium is the mandated typeface with dark letters on a light background (Hart 1985, 135). Some of the most familiar are: Chicago's O'Hare, ORD; San Francisco, SFO; Los Angeles, LAX; Dulles, IAD; Boston, BOS; Houston Intercontinental, IAH; Cincinnati, CVG; Nashville, BNA; Kansas City, MCI; and Atlanta, ATL.

10

Social Activities within Terminals

The new terminals are places where people engage in non-traveling activities, making them distinct spaces with attractions in their own right. The Pittsburgh airport mall and the gourmet dining at LAX are the kinds of facilities that draw people to the new airport centers, convince them to stay, spend time, and enjoy the environmental ambiance. Aerocity in the Kansai Airport near Osaka, Japan, is a mini-urban environment where travelers can actually live, complete with hotels, restaurants, and other services for daily needs. Furthermore, although few people would consider seriously the odds of winning at slot machines that are designed to extract the last remaining dollars from departing travelers, the gambling facilities at McCarran Airport in Las Vegas are a departure from traditional terminal space. Both Amsterdam and Frankfurt also have casinos in the airports.

The newly designed airports exploit their quality as public spaces. Precisely by capturing the multifunctional aspects of urban culture, new airports like Jeppesen or Kansai become interesting and successful. Being stranded at one of the dismal, older accreted air terminals can be a frustrating, tedious experience that adds to the stress of flying. In contrast, being stranded in a mini-city with no other alternative can lead to a host of interesting experiences, much like an unscheduled tourist vacation in its own right.

One important component of creating a sense of place is the way structures nurture a social life for people who purposely enjoy the attractions of the location. An excellent illustration of this emergent "place*ness*" is the phenomenon of *plane spotting*. A small number of people in our society are aficionados of air equipment. They engage in the practice of visiting terminals around the country in order to spot planes just the way bird-watchers travel to select sites in nature in order to catch a glimpse of avian species. In both cases, this hobby consists of finding suitable places for sightings and then recording them. Plane spotters like to visit airports as places. They even have their own websites (such as <www.airliners.com>) that report critical reviews of terminals for this purpose. Rating facilities from one to five stars, a recent review had this to say about the Jeppesen terminal at Denver International:

> When you really stop to look at it, it's amazing how much Denver International Airport has in common with a California counterpart, SFO. Both have beautiful interior facilities that rank among the very best, both are hub locations for United Airlines, and both are ranked among the country's 6 busiest airports. But unfortunately, that's not all they have in common; both are very, very difficult airports for plane spotting. Like SFO, most of the action happens far away from the terminal, and there are very few places to get a clear, solid view of what's going on. Thus, like SFO, DIA turns out to be a major disappointment for the hard-core spotter. (Plane Spotting 1999)

One airport that got a perfect rating, five out of five stars, was Los Angeles International Airport (LAX):

> If plane spotting were a religion, then Los Angeles International Airport would be its Mecca. LAX has everything that the plane spotter craves: crisp and up close views of takeoffs and landings, nonstop aircraft movements, tons of heavies and large aircraft, excellent facilities, plenty of places to sit and observe . . . it is an absolute plane spotting paradise. For the hard-core spotter, and even for some of those who might not be as fanatical, an afternoon spent plane spotting at LAX is like a trip to the amusement park. (Plane Spotting 1999)

Airports that scored four out of five stars were Salt Lake City (SLC), McCarran (LAS), and Phoenix (PHX). The new terminals are spaces that nurture a social life. The homeless, shoppers, diners, and plane spotters are populations that mingle with the crowds of passengers. This diversity creates an additional and unique dimension to the vocabulary of behaviors that characterizes contemporary air terminal culture. Despite the anonymity and potential placelessness of the airport, architects have demonstrated that the built milieu can still create a sense of place with all of its social consequences. Now the newest airports, like Kansai in Japan, exploit this city-like quality by expanding the ancillary consumer services on site. Kansai is an airport and a mini-city all at once. The triumph of airport architects in the last decade has been to create a unique vocabulary for terminal facilities that does two things well: they have provided a design vision that glorifies flight and created one that eases the transition from the earth to the air. Using elements that make cities great, they have also produced a lasting sense of place for what was once a totally transient environment.

Part 3

Life in the Air

11

Frequent Flying: What Fliers Want

> When Richard's wife and I waited for him to come home for dinner, we had to turn on the TV set. International arrivals were shown on Channel 6. The trouble was, neither of us knew which country he'd be coming from.
>
> Pico Iyer, 1998

The normative understanding of the airport is that it is a place of *temporary* habitation. Signified by its function, it is a transition space, a place for travelers to pass through on the way to other destinations. Social expectations dictate that we perform this act quickly. We are greatly inconvenienced, for example, by the demand of airlines to arrive one hour or more earlier than departure for check-in rituals. Waiting at airports is often perceived as killing time, and as a tedious interlude.

The previous chapters have demonstrated that, although airports remain dominated by their principal functions as gateways and transition spaces, they have evolved into multipurpose facilities. Many people spend productive time at air terminals whether they are shopping, working, attending meetings, or exploiting business and communication services enabling them to get things done while on the road. Architecture captures a new vision of the terminal, making space for this multifunctionality.

The same observations can be made of air travel. Our normative understanding of this activity comes from the past. Air travel is no longer a temporary, dead time in the air; the more time we spend in air travel, the more the experience

Aircraft of different sizes and ranges come and go as they service the increasing
number of travelers.

evolves in complexity. Travel time is a resource that allows for a wide variety of
activities. Perhaps the most important observation that can be made regarding
travel time is also the premise of this book—so many people across the globe
travel by jet plane that we can begin to speak of a *social life* in air space as a
separate dimension of living. We live in the air as well as on the ground. We are
progressively, irrevocably *humanizing* a realm that was for millennia the sole
province of birds and insects.

FREQUENT FLIERS

People fly so frequently that there are special clubs run by each airline that give
travel credits for miles flown. Cost-free tickets are issued after an accumulation
of at least 25,000 miles for domestic trips (though it used to be 20,000). While
many tourists are able to rack up large numbers, the top frequent fliers are un-
doubtedly doing it for business. Global capitalism and its multinational corporations have taken advantage of marketing, labor, and other cost savings by splitting the locations of headquarters, subsidiaries, manufacturing plants, research
and design facilities, and the like around the world. The practice has worked well,
but it has also necessitated the constant travel of business representatives to the
far reaches of corporate empires. Doing business with multinationals *means* travel.
As one observer noted,

> The gadgets that let business people fax, phone and surf the Internet from 30,000
> feet are from the same technology that once promised to eliminate bothersome travel

by heralding a new age of video teleconferencing and the information superhigh-way—businessmen talking to each other by E-mail and on television screens. In-stead, the opposite has happened. Advanced telecommunications have made the office portable, and have propelled more business people into a place called the *virtual office*—an office-in-a-bag that accompanies them as they work above the clouds. (Wayne 1995)

Many names have been given to these intrepid people: Frequent Business Traveler (FBT), Frequent Business Flier (FBF), the New Business Class (NBC), and Mega Travelers (MT). The one that seems the most descriptive, however, is *Road Warriors,* because there is something quite heroic about living in the air, on the go, through frequent flying.

In one account, a writer observes his friend, a global road warrior, as he un-packs. The scene is spectacular in its implied dimensions of competency involved in success with the new lifestyle:

> Richard began pulling out envelopes from his briefcase—I counted 27 in all—thick with bus tokens, coins and bank notes for the 27 countries he was likeliest to find himself in the next day. Then he began extracting a stash of crumpled, half-used plane tickets for Hong Kong–London, Hong Kong–Madrid, Boston–Tokyo and all his other regular itineraries. . . . He actually had to petition the Foreign Office to get permission to carry two passports simultaneously—he went through their pages so quickly—and in the previous year alone he crossed borders . . . 139 times. (Iyer 1998, 37)

Other periods in the historical development of capitalism as a world system have called forth individuals who have spent considerable time on the road in-volved in trading. "There have always been business nomads—from European merchants who traveled the spice routes to Asia to itinerant peddlers on the by-ways of Old Russia to the Willy Lomans on America's Blue Highways" (Wayne 1995). The new business class of frequent fliers heralds the emergence of the next stage in economic development, the global economy. With each transformation of capitalism, there has been a *new way of life*, a new kind of daily living. This is especially so for global business. The mega-travelers who increasingly popu-late the air are creating and sustaining the latest version of a new type of social-ity, in this case by using the functional props of our expanding air environment. Gone are the roadside rests, diners, motels, gas stations, corner bars, whorehouses, and "comfort inns" that comprised the world of the motoring salesmen who worked for corporations. (However, it should be noted that truckers in countries like America, Brazil, and Australia still sustain such a milieu in their wide open land spaces.) Modern corporate life relies on air travel, on literally living in the air, and this new frontier is peopled by frequent fliers.

Yet I suspect that they are something more than just supersonic versions of the old Phoenician traders or Bedouin merchants of old, and are separated from Willy Loman by differences of kind as much of degree. . . . In a post ideological world, they cannot know, as easily as the encyclopedia salesman surely did, exactly, where they stand. And flying from winter to summer in an afternoon—or waking up alone in 14th century Nepal and sitting down for dinner that night with the family in Century City—they face, and are forced to find new answers for the most basic human questions: where do they belong, what is their community and to whom are they most responsible? (Iyer 1998, 38)

Airlines and hotel chains love frequent business fliers because they spend proportionately more money on tickets and accommodations than do ordinary tourists or even first-class celebrity travelers. By altering the social and material landscape, they have become new agents of change.

The road warriors, a term coined by the travel industry, are a new class of superfrequent travelers, the top one percent of the 40 million or so people who travel for business each year. Minimum travel to gain road-warrior status is about 50 airplane flights a year and an equal number of hotel nights—an industry rule of thumb. At each airline there are about 20 million members in frequent-flier programs. And while numbers are sketchy, some 500,000 of those at each carrier travel at road-warrior levels and qualify for elite frequent flier bonuses. . . . Hard core road warriors, however, easily top those minimum levels: Hilton Hotel executives talk about the management consultant who stayed at their chain 330 nights in 1993—still a record. (Wayne 1995)

Road warriors cannot have much of an intimate social life. There are certainly not many who have families, but that is hard to determine because of a lack of information on this population. Truck drivers have been living a similar existence for some time and many of them seem to be able to raise children and sustain marriages. What seems to be an attractive aspect of the new kind of road life is less the frequent flying than the corporate expense account and the cushy hotels. Social status and business-class perks are the features that distinguish frequent fliers from truck drivers.

Being a road warrior means never having to make up your bed (housekeeping is there). Or worry about the price of a meal (expense account living). Or having to put gas in the car (it's a rental). And from the motion comes meaning. . . . "When you travel, you have a sense that you're doing something really concrete. You tease yourself into thinking that you've actually gotten something done." (Wayne 1995)

Or as another observer puts it,

The very point of business class is that it allows you to be screened off from the world at large, behind a curtain, from the riff raff. That such divisions are increasingly popular in the world where other borders are collapsing is evident from the fact that connoisseur class services are booming and have spun off cousins in hotels with their executive floors, and car rental agencies with their gold car lines. Virgin Atlantic calls its top deck and front of the plane seats "upper class." (Iyer 1998, 40)

Aside from anecdotal evidence, some surveys help to flesh out a picture of the typical business flier. One reported case came from a questionnaire distributed by Delta Airlines in 1998 on their shuttle flights in the Washington to New York to Boston corridor. The results of the survey (Wallis 1998) can be summarized as follows:

1. The typical business traveler is a married man between 36 and 45 years old who works for someone else and travels a lot. This group comprised 55 percent of the total. A third of the respondents were women and a quarter were under 35.
2. 53 percent took 21 or more business trips a year, 27 percent took 11 to 20 business trips, 15 percent took 6 to 10, and 5 percent took 5 or fewer.
3. 48 percent of the men looked forward to business trips; 67 percent of the women looked forward to business trips.
4. Asked to choose from a list of service improvements, a whopping 63 percent of frequent fliers wanted more comfortable seats. Only 5 percent wanted in-flight Internet access. Also on the list were "more leg room" and "no families."
5. The number of cocktails consumed on an average three-hour flight was: no drinks at all—55 percent; one drink—25 percent; two or three drinks—18 percent, and 2 percent of the passengers consumed more than three drinks.
6. Respondents were "fairly tolerant of standard problems like flight delays and mediocre food, but disapproved of armrest hogs, sitting next to chatty strangers, standing in line for lavatories, and having to shut their window shades for movies."
7. New York City was the most favorite destination, edging out San Francisco, and received rave reviews for its restaurants, museums, shopping, and nightlife. New York City was also considered the number one least favorite city.
8. Asked what was the first thing you do when you arrive at your room, "50 percent said they unpack, 15 percent said they freshen up, 12 percent phoned home, 6 percent nap, 5 percent turn on the TV or radio, and 12 percent said 'other'—which included getting naked, getting a beer, unpacking suits and hanging them in the bathroom with the shower running, and looking under the bed and in closets for intruders."

Frequent business fliers have changed the configuration of airplane seating because of their large numbers. Decades ago, there were only two classes: coach and first. Today, an increasing number of seats go to business class, especially on international flights. The new business class, invented by British Airways, has transformed the material configuration of air terminals, as we have seen. Work gets done in membership lounges like the Admiral's or Red Carpet Clubs of American and United, respectively. Airport terminals now offer business services and health club facilities, gourmet dining, and meeting rooms for conferences. Providing the latter means, in some cases, that business travelers *never* actually have to leave the airport terminal. Institutions on a tight budget find this resource very useful.

In the early 1980s, I was a professor at the University of California, Riverside, the only awful environment among the campuses of the entire California state system. Smog-saturated, dry, windblown, and deathly boring, Riverside was a place that I tried to leave at every available opportunity. One year I was placed on a system-wide committee run by the state administration that required meetings with representatives from every campus. This academic gathering would take place, I was told, in San Francisco. When I heard the location I was ecstatic—only to learn later that the meeting was being held at a hotel conference center adjacent to the airport. I came and went to San Francisco but never got near downtown or the fabled harbor and bridge. My experience on the ground was solely confined to the courtesy van that took me a quarter-mile from the airport to the conference room at the hotel. A friend of mine, a lawyer, has this experience often. He flies in for meetings at places like O'Hare, Denver, and Dallas/Fort Worth. Never the tourist, he puts in his time at the airport conference center, then leaves for home again, much like any other yuppie commuter.

Such business meeting facilities have become increasingly popular at airports:

> On the second floor of American's Admiral's Club [at O'Hare–Chicago], there is a 14,000 square foot facility that is routinely used by headhunters to fly executives in from around the country, by lawyers taking depositions, by sports agents hustling college or high school basketball players, even recently by the Dalai Lama, himself. Using the airport facilities decreases the need for meeting rooms, rental cars, directions, downtown hotels—all that messy stuff. (Rayner 1998, 42)

Conference centers combined with airport business service centers create a node that helps corporations and their executives make money. The more convenient airports themselves are seen in this process, the more they modernize with service centers that enable work to be done, and the more they will be used. Consequently, the global multinational economy's principal effect has been to generate a need for business service workers of all kinds. It may be the giant airports like Denver, O'Hare, or Dallas/Fort Worth that absorb the lion's share of this growth in the future, along with other more regional airports, rather than our large central cities, such as New York, Chicago, or Los Angeles. The marriage between air transport and business has created a new material realm, the megaterminal, which may actually be replacing the traditional city center. By calling national meetings inside airport facilities, corporations save on hotel, rental car, and ground transportation expenses. As new air terminals are constructed to nurture multi-functional travel space, they will begin to rival downtown areas of large cities.

12

Airplane Etiquette: Behavior in the Air

Unions representing flight attendants and ground crews around the world today declared a "day of action" against air rage, saying inappropriate passenger behavior is potentially dangerous and on the rise.

Associated Press, July 6, 2000

One of the most significant observations about the behavior of people in air transportation is that it is highly regulated by the experience. Air travel is exciting. No matter how jaded or frequent the flier, travelers respond to the situation of air travel as a special occasion. With rare exceptions, people are on their best behavior. Waiting in line, they are courteous; in terminal lounges, they are considerate; in bathrooms, they are polite; at baggage claim, they are helpful; and in flight, with few exceptions, they deliberately keep to themselves. Behavior during the air transport experience seems almost as if the fundamental forces motivating individuals in our society—ambition, greed, competition, paranoia, suspicion, contempt, pity, jealousy and awe—are all painstakingly, microscopically squeezed out of social interaction. The occasion calls forth a keep-to-yourself, minimally interactive mode of behavior that cannot simply be explained by any police or airport authority threat. In airports and on planes, people are simply *vectored*. They are going somewhere. Their destination is their own even if they are traveling with hundreds of others to the same location. Each trip is personal and it's nobody's business.

Consequently, people do not make the trips of others their business. With the purchase of a ticket, airline personnel meet their needs. Passengers do not require the aid of others. The environment of air travel is not so much a public space as it is an immense service-scape where people expect a respite from the interaction of everyday life. The norm is self-containment with regard to fellow travelers, and guarded anticipation with respect to the service personnel who will eventually address your needs.

There is, however, a flip side to this structured interaction and it may be the cause of some anxiety. Decorum and behavior on planes, and, indeed, our very fates, are under the strict control of airline personnel. In effect, we surrender the control we have over our lives when we enter the airport. Flying can be fatal. It is no longer up to us whether we live or die, but up to the pilot, the maintenance personnel, and the plane. Many people cannot easily handle putting their lives in another's hands; some even react with extreme anxiety to the mere prospect of a plane trip. Powerful people, in particular, who may function in complete control of their lives and the lives of others on a daily basis, are asked to surrender control once they board a plane. They react to this interlude at times with great difficulty and, in increasingly more frequent cases, unanticipated responses, especially if plied by a generous supply of alcohol.

AIRPLANE ETIQUETTE

Life in the air itself is even more intriguing. It is there, as a mass phenomenon, that people have humanized a new realm of the planet. We might instead anticipate the populating of the oceans; science fiction writers have already described great undersea cities like that of Captain Nemo. Aside from the few workers who operative offshore oilrigs, however, humanity's destiny does not appear to be moving in that watery direction. Already we populate the air, and on a mass basis. At this moment, American and Russian astronauts work away on a space station high above the earth, whether it is feasible to spend so many billions on this endeavor or not. We have no comparable "deep sea" station. The sky and the stars seem to be our destiny.

Unusual or obtrusive behavior on airplanes is rarely experienced. Slightly irritating behaviors of fellow passengers, amplified by the tight confines of jets, are almost always tolerated with a minimum of energy, rarely inflating into incidents that bother a passenger for any length of time. There is, however, a growing pool of public information sharing observations of behavior in planes. Recent troubling incidents with unruly, belligerent passengers and even some arrests and lawsuits that have occurred in the past few years have heightened everyone's consciousness about airplane etiquette. Now travel by air has produced its own genre of personal commentaries that are circulated in a variety of ways.

For example, Airplane Etiquette 2000, one of the principal sources covering airplane etiquette, can be accessed at its website <www.airportcitycodes.com>. It is comprised of individual passengers' comments and organized by an anonymous but energetic editor.

The top ten (plus one) poor etiquette things people do unknowingly on an airplane.

1. Grabbing the back of your seat as they get up or down disturbing you while you're enjoying a nap, reading, or drinking hot coffee.
2. Reclining the seat in front of you with great force, without notice or a cautionary look before hitting you in the forehead or crushing your laptop computer screen.
3. Hogging the armrests, and sometimes taking up a part of your seat as well.
4. Playing their Walkman so loud that although we can't hear the words or make out the song we begin to doubt the description—*personal* electronic devices.
5. Leaving the lavatory looking like the airplane just hit severe turbulence.
6. Standing in front of the movie screen.
7. Checking in at the check-in desk, then again at the gate despite being told that if they have boarding passes they can get right on board.
8. Failing to understand that OCCUPIED means that there is somebody inside terrified that they'll be exposed to all if you manage to break in.
9. Asking what drinks are on the drinks cart.
10. Coming through security with metal in their pockets, around their necks, fingers, ankles, ears, noses, or whatever.
11. When disembarking, stopping on the jetway right outside the airplane door to wait for their mother/father/spouse or other companion, thus causing a bottleneck.

From this list we can see that most of the violations of etiquette are minor distractions that many people might not even notice. Perhaps they are amplified by the current conditions of overcrowding. With the exception of people banging on your seat disturbing your peace, these intrusions cannot compare with screaming babies. This same website also lists ten things that people *knowingly* do. Again, the list seems more amusing than arousing—certainly airplane behavior seems comparatively decorous despite the cramped quarters and public mix of people:

The top ten poor etiquette things people do knowingly on an airplane.

1. Changing the baby's diaper in the middle seat of a crowded plane.
2. Standing up immediately before the seat belt sign goes off in an attempt to get off the plane quicker and finding 100 people doing the same thing. Note—a computer simulation shows that the plane will empty more quickly if people stood up and disembarked in ascending seat order.
3. Standing behind a flight attendant working a cart hoping that it will miraculously disappear, so they can get by.

4. Put their carry-on baggage up front so they don't have to carry it back, so those up front have to carry theirs back.
5. Complain if you move their bag in the overhead locker—Check it! If you don't want it touched by other passengers.
6. Yell at the flight attendants and other personnel about weather delays! Yep, it's their fault.
7. Farting.
8. Repeatedly talk to you while you're working, reading a great novel, or using a personal electronic device.
9. Pretending that they're world travelers and experts about air travel.
10. Cutting lines at check-in like they have some divine right . . . that's not what it looks like to us standing in line.

With few exceptions, during my many flights, no fellow passenger has intruded into my personal space in a negative way. By contrast, some flight attendants have, but now I possess a better understanding of these encounters. Perhaps the most irritating incidents involved little children who screamed, squealed, and cried at a loud enough volume to make the trip miserable.

I can, however, recall worse incidents than those above, for example:

1. People who bring too much carry-on baggage and then hit people in the head with it when they negotiate the aisle.
2. People who bring carry-on baggage that is too heavy and endanger people around them when they try to place it in the overhead bins.
3. Flight attendants who push their carts too fast down the aisle without giving people warning so that they smash into the kneecaps of tall passengers seated on the aisles. This often occurs in the later stages of the flights or at night.
4. Passengers who insist on reading all night with their lights on.

The last type of behavior is quite vexing. Airplanes design reading lights so that they supposedly fall within a narrow area focused on individual seats. In theory this might work, but in practice the bright stream of light is irritating to others sitting in adjacent seating, especially at night. Personally, I can never relax on a night flight when the passenger next to me has his bright seat light on.

Perhaps this effect explains the following. In 1992 I was flying on a red-eye from New York City to Los Angeles. It was a cheap flight that was fully packed. People were desperate for sleep; I know I was. Three people sat in the row directly in front of me. A woman who kept her reading light on occupied the middle seat. I could see her well because I was seated diagonally in the aisle behind at the window. She held an electronic organizer or a palm computer and was feverishly entering data and referring to notes that she pulled from her bag. Whatever noise she made was drowned out by the sound of the engines, but her light kept me from sleeping. I would doze off, wake up to the bright beam in front of me, and then have difficulty dozing off again. Probably I wasn't the only one inconvenienced by her. Halfway into the flight, she got up to go to the bathroom. When she returned she let out a scream. Someone had lifted her electronic organizer from her seat while she was away. "It's gone!" She yelled. Then she upset everyone around her by pulling out her carry-on bags and searching everywhere. Finally, she called the flight attendant and explained what had happened. We all listened intently with some pleasure. I am convinced to this day that one of her seatmates snatched the device and pocketed it away, not to steal it for their own use, but simply to stop this woman from working and keeping her light on. I can't prove this assertion; in fact, the airline personnel could not even help this woman get her device back. She slumped down into her seat, quiet at last, with the light off, until the end of the flight.

INCREASING PROBLEMS WITH AIRPLANE ETIQUETTE

As the number of airline passengers has stretched into the millions, and as flying has become a more frequent occurrence in most people's lives, the number of complaints about the experience has increased geometrically. Passengers are under considerable stress from crowded seating, travel delays, bumping, and a host of other inconveniences. Overbearing irritations now accumulate to affect the very interaction between travelers. A growing number of incidents seem to indicate that airplane etiquette suffers greatly under present conditions. Although the overt acts of air rage that have alarmed our society in recent years haven't increased,

> what seems far more pervasive, frequent fliers and airline personnel will tell you, is a widespread decline in just basic common courtesy. Overbooked planes, cramped spaces and frayed nerves, combined with delays, poor food, and stale air, have led to etiquette withdrawal. . . . Passengers who see jam-packed flights as someone's cruel lab experiment are becoming less considerate, more sensitive to slights and generally less patient. (Zoroya 1999, D-1)

Recent newspaper reports tell of increasing intolerance for crying babies, chatty seatmates, and the general crush of humanity on long flights. Armrest wars are now more frequent and passengers devise strategies for claiming space that should be shared. People are particularly vexed by businessmen who spread out in order to work while in flight, expropriating every available inch of seating space. Women tell of their intimidation by men seated next to them who inconsiderately cover the common armrest. One passenger reported that, rather than fighting over the armrest, she placed a pillow on it to increase its overall dimensions. According to one report, the most common clashes witnessed by flight attendants in recent years "have been over the simple issue of how far back someone reclines a chair" (Zoroya 1999, D-2). Some passengers have registered complaints about having their legs beaten black and blue by inconsiderate passengers in the forward seat. Tall people particularly suffer from the present arrangements. They seem to have a choice of either having their kneecaps smashed by the person who reclines the seat in front of them or, alternatively, sticking their leg out in the aisle where their kneecap will surely be smashed by the zealous flight attendant pushing the meal cart down the aisle at full speed.

Coincidentally, the increase in seat-back battles coincides with the recent decision of the major carriers to increase the number of total seats in the passenger coach cabin. This is especially true of seating in the Boeing 737 and 757 planes. Airline chairs are spaced on an average of 31 to 32 inches apart, hardly enough room for a normal-sized adult. An airplane seat "typically reclines between 4 and 6 inches lopping off valuable personal space" (Zoroya 1999, D-2). As the complaints have mounted, several major carriers announced in January 2000 that they were removing one or two rows of seats on their planes to increase legroom for passengers. Several bargain carriers, such as Vanguard Airlines, have reverted to more generous spacing arrangements as well. This change in policy will certainly help to alleviate what has become a frequent problem for travelers. Yet with so little relief in sight for the progressively uncomfortable and inconvenient experience of current plane travel, it can also be expected that the decline in civility witnessed in the air will also continue.

13

Drunks

As violent, unruly flyers turn the friendly skies into a high-altitude riot, airlines are finally clamping down on air rage.

Daniel Eisenberg, 1998

Most of the truly unruly behavior that has occurred on planes involves alcohol in some way. Belligerent drunks have become an increasing problem, causing some highly publicized incidents.

High-altitude altercations have involved the high, the mighty and the royal born: In October, police arrested investment banker Gerard B. Finnerman, after he disrupted a United Airlines flight from Buenos Aires to New York City. Finnerman, 58, allegedly was drunk and violent, shoving a flight attendant and threatening another. . . . Salwa Qahanti, a 43-year-old Saudi Arabian princess, was fined $500 and placed on six months probation for scratching the arm of a TWA flight attendant on a trip from Paris to Boston. (Feld 1996a)

Certainly one of the most harrowing incidents occurred in December 1995 on a Northwest Airlines flight from London to Minneapolis, when "eighteen members of a British tour group went on a rampage after they were refused additional drinks by attendants who said they already were inebriated" (Feld 1996a). The flight crew had to get help from passengers before the unruly drunks could be subdued. This incident, which took place seven miles up in the air, posed a serious danger to everyone on the flight. On another occasion in 1998, a drunk on a late-night flight from London to Spain ignored a flight attendant's warning not to smoke in the bathroom, then assaulted her by breaking a vodka bottle over her head. Inflicting a wound that required 18 stitches, the offender was subdued and then arrested upon landing by the Spanish police (Eisenberg 1998, 40).

It is difficult to determine the exact number of such incidents, but the 40,000-member Association of Flight Attendants claimed that there were "54 incidents of all kinds in 1993, which rose to 77 in 1994 and to 94" in 1995, i.e., the problem of abusive people on flights is getting worse (Feld 1996a). The Air Line Pilots Association gives a much greater figure. They estimated that the number of incidents in 1997 approached 1,000 (Eisenberg 1998, 40). In July 2000, a report was released by the Federal Aviation Administration on the dangers to flights and people caused by unruly, disruptive passengers. Examination of 157 incidents revealed that in 40 percent of the cases, the flight crew in the cockpit was distracted from their focus on flying the plane. In 22 percent of the incidents, a member of the crew was actually required to leave the cockpit in order to help out the cabin staff. At these times, the safety of the plane flight was jeopardized (*ABC Nightly News* 2000).

Experts point to several causes of abusive behavior and its increasing prevalence. Some say that crowded planes and schedule problems lead to such extreme behavior, just as we have seen them contribute to breakdowns in more basic courtesy and airplane etiquette. Others blame the pressures on business travelers. "For business people, the workplace itself has been extended and goes with them when they fly. . . . They are under more pressure more of the time in more places. And if they had control back at the office, they don't when they are on a plane" (Feld 1995).

Consumer advocate Diana Fairechild also considers low oxygen levels as part of the mix producing abusive behavior. However, for many, the principal culprit is excessive alcohol. According to a 1998 report in *Time* magazine:

> Airlines run a virtually free, open bar in first and business class, where some of the nastiest episodes occur. The booze is supposed to keep customers calm but may be having the opposite effect on some. Others say being deprived of a different vice, cigarettes, is a major cause of unruliness. . . . Then there are those who blame the airlines themselves. . . . "Flights are full, there are fewer flight attendants, and there's a general indifference toward the passenger." (Eisenberg 1998)

Something like these irritants must be the cause of breakdowns like the following:

> An Air New Zealand plane was forced to abort two landing attempts when a woman attacked two flight attendants and tried to open an external door, police said. . . . The Boeing 737 from Sydney was preparing its descent Friday into Wellington airport when the unidentified woman refused to fasten her seat belt. . . . When a woman

flight attendant approached, the passenger attacked her and locked herself in the bathroom. . . . Then she made a grab for the rear loading door. (*Buffalo News* 1999a, A-4)

Being in a situation in which you no longer have control, as noted earlier, is surely the single most active premise of air travel. Without much effort, we can imagine this existential dilemma and the need to trust to luck as the source of most of our anxiety. This aspect is compounded in personalities who work every day in environments that they control completely. It is not always easy for powerful people to suspend their privileges and surrender trust to other professionals. Flying for most people causes stress. For those individuals used to managing their everyday environment with tight control, air travel must produce pressures that few of us are willing to face.

From the scariest incidents of abusive behavior reported in the press, it is clear that alcohol is the single most important mitigating factor. Drinking alcohol may be a special treat on planes, and while excessive drinking on flights might be a way of alleviating stress, the fact remains that aggressive and abusive drunks have no place on a crowded flight. They pose a danger to everyone's safety. Unfortunately, flight attendants seem to do little to monitor drinking. Worse still, airlines actually encourage drinking in flight as part of their service, despite the ill effects on the body and the potential for creating abusive behavior.

I recall, for example, flying first class for the first time in 1995. The plane took off from Buffalo, New York, en route to Las Vegas. Even before all of the coach passengers were strapped in, the flight attendant began serving drinks to the first-class section. The person next to me was a well-dressed businessman who had pulled out a laptop and was busy at work from the moment he sat down. He ordered one scotch after another. The flight attendant supplied these to him with a smile. I stopped counting at four while we were in the air. All through the flight, I marveled at the ability of this man to hold his liquor, yet I was also horrified at the amount he drank. I concluded right there on the spot that first class was really for alcoholics.

The connection between unruly behavior in planes and alcohol served with a smile by attractive attendants has not gone unnoticed by the American Automobile Association (AAA). Recently, they released a guide called "Jetiquette" that addresses the issue of excessive drinking in flight (*PRNewswire* 1997). Meant for everyone, it also might help airline personnel deal with these matters before a passenger's behavior escalates into a dangerous situation.

1. **Be alert to potential disturbances**—At the ticket counter or in the aircraft, watch out for passengers who appear to be making unreasonable demands, use loud or abusive language, or demonstrate inappropriate behavior.
2. **If you are sitting next to an abusive passenger**—Since you're confined in an aircraft, it's not about "fight or flight." Stay calm, quietly gather your small valu-

ables, walk over to the flight attendant and explain the situation. If the flight is full, you will not be allowed to move, so do not ask the attendant to switch you with another passenger.

3. **Cabin air is pressurized**, re-circulated and very dry, and you cannot easily exercise. . . . Remember that alcohol, caffeine and soft drinks dehydrate, so consider ordering water or juice as an alternative or as a side beverage.

4. **Airline crews are well trained to handle on-board disturbances**—These skilled professionals are responsible for the safety and comfort of passengers, and they have ample experience in handling disruptive passengers. At a recent airline training seminar, one international flight attendant reported that more than a third of all the attendants had experienced some form of aggressive passenger behavior, ranging from head-butting a first officer to throwing objects at the crew to riding the beverage cart. For this reason, airline personnel carry police-style handcuffs and will not hesitate to use them if they perceive that other personnel are threatened.

These observations from the AAA seem to be of little comfort to the majority of passengers who are not problem drinkers. The key message is that plane personnel are always in control and have your destiny in hand. Yet they do not always handle abusive passengers in a way that suits the average traveler. Cramped quarters make adjustments difficult and often force personnel simply to ignore drunks in the hope that they will eventually calm down or "go away." Until alcohol on flights is more strictly controlled, there seems little doubt that ugly incidents 35,000 feet in the air will continue. As one analyst noted, "People believe they are entitled. They demonstrate the football-crowd theory: They bought their tickets and so they can do whatever they want to do" (Feld 1996).

14

Laughs

The accumulating material commenting on the passenger jet experience includes humor. Stand-up comics often make fun of the flying experience. This is the surest sign that it has passed over into the status of our everyday life, that it has been absorbed by our repertoire of common experiences. Television and nightclub shows making fun of flying are simply too numerous to mention. Ellen Degeneres did a routine that lasted for some time. She wondered about the grilled chicken that they serve on flights because it came with dark grill stripes. Maybe there was an open barbecue pit in the cockpit, she wondered, with a copilot standing over the grill. "Two more orders of chicken," the flight attendant might say, as the copilot plopped fresh breasts onto the fire.

Other sources of flying humor are written accounts. Shelly Berman, a comedian, published an extended essay that covers many of the funny aspects of air travel (1986). The table of contents is illustrative: The Overhead Compartment; Fear of Flying; All about Pooping; Understanding Your Flight Attendant; There Will Be a Slight Delay; Whose Voice Is That and Why Is It Saying These Things?; The Toy Meals; You Are the Only One Who's Freezing; On the Difference between Vacant and Occupied; Going into an Airport You're Not Too Familiar with and Wanting to Park Somewhere in the Vicinity of the Terminal So You Can Meet Somebody, For God's Sake!; Oh the Baggage Comes out Here an' Your Bag Goes Roun' an' Roun' Who-oh-oh-oh-oh-oh an' It Goes Out There; Who Can You Kvetch to When You've Been Dumped On?; Where Does Lost Baggage Get Lost To?

Berman's book seems to cover all bases, at least for the obvious aspects of air travel. Among other things, he says: "Do you think everybody suffers from fear of flying? No. But I think everybody suffers from fear of falling" (Berman 1986, 20). Or, "Ever try covering yourself with an airline blanket? You can cover yourself from your shoulders down to your waist or from your waist down to your knees. Hell of a choice. You gotta decide whether you prefer a chest cold or frostbitten genitals!" (17). And, finally, "Q. Before it actually happens, how can you tell a plane is about to hit turbulence? A. The Flight Attendant is serving coffee" (127).

The airline etiquette website (Airline Etiquette 2000) also reports humorous stories, although some are actually reports of personal experiences with frightening events in the air. As of September 21, 1998, one of the best of the lot was the following:

On a trip to Tampa, Fla., the woman to my right was shaking and drinking a lot of booze out of her purse. I asked her if she was okay and she said, "I'm *terrified* of airplanes and I haven't been on one my entire life. If my brother hadn't died so suddenly I wouldn't be here now. With my luck this thing will drop out of the sky." She started crying from all of her anxiety. The passenger on my left sits down and she is in no better shape, shaking and looking around like the devil was after her. She actually asked the woman to my right if she could share her bottle, which she did. I asked her if she was also afraid of flying. She said, "Oh, not at all, it's just that I am so late in getting to Tampa to see my lawyer. If I'm not there on time I lose a lot of money from the settlement we worked out from when I was in a plane crash."

Finally, recounting air travel humor would not be complete without a selection from the writings of Dave Barry, the nationally syndicated humorist who often tells about his trips. As he observes,

Air travel has become less and less pleasant, as more and more passengers are being crammed into planes that appear to have been configured to transport bait. This is why there is talk of an Air Travelers' Bill of Rights, which would require airlines to determine their fares on some basis other than lotto drawings, and serve food that is not made from the same material as flotation devices, and provide seats that allow for the possibility—however remote—that some passengers might have both arms *and* legs. (Barry 1999, E-4)

15

Meals

Some airlines hire chef consultants. They correctly perceive the situation as a public relations problem, but incorrectly believe that by attaching a chef's name to a bad meal, it will magically become a good one.

Mark Bittman, 2000

"**F**ree" meals are the onboard treat of air travel. Many passengers look forward to food and even obsess over it. Eating during flight breaks the tedium and boredom of travel, so people like to linger over their meals. According to a former flight attendant, "I can understand how airline meal services create a false sense of marking time. . . . I've seen how 'the service' even tempts people who aren't hungry! *Plane* boredom?" (Fairechild 1992, 23).

Shelly Berman has some pertinent observations about food in flight:

Most airlines haven't gotten around to serving catsup. This is because no airline serves French fries. It's a shame. French fries would be incompatible with the airline practice of serving *toy meals*. Airlines, in case you haven't noticed, serve miniaturized meals, but in such a way as to make it look like you're getting too much to eat. They give you little toy knives, little toy forks, little toy dishes, little toy vegetables, little toy steaks covered with little toy epoxy gravy. It's cute. (Berman 1986, 66)

Calling attention to the controlled portions of airline food is interesting because this kind of packaging is similar to meals in hospitals, where our lives are also in the hands of professionals. Unlike at home, we can only eat what is served on the plate. The presentation will not allow for second servings, yet that is always a possibility if you are hungry enough and you handle the matter properly with the crew. But Berman is also right, the presentation gives the impression that we are being served food in abundance. "It's all in the toy plates. Look at your next airline meal. See how the food slops over the edge of the plate. One touch of a fork will send food sliding off the plate. You won't think, 'This plate is too small.' You'll think, 'There's too much food here'" (Berman 1986, 67).

Airline food is also a principal way passengers are distinguished according to status. First and business classes have different service than coach. Many airlines, in fact, advertise gourmet dining for their most privileged passengers. Showcasing food is also a principal means of competition among air carriers—often in place of touting safety records and on-time service. To make up for the lack of quality of the coach meal compared with other flight classes like first class, airlines now offer an increasing variety of meals to cover individual taste preferences. The food may not be good, but you can have it fixed "your way":

> Apart from the children's meal, American Airlines offers these options: bland/soft (suitable for those with ulcers); diabetic; gluten-free (no wheat, rye, barley, oats, which people with celiac disease cannot digest); low calorie; lactose-free (no milk products); low carbohydrate; low fat and low cholesterol; low sodium; Moslem; Hindu; Kosher; vegetarian; and strict vegetarian (excludes milk products and eggs). (*Colors* 1995)

In short, the airline meal service is perhaps the most differentiated, most articulated aspect of the flight. With so many options now available, passengers are customizing their meals, although they might still prefer one typical first class service to all the different choices for coach. Meal options seem to be one way that airlines now *personalize* their service for coach passengers. This kind of individual attention is a simulation, and a way of obscuring the more fundamental class distinctions of air travel.

Despite the proliferation of meal types and the focus on food in the competition among air carriers, the question of eating on planes raises a number of serious matters about air travel that are almost universally ignored. First, most inflight meals are notoriously unhealthy. They are "typically high in fat, full of sugar and salt, chemically processed, bland, with pasty sauces, and lacking wholesome complex carbohydrates" (Fairechild 1992, 23). Second, cooking arrangements compound health problems. "In-flight meals are heated in a hot air oven at over 300° C—microwave is never used because it interferes with navigational equipment" (*Colors* 1995, 22). Or, as Diana Fairechild says, "Airline meals are only frozen dinners, not fresh food. They are heated in aluminum pans, not glass or copper pots. . . . Flight attendants are not trained chefs; moreover, since deregulation (1978), attendants are regularly handicapped by malfunctioning ovens and

*Food offered at terminals is progressing from typical franchised fare,
seen in the photo, to more elaborate options, as savvy passengers prefer
to eat off the plane rather than on.*

carts" (1992, 23). Hot air heating of food ruins many meals even before they are
eaten:

> Some vegetables, such as peas, may cause flatulence when reheated. Fried foods
> go soft and flabby; vegetables with high water content separate sauces served with
> them; during reheating, sauces that are too thin slide off entrees, and those that are
> too thick dry out. Because air pressure interferes with the palate, some airlines add
> sugar to their champagne and wines. (*Colors* 1995, 27)

Third, Diana Fairechild, a retired flight attendant and now consumer advocate,
calls attention to the most pertinent aspect of air travel with regard to eating in
flight: Airplanes fly at around 35,000 feet or seven miles high. At this altitude
the cabin must be pressurized for comfort. No airline pressurizes to sea level, because the cost is prohibitive; instead, most aim for a cabin pressure equivalent
to 8,000 feet high (1992, 23). This means that meals are taken as if passengers
were sitting on top of a high mountain. At this elevation, low air pressure means
gases build up in the intestines. Fairechild asks, "I've wondered how, in particular, first-class passengers can pack away an eleven-course meal in flight with their
organs already swollen from low air pressure! The choice, of course, is an individual one: arrive energetic, or drag heavy guts of undigested excess baggage,
then spend a week struggling with the body's demand for meals at odd hours"
(1992, 23).

In discussing Fairechild's claim with friends, they all were incredulous regarding the alleged figure for pressurized cabin elevation. Passengers don't *feel* like
they are at a high altitude when traveling by jet. In checking her figures on a re-

cent transatlantic flight, the pilot reported that the cabin was pressurized to 6,500 feet—lower than Fairechild's number but still quite *mountainous* in height. On other domestic flights, pressurization was always over 6,000 feet. Fairechild may have exaggerated the exact figure, but not the concept that we all fly at pressurized elevations comparable to being on top of a mountain. Why it is that we don't *feel* that way is an interesting question. The answer lies partly in the fact that the passenger cabin is supplied with more oxygen than available at that height on a mountain. This explanation seems to contradict an even more important claim by Fairechild regarding oxygen deprivation in economy class. Despite these complications, Fairechild's recommendations on how to eat on planes possess some validity. Passengers should correct their eating habits for height.

When considering which of all the available food choices are the most healthful for air travel, especially on long, international flights that involve the problem of jetlag, Fairechild (1992, 23) recommends fasting, i.e., not the vegetarian plate, the low-fat plate, or any other "healthful" alternative offered by the airline, but not eating at all. "There isn't really anything I would recommend eating on commercial jets except, maybe, the bread out of Frankfurt." Flying six to eight miles high means that people should approach eating on planes the same way mountaineers do with regard to eating at high elevations. "Among mountain climbers it is known that a pure carbohydrate diet gives one an 'altitude advantage' of about 2,000 feet, i.e., climbers have found that they can function on less oxygen on a pure carbohydrates diet. . . . So it makes no sense to eat any high protein meals" (1992, 24).

If you cannot fast on your trip, then still refuse all airline food and pack your own healthful carbohydrate-enriched snacks. Mountaineers and backpackers, for example, eat "gorp" or other high energy concoctions. "Or, consider bringing a raw potato to cook on board. You'll have to wait until the regular meal service is over, then ask a galley attendant to throw it in an empty oven, 450 degrees for one hour" (Fairechild 1992, 25).

Clearly, it would take an unprecedented alteration of mass consciousness for air passengers to give up their in-flight meals, regardless of the health benefits. Eating on board, having those specially wrapped and sealed controlled portions handed to you by the friendly flight attendant, is simply too much of a treat, too helpful a boredom buster, to be denied. Curiously, doing away with meal service might actually lower the ticket price for jet travel. A significant portion of the costs is wrapped up in food—its supply, preparation, and garbage disposal. According to one account:

> The 63 million rolls and 7.5 million croissants that Delta AirLines uses every year for in-flight catering are part of a huge shopping list. On average it buys, per day, 65,552 chicken breasts, 49,267 liters of wine and 93,646 creamers. Food and catering cost an average $5.50 per meal (all classes). (*Colors* 1995, 27)

Furthermore, as one example, British Airways has to dispose of 11,500 tons of garbage per year from its catering facility at Heathrow airport alone (*Colors* 1995, 27).

By dispensing with all food preparation in flight, the price of an airline ticket might drop and people might have fewer health problems from traveling. Why don't passengers consider bringing their own food on board, for example? As our discussion of air malls has also shown, there is an increasing number of gourmet dining options at large airports. Perhaps people who are concerned about in-flight meals can take advantage of eating possibilities either before or after their flights.

I have had several positive experiences of this kind. In 1992 I was returning from an international trip with my family and we had to change planes at Charles de Gaulle, outside of Paris. We had several hours to kill before our flight home. Looking around for eating options, I noticed an advertisement for a gourmet restaurant high above the terminal building with prices that were still reasonable. The entire family came. We found an elegant restaurant with wide glass windows for observing flights and white tablecloths on the tables. The food was absolutely superb. In fact, it was as good a meal as others I had eaten on our trip, although perhaps not the very best.

As air travel becomes a more accepted part of life and as terminals continue their functional differentiation as places to linger in as well as to leave, superior dining options will proliferate. LAX has already moved in this direction by inviting Wolfgang Puck and other gourmet chefs to open franchises at the terminal. Other airports, like O'Hare, offer alternatives to eating on the plane. Fueling up before a flight in a healthier eating environment, or bringing your own favorite food on board, may make more sense than perennially complaining about bad airline meals. According to people like Fairechild, it is also better for you.

16

Crashes and Air Safety

Running half a hour late, Pan Am flight 103 departed London's Heathrow airport bound for New York City on the evening of December 21, 1988. The 747 carried 243 passengers along with 16 crew members. . . . Passing over Lockerbie, Scotland, the aircraft disintegrated when an explosion occurred in the forward baggage hold.

Andrew Ayers, 2000

Caught unawares at breakfast, after work, or at a bar with the TV on in the background, we have all seen the headlines: "Sudden Death in the Air," "Absolute Irreversible Tragedy," "Plane Crash Kills 112." Whether smacking into a fog-shrouded mountain or plunging horribly into the cold ocean, the pictures of a commercial airline wreck are always gut-wrenching. We remember these events, perhaps because of their complete suddenness, their total loss of life, or the finality of the whole experience, in a way that is different from other kinds of deaths that we hear about or even experience secondhand. Images remain forever in the mind—the 747 forward cabin of the Pan Am jetliner sitting crushed but intact on the windswept field in Lockerbie, Scotland; the burnt-out hulks of two planes that crashed on an LAX runway in 1991 with all lives lost; the mid-air collision downing PSA flight 182 with all lives lost; the downing of TWA flight 800; and so on. One observer recently noted, "Of all transportation industries, airlines have endured an almost mythological association with catastrophe, inspiring decades of disaster movies and spawning a cottage industry in fear-of-flying courses" (Goetz 1999, W-1).

*The forward cabin of Pan Am flight 103 lies crushed and torn on a field outside
Lockerbie, Scotland, a victim of terrorism. (AP photo-file)*

As any professional connected with the airline industry can testify, crashes are
an anticipated risk of air travel. When they happen, they are truly unsettling events
that grip the nation's attention. Unlike auto accidents that result in a loss of life,
air travel disasters are investigated with the full authority and precision of the
federal government. Each fatal accident is presented as a kind of mystery to the
public. A cause must be found. According to public expectation, these investiga-
tions must result in better safety measures, even if all crashes can't be prevented.

Oversight and greater technological sophistication, coupled with more professional practices, are bearing fruit. Despite occasional and horrible tragedies, domestic air travel is safer than in previous decades. In 1998 not a single life was
lost through air accidents by major commercial American carriers. Considering
the hundreds of millions of trips taken, this is an unprecedented feat in an industrial society. Even in less-safe years, the statistics are clear—air travel is safer
than auto transportation. "Risk analysts at Lloyds of London have rated flying
nearly thirty times safer than driving" (Fairechild 1992, 113). During the very
same year (1998), more than 5,000 people were killed in auto accidents involving
tractor-trailer trucks. The carnage on American highways consistently reaches in
excess of 25,000 deaths a year.

CELEBRITY CRASHES

Despite the improving safety record and following a very quiet year, a number
of unsettling events in 1999 brought the issue of air travel safety into the national

spotlight once again. On July 16, 1999, John F. Kennedy Jr., his wife, and his sister-in-law took off from Essex County Airport in New Jersey on a flight to Martha's Vineyard. About 17 miles from their destination, the plane suddenly lost 1,100 feet in 14 seconds, indicating that something had gone very wrong, and it disappeared below radar coverage. "'A descent this steep is consistent with a nose dive,' federal officials said" (*Buffalo News* 1999c, A-1). The plane's wreckage was discovered at dawn the next day. All three bodies were brought up later from the ice-cold depths where the Long Island Sound meets the Atlantic Ocean.

The spectacular Kennedy crash has little to do with commercial aviation, yet it mesmerized the nation and provoked a fear of flying in countless people. Kennedy took off without filing a flight plan, something common for small, private planes. But he chose to fly in total darkness, and even riskier, he chose a route that was entirely above water rather than the safer one that hugged the Connecticut shore. Without landmarks, the flight is a difficult one for small planes even in daylight. Riskiest of all, however, was his choice of planes. Kennedy, a new pilot with less than a year's experience, traded up to a high-performance Saratoga II plane that can fly over 200 miles per hour. According to one expert, it is a "muscled-up, high performance airplane that requires a butterfly touch— something Kennedy may not have yet acquired. . . . With a velocity that can exceed 200 mph, it's a good 50% faster than many simpler planes. At that kind of clip, things can go wrong in a hurry . . . a deadly combination of too much airplane and too green a pilot apparently proved disastrous" (Kluger 1999).

The steep descent and the explosive force with which the plane hit the water meant instant death for all aboard. While the circumstances of excessive risk and limited training have nothing to do with commercial aviation, the way the plane crashed does. Kennedy died because of something called the "graveyard spiral," the bane of every pilot and a set of deadly circumstances that has occurred more than once, even to commercial and well-trained pilots. Flight experts

> believe that Kennedy fell victim to a flying error common among inexperienced "visual" pilots who run into bad weather—the "graveyard spiral." The widely dispersed wreckage pattern indicates that Kennedy's Saratoga was out of control and hit the water at an extremely high rate of vertical speed. The strong gyrational forces and intense speed of an "uncontrolled" impact would have led the Saratoga to explode upon hitting the water, dispersing its parts over a wide area. (*Buffalo News* 1999c, A-1)

The graveyard spiral results when a pilot flying visually and without a horizontal indicator inadvertently allows a wing to drop, causing the plane to enter an unnoticed turn. When this happens, the aircraft can suddenly lose altitude because of the loss of lift on the dipped wing.

> Sensing such a problem, an [inexperienced] pilot might return attention to the standard flight instruments and quickly apply back pressure to the control stick, trying

to regain altitude. But pulling back on the stick also dramatically tightens the plane's turn. [The correct course of action, instead, would be to slowly increase the throttle and steer away from the turn until the plane was level again.] To compensate, a confused or panic-stricken pilot then "over-controls" applying even more back stick, making the turn, and thus the loss of altitude, more severe. The banking that results can corkscrew the plane into a descending and sometimes unrecoverable "grave-yard spiral." . . . Kennedy was not trained to use flight instruments, so he could have dropped into a nosedive without realizing it. (*Buffalo News* 1999c, A-4)

Who Kennedy was and what he represented to the American people made this crash an event of profound grief for the nation, even though the circumstances of excessive risk-taking are also now clear. Celebrity accidents turn an otherwise disastrous event occurring to anonymous people into a true national tragedy with extensive media coverage and commentaries. The story is told again and again with different nuances that reverberate all the way down the line of our mass media to the dreadful exploitative newspapers at supermarket checkout stands.

Shortly after this incident, on October 25, 1999, another celebrity—golf pro and legend Payne Stewart—died in a bizarre plane crash. Taking a Lear jet with a crew of two and three others, Stewart left Miami's Dade County Airport on a routine flight to Dallas/Fort Worth. Twenty minutes later, there was radio silence and all attempts to contact the plane failed. The jet kept flying on its original heading to the northwest for four more hours. At its cruising altitude of six miles high, the plane had turned into a ghost flight on automatic pilot with everyone aboard either dead or deeply unconscious. Traveling 1,400 miles further until its fuel ran out, the jet plunged 30,000 feet into a dirt field near Mina, South Da-kota, and hit the ground at an estimated 600 miles per hour. According to press accounts, the plane carved a 10-foot crater in the ground and its flight voice re-corder broke, even though it was guaranteed by the manufacturer to function up to a stress of 100 g's (Morse 1999). Investigators hypothesized that the seals to the cabin malfunctioned and the plane depressurized so rapidly that all aboard were knocked out or killed. Apparently, other Lear jets in recent years suffered a similar problem although the plane is widely used and very popular (Morse 1999).

The death of Payne Stewart held few lessons for commercial aviation but the public could not miss the details of the crash or the aftermath of the deaths. Stewart's biography and quickly edited testimonials were all over the nation's media on subsequent days. Any crash, no matter how strange, is unsettling and tragic. By personalizing the event because those involved were celebrities, the entire public bears the shock just a little more deeply and the fear of flying is renewed in our imaginations.

COMMERCIAL CRASHES

Six days after Payne Stewart's death, and not too far from Kennedy's demise off the island of Nantucket, another fatal accident occurred on October 31, 1999.

EgyptAir flight 990, a state-of-the-art Boeing 767, dropped from a height of 33,000 feet minutes after takeoff from New York's JFK and exploded on contact with the ocean, killing the more than 200 people aboard. Investigators determined that the big plane's engines were cut off in mid-flight, and that a fight had occurred between the copilot who had the controls after take-off and his pilot who was valiantly trying to regain them. Despite the objections of the copilot's family and Muslim clerics in Egypt, it is still widely believed that this man committed suicide and brought the plane down with him (*Buffalo News* 1999e, A-1).

The EgyptAir incident does concern average travelers. There are two aspects of the disaster that are most troubling. First, it was the last in a trio of widely publicized crashes in 1999 that occurred while the plane was en route. Accidents, if they do happen, usually occur on takeoff or landing—these are the times when both pilots and seasoned flyers are the most wary. Yet the tragedies of last year pointed to deadly circumstances that emerged during the relative safety and calm of mid-flight. Until the EgyptAir event, commercial jetliners did not simply drop out of the air from their cruising altitudes. Although the precipitating factors of all three crashes seem way out of the realm of possibility for most, if not all, commercial flights, these after-takeoff, in-flight disasters remain unsettling.

Even more pertinent, however, the EgyptAir crash highlights a set of circumstances that affects us all. As more countries rev up their commercial service, there will inevitably be more fatal accidents involving mass deaths. The record of all top carriers remains a good one, but the number of people flying throughout the

American Airlines flight 1420 lies broken in pieces under power lines after overshooting the runway on June 1, 1999, in Little Rock, Arkansas.
(AP photo/Danny Johnston, file)

world continues to increase week after week, month after month. More flights and more crowded skies are the inevitable outcome in the near future, and as more carriers get involved, we can expect more tragedies.

According to Walter Boyne, by the year 2015, and considering all airline trips across the globe, "we can expect to see at least one major airliner crash per week" (1999) Boyne adds,

> By 2015, the number of airliners flying is expected to grow from the current 14,000 to approximately 24,000, while the number of airline passengers will grow from 1.5 billion to more than 3 billion annually. These figures mean, in essence, that while it will still be as statistically safe to travel by air for an individual, that individual will be subjected to a weekly barrage of bad news about 200 or 300 other human beings whose lot it was to be the statistician's fodder. (1999)

In making this sobering prediction, Boyne has assumed that today's excellent safety practices will be maintained. Should they falter, the expected weekly death rate will climb farther. We already know that a number of foreign carriers are simply not to be trusted. Russia and China have particularly poor safety records. Other countries are perilous for travelers on domestic flights. Despite all this potential for disaster, flying remains a very safe mode of transportation. More importantly, the issue of safety for the American industry has led to a number of distinct improvements. Both management and government administrators right-fully feel that, because domestic passenger trips are expected to double over the next 10 years, improving safety records means a reduction in fatal crashes. Consequently, rather than expecting the domestic record of airline safety to remain the same, it is actually improving, thus making accidents within the United States even more rare in the future.

IMPROVING AIR SAFETY

In recent years, the Federal Aviation Administration (FAA) has mandated in-creased flight crew training. Navigational charts have improved, helping pilots identify ground obstacles more easily. Furthermore, "safety experts also point to a recent industry and FAA decision to allow pilots to abort landings if they aren't ready without having a mark on their record" (Goetz 1999). In fact, the industry has looked closely at past informal practices that penalized personnel for report-ing possible risks. An industry-wide initiative called the Aviation Safety Action Program was adopted in January 2000. "Pilots, mechanics and airline workers will be able to report everyday errors and problems without risking disciplinary action under a safety plan announced Friday by the Government and the airline industry" (Zaldivar 2000).

According to this report, American Airlines originated the change of policy in 1996 on a voluntary basis. Since then, thousands of reports on potential problems have helped prevent accidents. Many of the personnel are now eager to help notify management about the small details of operating commercial aircraft that have, in the past, fallen through the cracks of safety concerns, but can nevertheless cause fatal accidents.

> FAA officials said that the reports typically involve such things as confusing runway markings that might cause pilots to make a wrong turn, miscommunication among pilots and controllers, and a variety of in-flight glitches. The reporting at American has led to better signs and lighting at some airports and some new procedures. . . . Instead of trying to find a single cause of a major accident after it happens, they are now finding all the little things that might lead up to an accident beforehand. (Zaldivar 2000, A-3)

Another dimension that until recently has been relatively ignored is the accident response time at our domestic airfields. In many accidents that are the result of "runway incursions" of all kinds, people die not because they are killed in a crash but because of smoke inhalation after they have survived the initial impact. Therefore, if airports can accelerate their response times to accidents, more lives can be saved.

Recent reports indicate that at some airfields in the United States, response times are much too slow. On June 11, 1999, flight 1420 arrived at the Little Rock, Arkansas, airport, crashed, and slipped off the runway. It took 19 minutes for rescue crews and firefighters to reach the plane—an excessive delay—and 11 people died of smoke inhalation. The poor record prompted an investigation that revealed that many medium-sized or small airfields need to improve their rescue response times (Levin and Morrison 2000, A-8). As a result, greater attention is now being paid to quick rescue measures that can pull smoke-felled passengers from crashes at airports.

Due to the persisting improvements in air safety and the already low rate of incidents for domestic flights, the fear of flying seems exaggerated compared to the risk. Yet that fear remains primal as it lurks just beneath the surface of every flight. Fear of flying is part of our culture, our social consciousness, even as we advance to an age of flight unprecedented in history.

17

Fear of Flying

Despite the air travel industry's sterling safety record compared to other modes of transportation, the life-or-death aspect of flying frames the experience. Recent reports indicate that 25 percent of all American fliers have some fear of flying (Hunt 1999, W-1). In fact, risking death is the very essence of flying for most of us. One website—Plane Spotting—lists nicknames or acronyms of air carriers. Almost all of these sobriquets reference the act of crashing. Air BC is "Air Burn and Crash"; Air Cambodia, "Air Forbodia"; Air France, "Air Chance"; American Airlines, "Always Awful"; or "Abort, Abort"; British Airways, "British Aircrimes"; TWA, "Try Walking Again"; and United, "U Need Insurance That Exempts Death" or "U Never Intended To Eat Didya."

Behind the humor lies the frightening reality of air travel. Your life is in the hands of the pilot and maintenance personnel. Unlike almost every other kind of experience with professional services, traveling by air requires us to surrender *total* control of our existence. This is a primal act that provokes primitive fears for survival and it can be compared to entering the hospital for major surgery. The same surrendering of control over our lives to doctors usually compels people to choose their surgeons and hospitals carefully, as well as to take other precautions. Major surgery is often a profound *religious* experience for many people. In this sense, the situation of air travel is approached by the masses in a comparatively blasé manner. Many people find the unbounded nature of the demons let loose by being a jet plane passenger more than they can bear and they simply do not fly. Others deal with the anxiety through drinking on the plane or through a host of personal rituals that are invoked every time a trip is taken. Only the most seasoned travelers, the core of frequent fliers, seem to be immune from this life-or-death, primal dimension of air travel. They sit down and take out laptops or yellow pads and get to work. How much of this compulsive behavior is a coping mechanism for loss of control and fear of flying, we can never know. We do suspect, however, that the obvious white-knuckle riders are in touch with their feelings.

Diana Fairechild, the former flight attendant with over 20 years of flying experience, documents how the terror of facing death on a plane trip lies so slightly beneath the surface that, despite the façade of calm, it can be called forth with the slightest provocation:

> Many people reason with themselves that it's safe to fly, but they still feel fear. Sometimes a little mechanical trouble with the safety video prior to takeoff is enough to trigger the darkest sense of foreboding in some passengers. . . . "Ladies and Gentlemen," I said to a full first-class cabin one morning, "I have something to tell you." All passengers suddenly grayed. A hijacker? Engine trouble? I hadn't meant to distress anyone; I was simply in a hurry. So I quickly resumed, "Sorry to startle you; there's nothing to worry about. We have no knives and forks on board, that's what I need to tell you." (Fairechild 1992, 112, 115)

Air travel is unique because, deep down inside us, it is a "near death" experience. It is the most common way individuals surrender control and voluntarily place themselves in harm's way in contemporary society. If they drive, they are also at risk, but they remain in control behind the wheel. Air travel is a necessity for those people who seek a modern life that includes tourism and, increasingly, a professional, high-paying job with a global corporation. For this reason, flying is the example *par excellence* of the new mode of living in an advanced industrial society that mixes the dimension of *risk* with our belief that social evolution derives from life chances based on the distribution of wealth. For most of human history, our life chances have been almost exclusively a function of personal class status. Barring the unforeseen case of violence, robbery, war, or act of God, the principal way people prosper in life has always been through access to money. The richer you are, the better your opportunities for medical care, entertainment, leisure, work, education for your children, and positive living arrangements.

Now society has worked in a separate aspect to the determination of life chances. It is based on risk. We are no longer clear on how to achieve success in corporate life. We no longer know what the healthiest foods are to eat, or where the healthiest places to live are located. The professional work world requires taking greater chances. Finally, our choice of mate has grown increasingly complicated, as is the prediction of family success, especially with teenagers. All of these areas belonging to everyday reality bring distinct levels of risk.

Air travel personifies the risky activities that people pursue in order to live the types of lives expected of them in our society. People travel a lot for both business and pleasure, and the easiest, quickest way to cover these distances is by air. Sociologists talk of the *risk society,* where success or failure is often a product of chance factors. We achieve goals sometimes by sheer fate or serendipity as we move through complex social interactions. Recognizing the important role of chance in daily life exposes the fallacy of believing in traditional cause-and-effect paradigms that explain existence. This chance, or probabilistic quality of the quotidian, is often considered a feature of postmodernism, especially in the work of author Thomas Pynchon.

Pynchon's (1973) cosmology elevates the role of random, stochastic processes to the level of a dominant causal force. Chance, for Pynchon, is behind the workings of the universe itself. We are alive simply because, in the entire universe, random events eventually took the form on this planet that produced life. Our fate and our quality of life remain tied to those same stochastic processes. In our daily existence, it is precisely the chance moments that contain possibilities. Everything else is routine and predictable. We meet people, collect information, and connect with opportunities more through chance than design. Air travel is filled with these serendipitous encounters and this is especially true of air disasters. All planes are maintained according to the book. *There is no way of predicting when a crash will occur.* Because someone took a particular flight at a particular time, however, they die. Oxygen-producing equipment may have been carried in the cargo holds of jets for years, but it was only with the storage arrangements on the now defunct carrier ValuJet that the chemical reaction brought the plane down in the Florida swamp with total loss of life. Many random factors had to have been at work converging on a particular time and a particular place to make the probability of an accident tip over into a certainty. Such disasters are best explained by chaos theory (Langewiesche 1998, chapter 7).

To understand the risks of air travel, we have to give our minds over to chaos theory, to Pynchon's randomness, as the prime force in the universe, and abandon the old cause-and-effect way of thinking. According to Pynchon, the universe is guided by the laws of entropy. Things run down or break down. When they do so with a confluence of factors, a disaster occurs; we have no way of knowing beforehand with any degree of certainty when misfortune will strike. We can only gauge risk and likelihood. Air travel symbolizes this new, postmodern world, where God no longer writes the scripts of individual lives, where terrible tragedies occur because of massive system breakdowns rather than "evil" intentions, and where probability and not simple cause and effect explains success or fail-ure in life.

FEAR-OF-FLYING SEMINARS

Fear of flying limits the market for jet travel even to this day. Airlines are par-ticularly sensitive to the problem when it constrains their use by business. People who need to fly, yet remain horrified at the prospect, often resort to counseling and therapy to help them manage their terror. According to one report,

> Millions of the fearful refuse to fly. Among the notables are Aretha Franklin and sportscaster John Madden. The serious cases have panic attacks, sometimes just before the plane is about to take off. With waves of fear their hearts race, they sweat or feel hot, they can't breathe, they jump up and demand to be let out of the plane. (Clarke 1994, 164)

Lately several carriers have introduced structured seminars on coping—teach-ing the terrified to fly by managing their fear. American Airlines offers a semi-nar called AAirborne that costs $350 for two days; USAirways offers a Fearful Fliers Program that consists of five three-hour sessions during one week for $325. There is also a private company, Pegasus Fear of Flying Foundation, which holds seminars at airports and corporate offices.

According to one participant, the American Airlines seminar was helpful. It combined practical advice from professionals with old-fashioned therapy. Part of the cost is meant to cover an actual "graduation flight" with participants board-ing and flying round trip by air to practice their newly acquired coping skills.

> Our first session was a 10-hour marathon of myth-busting led by a pilot, a flight attendant and a mechanic. "Airplanes do not drop, dive, plummet or fall," they de-clared. A psychologist came next and taught participants to use everything from creative visualization and rhythmic breathing to snapping ourselves with a rubber band every time we imagined the plane taking one of those impossible dives. (Clarke 1994)

This report also mentions publications addressing the fear of flying: *The Fearful Fliers Resource Guide*, edited by Barry Elkus and Murray Tieger, available from Argonaut Entertainment, and *How to Fly* by Natalie Windsor, Corkscrew Press.

Becoming more aware of the comparative dangers of flying is also another way to cope. Air carriers vary according to their safety records. Some airports are safer than others. Statistics on these matters are available. Prospective passengers do have the option of researching the current records of air carriers and airports, though they are unlikely to do so. For example, "Serious errors at airports are called runway incursions, an all-encompassing term that could mean anything from planes taxiing too close to fatal collisions such as the one between two Northwest Airlines jets in Detroit in 1990. Runway incursions reached a five-year high of 281 in 1990, but fell to 204 last year [1995]" (Feld 1996b, 42).

International travel poses its own set of safety issues. Foreign carriers vary greatly regarding their safety records. Because our own country does not regulate them, records are not available from the Federal Aviation Administration, nor is the FAA obligated to inform consumers about the records of foreign carriers. "Countries that have air safety standards far below those of the U.S. include China, the former Soviet Union, India, Korea, Central Africa and Colombia. Unqualified staff, political problems, minimal security and poor maintenance lead to air accidents in these locations" (Murdoch 1994, 2).

Probably the best source of information on foreign travel risks comes from the International Airline Passengers Association, a consumer advocacy group. Their mailing address is P.O. Box 870188, Dallas, TX 75287.

According to Guy Murdoch, writing in *Consumers Research Magazine* (1994):

> Two countries . . . have horrendous air safety records: the former Soviet Union and China. In each of these countries, a recent explosion in the number of airlines accompanied by corrupt or nonexistent supervision, civil strife, and ancient infrastructure has created circumstances where passengers take their lives in their hands when they travel by air.

Murdoch is wrong on one account. Passengers *always* take their lives in their hands—that is the very essence of air travel that differentiates it from other professional services, except surgery. Still, information on foreign records *before* traveling helps. Tourists in Russia or China might be safer if they took the train, although who can really say? Murdoch also mentions other countries:

> In India, all domestic flights are considered unnecessarily dangerous. The same is true in Korea for all flights except those into Seoul by "honor roll" airlines. Also unacceptable are flights that pass through the Andes in South America. . . . Finally, most of Central Africa has conditions including political problems, poor air-traffic control systems with unqualified personnel, inadequate airports, minimal or no security at airports, and poor maintenance of aircraft that make air travel dangerous. (1994)

No one can predict whether we will become an inevitable statistic on our next flight, despite the fact that our chances for involvement in an accident by air are quite small. The fear of flying remains a pervasive one in our society. People can cope by learning more about flying, about statistics on safety, about safety measures themselves, and about safe and unsafe airlines, airports, or routes. Those that need the most help can also find it through participation in counseling, seminars, or other kinds of therapy. In the end, if your fear of flying remains (as it does with a number of celebrities), there is always the train or bus.

18

New Horrors

"We see lots of passengers," says [the] medical director for Kennedy International Airport. . . . Chest pain and heart attacks account for most medical incidents, followed by food-borne diseases, gastric upsets, ear problems and dehydration. "We've also had our share of deaths. I'd say we get inbound flights with dead bodies on them between five and ten times per year."

Brian Alexander, 1998

IT'S THE AIR IN THE AIR

People are stressed when flying, or afraid to fly, because they are making a life-or-death decision. Facing death provokes primal fears, yet air travel is statistically safer than driving a car. Recent safety records of U.S. carriers are truly impressive considering the intricacies of running complex organizations of this magnitude. In 1995 a record 548 million passengers flew on domestic flights. "The FAA sees the total headed toward 679 million by 2001 and 830 million by 2007" (Feld 1996b, 42). Ironically, the fear of flying that comes from facing death is minor compared to other horrors about air travel that have only recently been brought to light. As life in the air has become more commonplace, observers and analysts of all kinds have begun to examine the overall quality of the experience and have uncovered new terrors. Writing about alarming factors involved in flying is only an extension of our increasing concern about the general quality of our living and working environments. Information on hazardous aspects of air travel *within* the airplane is relatively new. One of the most compelling concerns involves the quality of cabin air.

120

Cabin air quality was not always seen as the problem that it is today. Airline passengers once breathed fresh air that whooshed through the cabin every three minutes, but beginning in the mid-eighties the airlines, in an attempt to boost fuel economy, began mixing recirculated air with fresh air, and only changing the air on an average of once every seven to nine minutes. The airlines have managed to save an average of $60,000 per plane annually because of the use of recycled air, but critics claim the high preponderance of recirculated air in the passenger cabins makes people extremely uncomfortable, if not downright sick. . . . In Canada alone, one in every 35 air travelers files an insurance claim relating to illnesses they believe they contracted during or after air travel. (Hanson 1997)

There are two distinct aspects to the problem of bad cabin air. First, recycled air has low oxygen content. Passengers breathe rarefied air. According to some doctors, on a long flight this can lead to a condition known as *hypoxia*, too low an oxygen level for the central nervous system to function properly. Symptoms of hypoxia are similar to high altitude sickness—lightheadedness, shallow breathing, and fatigue (Fairechild 1992, 74). Other symptoms include feeling clammy or stuffy, a common complaint when the plane is taxiing or idling on the runway. Oxygen deprivation can lead to a rapid pulse as the body tries to make up for the deficiency; on a long flight, this effect can be quite fatiguing. According to Diana Fairechild, "Many passengers notice the diminished oxygen in the cabin, but they don't speak up until after landing. Commercial airlines' ventilation/temperature was rated 'less than good' by 21% of 140,000 readers of *Consumer Reports* in 1990" (1992, 75).

The supply of oxygen on an airplane is determined by social status. Passenger planes carry several oxygen packs that pilots can use to enrich circulating air. These are usually turned off for coach. The cockpit purportedly has 10 times the oxygen level of coach (Fairechild 1992, 74). Clearly pilots need proper ventilation and oxygen levels to do their job with utmost safety, but even the first class section has more oxygen than coach. "'Are there any important advantages in flying first class? I believe there are none,' wrote the World Bank's Health Director. . . I have to disagree with the doctor. First class is not about gourmet fare; it's about air—approximately three times more per passenger than in economy." (Fairechild 1992, 76).

The second problem arising from heavily recycled air is the spread of germs and contaminants within the cabin. Internal airflow is filtered, but the system used in commercial aircraft does not block germs. Filters are notoriously gummed up from constant use. Fairechild quotes information that appeared in the *Journal of the American Medical Association*:

During the colder months, frequent fliers complain nonstop of upper respiratory tract infections. Severe infections are almost inevitable sequelae to intercontinental air travel presumably from prolonged recirculation of mixed viruses from 450 people in a confined area. . . . Airborne, biologically-derived particles include bacteria, viruses, and fungal spores. All can be present in aircraft cabins. Anything smaller than anthropod fragments [pieces of bugs] is not likely to be caught by the aircraft filters. (1992, 70)

Because ventilation may be turned off completely when planes are delayed at the gate or on the runway, the threat of being infected by other passengers increases greatly. These events occur more frequently during the winter months when bad weather plagues many airports.

Despite the recognition from medical authorities that air travel exposes passengers to potential illness, there is little documentation of precise effects. Perhaps the most important reason for this lack of information is the very nature of both travel and disease. On the one hand, people disperse after flights to a wide variety of local destinations. On the other hand, illnesses usually take time to incubate. Often someone infected on a flight might not become ill until days after landing. In addition, some physicians discount the possibility entirely that it is airplane cabin environments *per se* that cause disease. A federal aviation flight surgeon, for example, has claimed that it is actually the stress of traveling by air that produces ill health. Many others, such as the Association of Flight Attendants and consumer advocates like Fairechild, refute this argument and have been lobbying for years for better air quality.

The likely possibility of disease transmission by recirculated cabin air has been inadvertently substantiated by an irrefutable source. Recently, in the 1990s, the Centers for Disease Control in Atlanta documented several cases of passengers being infected with tuberculosis by fellow passengers carrying the disease while in flight (Hanson 1997). Diana Fairechild suggests that if you are seated near someone with a bad cough, you should ask the attendant for a change of location. On a crowded flight, however, attendants may not be able to accommodate you. In the long run, lobbying for better air quality and less recycled air on jet planes is recommended.

The issue of air quality on planes has become part of the new agenda of air travel concerns among consumer and professional organizations. Increased awareness—and the lobbying efforts that derive from it—constitutes one more dimension of living in the air that has important political implications.

19

Medical Emergencies

Another horror recently surfacing in press accounts and commentaries on life in the air is the special problem of medical care. Constrained inside a jet more than 30,000 feet in the air, any serious medical emergency can be lethal. Consider the following account:

> A young woman was in a motorcycle accident, but not thinking herself seriously injured continued on and took her flight. An hour into the Hong Kong to London flight, she developed chest pain and difficulty breathing. Two doctors were on board. They diagnosed a broken rib and pneumothorax, which is air in the chest cavity. The urgency of the situation demanded immediate treatment so a drainage tube was surgically inserted. The doctors used local anesthetic, a scalpel, surgical scissors, and a urinary catheter from the airplane's emergency medical kit and they improvised other surgical necessities from hand towels, a coat hanger, and a container of bottled water. Brandy was used to sterilize instruments. Once air was released from the chest, recovery was rapid. (Wallace et al. 1995)

The young woman in this case was extremely lucky. If there had been no doctors on board, she would have died.

For many years, airline policy has recommended that when a medical emergency develops, it is best to land the plane at the nearest airport. Consequently, flights were only provisioned with limited emergency kits containing the most basic items. On international flights over the ocean, however, any emergency could prove fatal because the plane simply cannot land. According to one estimate, the number of fatalities on planes worldwide remains low relative to the total volume of traffic and averaged 72 passengers a year as of 1988 (Woodyard 1995).

Despite this record, many emergency health incidents also occur that require quick medical treatment. One report claims 462 serious injuries in the three-year period prior to 1998. It stated: "90 percent of these were head injuries—mainly to those seated on the aisle—and 160 of which required medical attention" (Alexander 1998, 40). Another report by the Air Transport Association said "there were 10,471 medical incidents on the nine largest U.S. airlines during 1996" (Alexander 1998, 41). Unless there are trained medical personnel flying as passengers, little can be done until the plane lands.

> Airlines and the government are looking at ways to improve a difficult situation. Right now, the FAA requires that airlines teach flight attendants how to handle routine passenger illnesses or ailments such as fainting or epileptic seizures, but does not specify training other than familiarization with the medical kit. . . . Pilots are instructed to call medical base stations to consult with physicians and are authorized to divert the flight to the nearest airport where paramedics are standing by. (Woodyard 1995)

The worst medical emergency on an aircraft is a passenger with acute heart problems. Until recently, only a few transoceanic carriers, such as Qantas of Australia, carried defibrillators. Recent awareness of the problem, with people dying before the eyes of personnel and passengers alike, and the development of ultralightweight, easy-to-use machines, have led to improved availability of care. American Airlines has become the first U.S. carrier to stock defibrillators on many of its flights. Soon after their introduction in 1999, their use by the flight crew saved a life. "An American nonstop flight from Boston to Los Angeles was an hour east of Denver Thursday morning when Michael Tighe's heart began beating irregularly, no longer able to pump blood to his brain." Successfully employed by the crew, this was the first case of a defibrillator's use, two days after the machines were placed on the aircraft. "Except for that singular coincidence, Michael Tighe would have died in the aisle of a Boeing 757 somewhere over the eastern slope of the Rockies" (Crewdson n.d., A-18).

Like the issue of bad air, medical care is a contentious topic. Federal agencies, consumer advocate groups, corporate representatives of airlines, and professional organizations are pushing for changes, although different perspectives have brought forth contrasting and sometimes conflicting positions. Along with the voluntary introduction of defibrillators, other improvements are proposed. One new product is the smoke hood, which, although costly to provide on a mass basis, can save the life of any passenger who survives a crash. Consider the following account:

> On hands and knees in the smoke-filled cabin of the Boeing 737, David H. Koch knew he had to get out as fast as he could. "I stood up and put my head in the smoke and started coughing violently," Koch recalled. "I could feel the smoke starting to overcome me." His USAir flight had hit a commuter plane while landing at Los Angeles International Airport in 1991, and the burning craft pinned below was generating thick, black smoke. Seeing a sliver of light, Koch went for it. He was lucky; it was an exit. Twenty of the 23 fatalities on Koch's flight were attributed to smoke inhalation. Koch believes that most of the victims would have survived if they'd had smoke hoods, loose-fitting bags that are pulled over the head and provide clean air to breathe. (Kramer 1998)

Like other possible safety measures that cost money, airlines are reluctant to deal with the matter, but greater awareness is bringing change. Smoke hoods have been in and out of discussion for 30 years. The FAA claims that in an emergency warranting fast exiting of the airplane, passengers would waste precious time putting on the hoods (Kramer 1998). Proponents claim that the issue is about money. In 1993 the FAA turned down a proposal to make smoke hoods available on commercial aircraft. "In denying the request, the FAA cited an association analysis that put the cost to buy and install the hoods industry-wide at $127.7 million" (Kramer 1998). Proponents argue that the expense is much less than other safety systems that commercial carriers have already installed, such as onboard, computerized warning systems or cargo hold fire-suppression systems following the crash of ValuJet. This tends to support the corporate argument that the issue is about evacuation times, not money.

In short, the issue remains hotly contested with the federal government, consumer advocacy groups, professional service associations, the media, and ordinary citizens involved. Most likely some compromise will occur in the future and a form of smoke hood safety device will be a fact on flights. In the meantime, fliers interested in having one can purchase smoke hoods from vendors, such as Brookdale International Systems, Essex PB&R Corporation, and others. Prices ranged from $70 to $160 in 1998 (Kramer 1998).

20

Dehydration

In a discussion of medical ailments caused by flying, the director of the medical offices at Kennedy International Airport in New York City mentioned that dehydration was one that they treated (Alexander 1998). Because drink service is such a basic feature of air travel, this fact seems quite odd. How can passengers become dehydrated when flight attendants ply them constantly with both soft and alcoholic drinks? The answer lies in the lack of moisture content of cabin air and the failure of passengers to hydrate themselves. The issue raised here is not about poor quality cabin air per se, but the quality of the air—in this case, its incredible dryness—of which all passengers should be aware.

"Inflight cabin air is dryer than any of the world's deserts. Typically, relative humidity (the moisture content of the air) is 20–25% in the Sahara or Arabian deserts, while optimum comfort is around 50–55%" (Fairechild 1992, 57). Diana Fairechild quotes a report that appeared in the journal *Aviation, Space and Environmental Medicine* claiming that, on long distance flights, cabin humidity levels drop to "well below 10%, in many cases approaching 1%" once ground-level humidity has dissipated.

On long flights then, passengers run the risk of suffering dehydration, which is known to severely stress bodily organs. Effects also have no class distinctions. Dehydration problems are as much a bane to the flight crew and first class as coach. Fairechild has an interesting solution to the problem, but I don't think many passengers would be willing to follow her advice:

> For humidified breathing air: cover your nose and mouth with a water-saturated large cotton hanky. Fold on the diagonal and wrap ends around ears. The speed with which moisture evaporates from this hanky will give you some idea of the degree of the aircraft's dryness. On twelve-hour flights, for example, a passenger may want to wet the hanky a dozen or so times for comfortable humidity. (1992, 58)

A less humiliating and less obtrusive solution is simply to drink plenty of water while in flight. Imbibing in this fashion runs counter to the socially expected norm of alcohol consumption, especially in business and first class. Alcohol only compounds the problem of dehydration, as well as causing other ones that are associated with "bad" passenger behavior. Currently, however, airline beverage service enforces a norm of drinking as "treats," whether it is sugared and caffeinated beverages or wine, beer, and hard liquor. According to Fairechild, "Frequent fliers know that alcohol and altitude are not compatible. Alcohol poisons the tissue cells so that we cannot utilize oxygen properly. With the already reduced oxygen supply in jets, this ill effect is even more pronounced" (1992, 60).

Technology does exist to humidify jet cabins. The main drawback to deploying such equipment is the amount of water passenger planes would have to carry in order to operate the hardware. "For example, to sustain a relative humidity of 35%, a 747 [aircraft] will need to weigh 2200 pounds more on takeoff—translating into about fifteen passengers left at the gate!" The cost, then, is prohibitive. Because every passenger has the ability to overcome the low cabin humidity by drinking water, unlike the case of low oxygen content in the air, this matter is not likely to become the kind of issue that other negative aspects of air travel have already assumed. There are no regulatory conflicts nor are there any consumer groups advocating more humidity in flight, the way they are with oxygen. Despite the medical concerns and the well-known ill effects of potential dehydration, most airline in-flight service will probably retain its norm of celebration with soft drinks and alcohol served in abundance. However, if future travelers encounter a seated passenger with a wet hanky covering his or her face, they will know that this person has probably read Diana Fairechild's book and taken it to heart.

Jetlag: Flying and Folk Religion

Jetlag is definitely not psychological; it is cycle logical. The reason we experience jetlag is because all our internal cycles—such as temperature, sleep patterns, sexual desires, cravings for sweets, reactions to medications, susceptibility to illnesses and more—are disrupted when we travel.

Diana Fairechild, 1992

$\mathbf{F}$or the average consumer, taking a plane trip is framed by the fear of flying, involving nothing more nor less than a fear of crashing, whether it is on takeoff, landing, or caused by turbulence. People are afraid of turbulence in flight; many have a fear that the wings of the jet will fall off, or perhaps worse, that the plane's cabin will be ripped open and that they will be sucked out—this happened several times because of aging jet bodies, although it is a rare occurrence.

If there is a spiritual component to air travel, its most obvious incarnations are the rituals performed by superstitious travelers that are intended to ward off a crash or disaster of some kind. I have seen people pray before takeoff or watched a seatmate adjust body and harness and then assume a distinct position with eyes closed prior to flight and landings.

THE NEW TERROR ZONE

Regardless of the depth of this fear and its diverse manifestations, Diana Fairechild's book virtually dismisses such worries. Fairechild has no fear of flying in the common sense. Instead, she lays out problem after problem in chapters that create a new universe of fear by *redefining* the airplane itself as a terror zone. Sitting on a plane, we are really less the captives of our own fear of flying than an imprisoned passenger subjected to extreme environmental threats to the body and mind.

People are already aware that their environment bombards them with constant hazards. Consciousness has been raised about the food we eat, the air we breathe, and the water we drink. We know that plastics often contain toxic chemicals that are carcinogens, that sunlight can cause cancer, that smog and industrial pollutants damage our lungs, and that environmental stress attacks the immune system, making us susceptible to more common illnesses. Fairechild transposes this domain of everyday terror from life on earth to the experience of air travel. Furthermore, she extends her discussion to cover the emotional and mental stresses of that experience. These two areas of concern she calls *jetsmog* and *jetlag*.

Jetsmog is the internal environment of the airplane. According to Fairechild, it is almost unfit for human life. It has little oxygen, is filled with the germs of other passengers, and contains fungus spores and chemical pesticides at toxic levels. Finally, the entire cabin is bathed in low-level electromagnetic radiation from flight equipment and x-rays encountered at high altitudes. The longer the flight, the more the exposure. Passengers on the chic, supersonic Concorde are practically in outer space at 60,000 feet. They are subjected to x-ray and cosmic radiation, as are astronauts. If these concerns are not enough, Fairechild exposes the practice by some airlines of spraying noxious chemicals into the air supply of the cabin to act as a pesticide prior to landing. This procedure occurs on international flights by some carriers to countries that require it as a precondition for landing. Most Americans do not encounter the practice unless they travel to these destinations, which are listed in her book. During her career as a flight attendant, Fairechild was exposed to pesticides so often that she developed toxic poisoning and was forced to retire.

Jetsmog leads to jetlag. The body and mind are weakened by hazardous environmental exposure. People on long flights require downtime at their destination to recover, sometimes to excess. As Fairechild points out, the negative effects can occur quite frequently even if no time zones are actually crossed, for example, in travel from the East Coast of the U.S. to the interior of South America. It is the length of time in the cabin environment, rather than the sheer effect of time changes alone, that leaves the body and mind depleted. The majority of Fairechild's solutions to jetlag—she lists over 200 of them—consist of New Age thinking applied to environmental stress (1992). We are told to immerse ourselves in water immediately after a long flight to eliminate the negative electrical effects of travel. We are advised to commune with nature, to eat natural foods, to drink pure water, and to meditate. Fairechild has a veritable liturgy of meditations dispersed throughout her book.

The most fascinating aspect of her discussion is her reinterpretation of those aspects of air travel that we most desire. As we have seen, drinking alcohol is one of the very worst things you can do on a plane. Another debilitating activity is to eat airline food. Partying in the air leads to prolonged jetlag on the ground.

Fairechild is a sincere person. Her advocacy of more oxygen for coach passengers is a blessing to us all, as are the tips she has for managing jetlag. We would probably be better off if we prepared our own snacks to eat on the plane and certainly airlines would save a lot of money if they went out of the catering business. However, some of the truly frightening hazards Fairechild mentions are simply beyond our control and only add to the fear of flying. Exposure to radiation, to pesticides, and to cabin carcinogens are no doubt real events of travel, but they can hardly be avoided at present. We can applaud her call for increased consumer lobbying to change the present conditions, but in the meantime, we all have to fly. The same can be said for our acceptance of exposure to these same threats in daily life on the ground. To this extent, air travel is an extension of our everyday traumas and their presence in the air deflates the wonder and allure of travel. These environmental terrors are part of the risks we all bear whether we are flying or simply earthbound.

By calling attention to the hazards of air travel, Fairechild extends the domain of terror already enveloping life on earth. Out of our control, they only add to our feelings of helplessness. What may be worse, knowledge of the risks creates a conflict situation with our own plans for vacations and leisure. This is not Fairechild's fault, because her sensitivity to any kind of damaging environmental exposure is part of the cultural sensibility of a large segment of the population that now examines every conceivable fraction of our existence for potential dangers to life. We live in a culture of everyday terror that is only amplified by air travel. This is ironic because in the United States flying itself is incredibly safe. With enough reminders, consumers and professional associations may create healthier jet environments and more governmental regulations, but the attractiveness of flying will remain regardless.

Despite her contribution to the culture of fear, Fairechild has provided an important interpretation of frequent flying that remains useful. Because air travel is a kind of near-death experience, it should be approached *spiritually*. Jetlag, the bane of frequent fliers in particular, can be dealt with by meditating on the positive possibilities of flight. Attention to the eating, resting, and stress reduction prescriptions of her book probably does reduce the physical and mental stress of long trips. Who better to know how to manage this experience than veteran crew personnel? The ultimate guide to *all* the terrors of jet travel and to those of daily life is proper mental attitude. Consider these observations:

How we adjust to the multiple stressors of jetlag, jet-smog and jet-tag impacts our journey at every stage and on every level. . . . Picture yourself accomplishing the following tasks; as you observe yourself, imagine you can feel your level of stress. What are you like as you research airfares? Make decisions on climate, hotel, transportation, and recreation at your destination? Is packing and handling baggage a struggle or a juggle? Do you leave your house a certain way, or in disarray? . . . At the airport, how do you greet the agent? Do you face delay with equanimity? Bristle at security? (Fairechild 1992, 123)

For Fairechild, jet travel is simply an extension of daily life, but because of its unique level of stress, it is also an occasion to reexamine and deploy mechanisms that will aid us in living. Such wisdom may not be relevant to the occasional traveler or tourist who might prefer to treat an impending flight by reveling in stress precisely because it marks an extraordinary event. The majority of frequent fliers who must travel for a living, however, require some help with the rigors and stresses that accompany flight. Both crew personnel and business people who suffer unduly from jetlag can court failure on the job and in their important interactions with others. They require enlightened coping mechanisms. Where they find the kind of help they need is less important than the recognition that flying is in many ways simply an extension of life on the ground.

Despite the current efforts of airlines to create an atmosphere of sheer indulgence and celebration with gourmet meals and plentiful alcohol, the more people learn about managing the stress of travel, the more they will adjust by creating a more suitable type of healthy behavior. In the future, if consumer advocates have done their job, the air cabin milieu of excess and the carnival abandonment to food and drink, which airlines use to compete with each other in first and business class, may be replaced by a more sober, more spiritual, and more contemplative time in the air. Perhaps Fairechild is right; she certainly has had enough air flying time and has given the matter much thought When flying across time zones, bring your own food, be prepared to meditate, to sleep, to read, to sit quietly, and to think about the wonder of it all.

COMBATTING JETLAG

Someone I know is the principal violinist for an internationally famous symphony orchestra. She mentioned one day that on a recent trip halfway around the world, the symphony played disastrously and was given a terrible review in the local press. When I asked her to describe the nature of her flight experience touring for the symphony, she mentioned that plane trips were always a time of excitement and symphony members took the occasion to socialize. This orchestra's trips were busy events of drinking, eating, and talking. She also mentioned that the members suffered badly from jetlag. The poor performances they had recently given were a result of fatigue from travel.

Astoundingly, the management of the symphony failed to put these two pieces together. Taking long international flights while spending time socializing and drinking, without sleeping, is a recipe guaranteed to produce a monstrous and debilitating case of jetlag.

As a consequence of writing this book, I have tried out several techniques recommended by Fairechild and others who fly frequently and who write about the negative effects of crossing time zones. Here are my suggestions for combatting jetlag:

1. Long flights are for sleeping.
2. Never drink alcohol. Use a sleep aid or a doctor-prescribed tranquilizer to put you under.
3. Wear earplugs. Get the ones that equalize air pressure for greater comfort.
4. Use more than one pillow. Take them from the overhead bin, if they are available, or ask the flight crew for extras. Place pillows in spots to support your body. Then, wrap yourself in a blanket and, lastly, attach the safety belt around you so that it shows. This way, the flight crew will not wake you if the plane encounters turbulence.
5. Do not eat food until you have spent the major portion of the flight in sleep. Give instructions to the flight crew not to bother you. When awake, drink plenty of water. Keep hydrated. Bring your own food and snacks. Prepare your favorite sandwich to take along. After sleep it is OK to eat an airline breakfast meal on board.
6. On arrival, expose yourself to sunlight as soon as possible. Taking walks is best. Get out in the sun, if it is available, every chance you get at the new destination. Experiment with melatonin to see if it helps readjust your body clock. Start with the smallest possible dose.
7. Good luck.

Part 4

The Compression of Space and Time

22

Industrial and Corporate Changes

> [W]e have been experiencing, these last two decades, an intense phase of time-space compression that has had a disorienting and disruptive impact upon political-economic practices, the balance of class power, as well as upon cultural and social life.
>
> David Harvey, 1988

Social scientists consider time/space compression an important characteristic of contemporary society (Harvey 1988). Much of the academic discussion concerns the way business enterprises have changed to meet the realities of profit-making at the beginning of the new millennium. In the past, producers of manufactured goods possessed a more localized horizon. Managerial, factory, and even marketing centers were located near each other. Competition among producers making the same product took place through advertising, which increasingly appeared in new media such as radio and television. Cost-cutting considerations and effective advertising remain key concerns of business, but now corporations use space and time to produce profits as well. Factories are dispersed according to the needs of markets and the cheapest supply of labor. Often this means that production facilities are located in foreign countries where there are no unions and where the labor force works long hours for much less pay than their American counterparts. Management centers are also separated from production units. At times, these are located where professionals prefer to live—in rustic settings, in places with "good" climates, in low-tax suburbs, or in large metropolitan centers where like-minded businesses congregate to share knowledge. Decisions about location—the creative use of space—have become one means of acquiring a competitive edge.

Corporations also use time to their advantage. Electronic modes of communication shorten the lag time between messages. Technical knowledge is downloaded at production sites through computers and automation. Suppliers, subcontractors, and distributors are all linked with producers in real time so that waits between steps in the manufacturing process are kept to a minimum. Among the many variations of this new mode of organization, the Japanese *koban*, or "just-in-time" system of supply, has been the most widely emulated. Producers abandon the function of stocking inventory and jettison in-house units that manufacture selected parts that can be built by other companies at lower costs. They then create a network of independent suppliers and subcontractors that pledge to deliver needed inputs to production "just in time." In this system, the principal company organizes time in great detail and it is the outside suppliers who bear the cost of providing inputs. Organization of a manufacturing enterprise along these lines often utilizes packaged systems such as CAM (Computer Assisted Manufacturing) to ensure that all parts of the puzzle come together when expected, while inputs are shipped using the most up-to-date and swiftest means.

With space/time compression, production ranges across space searching out the cheapest costs, times are shortened, and the speed of resource utilization is maximized. The result is a corporation that is capable of quicker responses to a changing environment than in the past (Piore and Sabel 1984). Social scientists use the word *flexibility* to describe the principal characteristic of this new mode of business organization (Harvey 1988; Gottdiener and Komninos 1989). Successful corporations strive to become more responsive to consumer demand, to have greater flexibility in forms of management, to have the capacity to switch labor sources according to costs, and to rapidly coordinate marketing and distribution across increasing distances (Lash and Urry 1994; Castells 1996). While not every sector of industry has been equally affected by these changes, the sum total of their influence has been characterized by social scientists as *globalization*. As Scott Lash and John Urry remark, "Capital circulates not only along routes of greater and greater distance, but also—especially with the rise and increasing capacities of electronic networks—at ever greater velocity" (1994).

According to many observers, the global scale of production and marketing has been made possible by the ability of business to use telecommunications and computer technology to effect an efficient and profitable organizational hold on dispersed subunits of the corporation. According to Manuel Castells:

> The international/global economy is organized around command and control centers able to coordinate, innovate, and manage the intertwined activities of networks of firms. Advanced services including finance, insurance, real estate, consulting, legal services, advertising, design, marketing, public relations, security, information gathering, and management of information systems . . . are at the core of all economic processes. (1996, 377)

Consider the case of sneakers. They are typically manufactured in developing countries with cheap labor. They are distributed and sold in other countries at a hundred times what they cost. Advertising and marketing through global media such as satellite television and mass magazine publications jack up the price. Celebrity endorsements, such as ads featuring famous basketball players, make the foreign-manufactured sneakers "must-have" items, especially among children who can least afford them. Magically, large companies like Nike and Adidas can manufacture an incredible diversity of products—not just any ordinary sneaker, but shoes of such varied design and function that they literally challenge the consumer to reject the possibility of making a choice. All of this, the entire operation stretching from locations around the globe, can be coordinated successfully from a single command and control center through the use of electronic telecommunications and computers. Even so, this much-celebrated, new mode of global operation cannot succeed without frequent air travel.

23

The Need for Air Travel

The new emphasis on space and time as flexible and controllable factors in corporate profit making and the increasingly far-flung scale of corporate operations called globalization have created a need for a select segment of the work force to travel more frequently and over longer distances than has ever been imagined. Social scientists who study the new trends consider the 1970s a critical point when such sweeping organizational changes began to occur in American businesses. At about this time, air travel also entered a new phase where a mass market of passengers was produced through societal conditions. A social infrastructure surrounding the use of jet planes for travel by average citizens became increasingly normative. As flying became a more frequent occurrence for an increasing number of people, both business and tourism adjusted their operations to accommodate the airplane user. Important but subtle interactive social changes followed to make flying a regular and reliable event.

Among the reasons for the appearance of mass air travel in the late 1960s are the following:

1. During the 1960s, an extended period of prosperity kicked in, after the recession of the 1950s, that resulted in rapidly rising real incomes. By the

1970s, American workers had an unprecedented *real* wage. (After declining substantially in the 1980s, it has yet to be matched during the boom period of the 1990s.) More disposable income meant more people in the market for air transportation both for personal and business purposes.

2. Beginning with the postwar period, an immense and unprecedented population shift brought millions of people to the Sunbelt and the West Coast. Population in the United States had been concentrated in the Northeast and Midwest. Trips previously could be taken by car, rail, or bus with enough convenience. In the 1960s, the growth of metropolitan areas in the Sunbelt, coupled with the shift of business to the West and South, created a *national* system of manufacturing and a subsequent, very profound, dispersal of population by the millions, making air travel a necessity. Wars in Asia—first with Japan, then with North Korea—had compelled the federal government to pump billions into infrastructure with subsidies that benefited the Sunbelt enormously. With the unparalleled amount of military spending during the war in Vietnam, and the effective operation of "pork barrel" programs by politicians for their home districts, the wealth was spread around. Growth of economically successful areas in the once sparsely populated regions of the country exploded. It became a norm for people around the nation to use air transportation to visit relatives, reunite with families during holidays, conduct business, and engage in leisure activities like vacations.

3. Creation of the 727 workhorse jet airliner by Boeing provided airlines with a durable, comfortable plane that fit mass air travel needs. Combined with cheap fuel and a surplus of pilots/mechanics due to the earlier military endeavors all the way from World War II to Vietnam, it was possible for many corporations to enter the business of passenger flight despite its economically risky nature. Major players of that time, like Eastern, Pan Am, and Braniff, for example, no longer exist today; others, like TWA, are shells of their former selves.

4. In the 1960s, the famous IBM 360 computer was introduced and perfected as *the* business mainframe. The 360 revolutionized booking, accounting, scheduling, and cost management for airlines in particular, and all big business in general. Computer booking systems developed by IBM, such as SABRE, gave the airlines that used them a competitive edge (Petzinger 1995). Other air carriers that had entered reservations manually soon joined the computer revolution, making the entire national system more efficient and thereby increasing its capacity.

5. Along with business and personal travel, the 1960s ushered in a period of tourism that grows even today. Specialized places for leisure and recreation were developed in an expanding domestic tourist industry at the same time that foreign travel, often organized as tours, became more feasible for the average person. In the United States, tourist meccas began to emerge in Las

Vegas, South Florida, Los Angeles, San Francisco, and New York. More specialized places for leisure, such as the skiing industry in Colorado and Utah, or the snowbird migration each winter to the beaches of Florida, Puerto Rico, and the Caribbean, complemented the increasing variety of tourist destinations during the entire year.

Pushed by these and other changes in mass travel by air and the increasing global reach of business, airplane trips not only became the norm for business and tourism, even for short trips between locations, but more people who may have been reluctant to fly, either because of the cost or the risk, welcomed the chance and joined the ranks of passengers by the 1970s and 1980s. Space/time compression became a common experience for an increasing majority of Americans. This change required a shift in sensibilities and modes of service occupations that has not been widely recognized. People who travel by air must trust the social institutions involved. Airlines had to be trusted. Hotels and rental car companies had to deliver reliable products. Services for tourists and business travelers alike had to achieve a level of reliability and standard of practice that would satisfy customers and preclude unexpected or unnecessary inconveniences. The *mass* phenomenon of travel would otherwise not have evolved.

People who fly by plane require that their trip be comparatively "normal," and furthermore, when they arrive at their destination, they expect that arrangements on the ground also suit their purpose. Hotels and rental car companies, for example, had to develop reasonable, predictable services. Companies in locations around the globe connected to this emergent social infrastructure catering to travelers by providing products that could be understood, used, and relied upon beforehand. *All* expectations had to be met. The result of this new social practice of mass travel by air is the infrastructure of hubs, spokes, vectors, terminals, hotel destinations, ground transport, tourist offices, banks, travelers checks, easily available tourist guide books, and corporations that we observe today as mutually connected in a globally functioning economy.

One of the true pioneers of this transnational travel infrastructure was the Thomas Cook & Son Company, which invented traveler's checks and made trips to exotic locations feasible and practical, if not also enjoyable (Lash and Urry 1994). Today commercial aviation relies on an extensive, global infrastructure representing billions of dollars. We can fly virtually anywhere in the world and be reasonably certain of both safety in the air and comfortable accommodations once we arrive.

24

Experiencing Space/Time Compression

Space/time compression through air travel has special dimensions when experienced personally. It is different from the phenomenon regarding the way business now deals globally. Personally experienced, flying from one place to another different location brings on a *cognitive* form of space/time compression that is similar to culture shock. This is best understood by the frequent flier. Of all the effects of air travel—including jetlag, unknown illness, serendipitous meetings with the opposite sex, lost baggage, unhappy flights, and delays—the most powerful is the compression of space and time through bi-coastalism. Cosmically speaking, switching spaces through jet travel means *literally* living in two places at once.

THE BI-COASTAL CONDITION

Most people who fly ignore the compression of space and time. Traveling only occasionally, a trip by air is still a special event. People mark the time as a definite transition and behave accordingly by focusing on the trip as a unique occasion.

Upon arrival they sleep in and allow themselves downtime to adjust. Their destination point is viewed as something fundamentally different from their place of departure, even if they stay in the kinds of franchised hotels that are similar everywhere. Through a mental device, we preserve the uniqueness of locations. If we are tourists, we accomplish the task in a relatively easy manner. We change identities by flying and arrive as a person on holiday. We then behave in a holiday mode. We take photos so that we can document and remember the physical accomplishment of changing places. Our new location is defined as different from the one where we spend daily life. It is a space of leisure, travel, and rest. We consume the tourist services and "commodified" exoticism of our vacation spot.

People who travel for business—the road warriors—have a different experience. One place is tied to another by the normative, expected ways of doing business. Arriving after a flight, business travelers must find their way to the plant or office and get to work. Their visit is an extension of daily life at the point of departure, not a separate, distinct location that allows for a change of identity or respite from the world of work. Travel under these circumstances is more ordinary, more routine.

Being bi-coastal is like being a frequent business flier only the experience is amplified, made more extreme.

For over a decade I lived in Southern California, in and around the city of Los Angeles. My wife and I started our family there. Wanting to leave the area because we had grown tired of the Los Angeles way of life, I accepted a position in Manhattan in 1992. Unsure whether we truly wanted to make the move, my wife and children stayed in California. In short, like many people before and since that time, I became bi-coastal. Despite being away from my home and family, I had to establish a home in my new location and that home had to have enough conveniences of daily life to make staying there comfortable. It was *habituated*, perhaps not in the same fine-grained way as my house in Southern California, but nevertheless, it was a place that over time took on the trappings of a space where I spent an everyday life. I was, in short, in two places at once.

With two small children, I resolved when I took the new position to see them as often as I could. My new job was like my old one. I was a professor at a university. I was expected to teach and conduct research that would be published. I had the normal teaching load, two courses a semester. Because of my situation, the new institution allowed me to have a Tuesday/Thursday schedule. When conditions at work allowed, I traveled back to the West Coast after classes on Thursday and visited my family until the following Monday evening. There were no flights early enough on Tuesday morning to make up the three-hour deficit from the West to the East Coast and get me to New York in time for my Tuesday classes. I went home an average of twice every month during each semester, with holiday times such as Christmas and intersession spent totally in Southern California. During the semester, then, I was flying back and forth once every two weeks.

The graphic contrast between Los Angeles and Manhattan could be the subject of an entirely separate discussion because the two coasts have such different lifestyles, yet are so similar in other ways. More relevant to the subject of frequent flying, however, was not the experiential contrast in locations per se, which is also common to tourism, but the cognitive or emotional contrast created by the compression of space and time, of literally *living* in two places at once. On Thursday I would be teaching a class of New York kids, dealing with their "stuff," riding the subways under Manhattan, interacting with store clerks and service workers who lived in the Bronx or Brooklyn or Queens and had New York lives of their own. That very evening, after taking advantage of the three-hour time difference between the East and West Coasts, I found myself eating dinner in the kitchen of my house in suburban Los Angeles surrounded by my wife and children. Reversing the experience, with dinner at home and a quick drive to the airport for a red-eye flight back to Manhattan on Monday evening, did not detract from the strangeness of the experience.

Each time I made the trip, it was the compression of space and time that affected my mental state most. While living in my apartment in Manhattan, it was very much like I had no family. My life in Southern California, with wife, children, and home, was just a vivid memory. When I was back home, the thought that I was also a professor at a university in the very dense environment of Manhattan, with a teaching schedule, committee assignments, and a daily routine of shopping, commuting, and working, seemed like some very bizarre dream of someone else's life. In between these times and feelings, I became confused, depressed, disoriented, and easily panicked, as if some trap door into a black, immense universe could be kicked open beneath my feet at any moment. I suffered from bi-coastalism. At least one other person has reported that it gives you "bad dreams" (National Public Radio 1997). Believe me, it does!

Because I was traveling every two weeks, I quickly withdrew into my other life whenever I was hassled by something within a few days of departure. In a sense, I made the trip to the opposite coast in my mind, before I stepped onto the plane. With withdrawal so easy, I was able to cope, and I also had the luxurious option of screwing up if I wanted to. Most of the time I took my role as parent very seriously—perhaps out of guilt at being away. Back home on my frequent weekend visits I became super-dad, catering to every whim of my wife and children. I would drive the children around, go to their school athletic events, take them to the library, be on call as their chauffeur, teacher, and guide. My wife was treated in the same way. I was her attentive, patient audience for the minute, detailed accounts of her day-to-day job and family activities. I did the grocery shopping and worked on the house. At night we renewed a loving, intimate relationship that was strained by my absence. But when some explosion occurred between the kids or when the boring details of running a household, the bane of every housewife, got too much, I relaxed by drifting away, by thinking of my small apartment in Manhattan, a dark and comparatively quiet space.

At work on the East Coast, I resorted to this mechanism more often. Stresses always popped up. The insanity of trying to run a public university within the context of New York City politics and social unrest burst into the academic reality of classes, faculty meetings, and administrative announcements a hundred times a day. Most professors did their best suffering through the humiliation of dealing with complaining students and carnivorous administrators looking to cut costs.

A respected colleague of mine invited me out to lunch one day. At the table during the meal he brought up the subject of his graduate days at UCLA 25 years before and how much he loved California.

Lowering his voice he then mentioned that, before taking the job in Manhattan, he had purchased a small house in Venice, California, "just a few blocks from the beach." He proudly added, "And I never gave it up. I rent it out every year, except for July and August, and that's where I go for my summers." He paused to allow me the chance to visibly appreciate his position.

I encouraged him with a look of awe. Then he added, in an even lower voice, getting quite close to me, that he still kept his California driver's license and never got a New York one, even after working in Manhattan for 25 years. Pausing, he pulled out his wallet and showed it to me. I looked at it and noticed his picture taken when he was quite young. "Spending my summers in California is the only way I can tolerate New York," he added. Apparently, I wasn't the only one that used bi-coastalism to effect a mental distance as a survival mechanism for teaching at the City University. This professor had been doing it for over two decades!

Bi-coastalism is a more conceptual, more cognitive, and more emotional response than a physical one. When flying goes right, you can get used to the trip itself. With delays, missed flights, the dash to the airport, long check-in lines, and screaming babies in the next row, the stressful and physical aspects of flight can, however, be overwhelming. Whether you suffer terribly on the trip or not, being bi-coastal leaves you with having to confront two separate realities, to actually live in two separate realities, and you must be able to function in both. Because being bi-coastal means having a daily, everyday life in two distinct locations, you can't play the role of the tourist. You have to function and you have to meet people's expectations in both locations. Yet you also have to behave *as if* you have been living in only one place all along. Most of the time this is not a difficult task. In fact, it can be quite stimulating because the bi-coastal trip breaks the routine of ordinary activities at home. At times, however, when the stress of daily living gets too much, it becomes easier to simply withdraw, to put distance between yourself and the people asking too much of you or bothering you in some other way, and to project into your "other" life.

Something about the stresses of daily life in our largest cities makes having more than one home a survival mechanism. People who can afford it purchase a country place, while living and working in the city. Another aspect of this emergent social culture with people living in two places at once involves immigrants, or rather the new breed of immigrants (Appadurai 1996). In the past, when people left their native land to live in another country, it was usually a total commitment. Although they may have visited their former homeland, they did not reestablish a life there. Now, many of the new immigrants that have settled in the United States, for example, retain close ties to their place of birth. They may continue to own property there and to live in both places at least part of the time, such as summers. This particular facet of our new global culture is not the same as the common practice of keeping a city and a country home. For the middle-class professional immigrants who can afford it, it is a specific way of life meant to retain an everyday identity in two distinct cultures.

Comparing it to tourism may help to explain the effect of space/time compression on bi-coastal people. Visiting a foreign country for the first time usually means culture shock. The particular cognitive or emotional changes that are induced by tourist travel are often discussed using this conceptual frame and there is even a series of books called *Culture Shock* marketed for people who wish to prepare for a trip to another country. Among other things, cross-border travel creates stress when visitors have to contend with a foreign language, foreign food, particular customs that are different than those at home, ways of interacting with people who are different, religious distinctions, and the like. Even at home, it may take us months to find the restaurants that we like best, for example, often after eating in several places that we detest. How difficult, then, it must be to find a good meal in a strange city shortly after arriving. At home, we know the norms and mores of shopping on an intimate basis. What happens when we visit another culture with an entirely different set of social understandings surrounding the purchasing of commodities? What happens when we travel to a place where the people have a different body language and can misinterpret our own? How do we protect ourselves from crime in strange environments?

Because of these and other fears, many tourists opt out of encountering the shock of a new everyday life by traveling on a tour. They purchase a package deal that includes being met at the airport, being guided around town in relative safety, having hotel accommodations made for them at "approved" places, and having a guide instruct them on the ways of eating and on restaurants that are also "approved" or "recommended." Packaged tours include trips by secure bus or car to the countryside and other cities or sites. Guides always speak English and act as the interpreter, so the shock of a new language is dampened, if present at all.

Franchising also plays a role in minimizing the culture shock of travel. The common, familiar commodities that are marketed through franchising constitute a solid base for our emergent global culture. We are all used to negotiating hotel lobbies and upscale restaurants. Today there is a kind of franchising culture that homogenizes experiences in different places that sociologist George Ritzer refers to as *McDonaldization* (1992). When traveling we can stay at familiar hotel chains. Their logos and services are already well known and so provide both comfort and convenience. People are also more familiar with the cuisine of different countries. As tourists we seek out the images of restaurants and foods that we already know from watching television or movies. In short, there are many mechanisms that people use when traveling which minimize the culture shock of visiting a foreign country. When truly panicked by an encounter with the new, tourists in most big cities of the world can always go to a McDonald's for hamburgers and French fries.

In contrast, bi-coastalism produces a shock of space/time compression that is all the more heightened when we are intimately familiar with our destination. In many ways, it is an entirely different, almost opposite, phenomenon than the culture shock of tourism. The effect arises from possessing a daily life in two or more places separated by a great distance and the realization that when we are immersed in our everyday life at one location, the other seems as if it is not real, as if it is imagined or dreamed. We dream the life of another person, but we are that other person. Soon after encountering this kind of strangeness, we travel to the other location and have the same feelings, only in reverse. Being bi-coastal means always being caught in someone else's dream that is also a dream of our own.

Bi-coastalism produces radical dislocation and severely undermines the taken-for-granted reality of daily life. It is the very epitome of *de-territorialization*, the phenomenon discussed at the beginning of this book that is most characteristic of jet travel in a global age. With one life in a single location, the daily grind may be boring, but it is still experienced as the most real, the most defining reality for our minds. We are secure not only in our attachment to people and activities but also to a sense of place, of a territory that nurtures us. It is these combined feelings of people and place that give our opinions about society and life in general a degree of certainty. Being bi-coastal kicks out this elementary foundation from beneath the mental edifice of daily living. It is disorienting and de-territorializing. Reality becomes comparative, relative, and no longer absolute. We are no longer certain what is true, culturally imperative, or real. We live two different lives simultaneously, as a dream that is interrupted only by jet flight.

25

Bi-coastalism and the Fear of Flying

Some degree of trauma is an almost inevitable aspect of flying. People suffer from the trauma of waiting before they get to their assigned seats on the plane. Each time when the boarding announcement is made, there is a predictable crush of passengers lined up, each seemingly determined to be first on the plane. The tension mounts as the rows are called, like some lottery or bingo. Once seated on the plane, this tension does not go away. The fear of flying becomes a thick atmosphere that every passenger breathes, a veritable climate of fear and stress, that is relieved only when the plane becomes airborne and then only temporarily until descent when this cycle of panic and release sets in once again.

Is there something very wrong with losing the "terror" of flight, or rather, the feeling that flight is a special occasion in life? Why do people have to scare themselves half to death while taking a vacation? Why should flying have to be stressful? The same flight an ordinary person approaches as a near-death experience, or just as a very special event, is only one of hundreds of flights that take off and land at that airport that very same day. Planes are constantly in the air, ferrying millions of passengers, every second, every minute, every hour of every day, to their destinations. On average, three million passengers fly daily in the

United States. Why must the flight that we take be so singularly important, or, for that matter, be selected especially by God for destruction? We incorrectly assign the same divine interest to our lives, our planet, and even our universe by projecting ourselves as the center of attention. Perhaps the main mental trick of bi-coastalism is overcoming this overwhelming fear of flying.

Previously, when I traveled only occasionally, every trip by air was an exercise in stress. I obsessed over packing, having my tickets in order, getting to the airport on time, getting on the plane, and, most obviously, making it to my destination without dying. Mad dashes to the airport in traffic are vividly remembered, especially all those times when I was stuck in a traffic jam while the clock was ticking. I often left the house hours early, in order to catch a flight without the agony of needing a last minute, high-speed ride to the airport. The fear of flying and its attendant stress was psychic damage that I simply could not afford.

When I became bi-coastal, I emulated the flight attendants, not my fellow passengers. Packing was easy because it had become routine. The drive to the airport was relatively stress-free because I had learned exactly when to do it in order to be there in plenty of time to check in. Once at the terminal, I was content to know that within a short while I would be back in the air, going to my "other" life. I was never in much of a hurry to get to that other life, or rather, getting there was now something *inevitable*, not like the expectation before a vacation trip or a special journey for business, which produces excitement, anticipation, and apprehension. Bi-coastal living means taking the plane to work *as if* it were a bus or train. The best thing to do was to ignore whatever dangers lurked, curl up with a newspaper or favorite book, or go to sleep, until the trip was over. I got to know many professors in Manhattan who commuted by train from far-flung suburban communities in upstate New York or across the Hudson River in New Jersey. They all had one- to two-hour commutes each way. My six hours in the air was just an extension of that same *quality* of time, commuter time. Commuter time is not the proper occasion to fret over the dangers of the trip.

I eventually lost my fear of flying. What was once an unusual occasion that provoked anxiety, expectation, and great stress was now a mundane, ordinary detail of my otherwise normal life. I would get on the plane and prepare for flight without any special ritual or any particular attention to the unusual nature of jet travel. People never get into a car, for example, and marvel at the miracle of the internal combustion engine, yet many still consider flying unnatural. I lost this conceptual association when I had to fly frequently. Air travel became as natural, as ordinary, as driving in my car. Statistics say it is also safer. I'm sure that flight attendants and pilots feel the same way. It's a job, *not* an adventure.

I do not want to give the impression that every trip I took in my bi-coastal period was free of stress or fear—quite the contrary. There were several times, especially during the winter or early spring months, when the weather forced delays, missed connections, or cancellations, that I learned to cope with these *unexpected* aspects of flying, but not without suffering from stress. Most disturbing were those rare moments when a bit of severe turbulence occurred, when the dreaded announcement by the pilot that we were headed for some serious weather, would unleash overwhelming fears. I can easily recall, as I now sit safely on the ground, times when the "fasten seatbelt" warning light would come on unexpectedly with a thunderous "boing" of its bell. Then the pilot would announce "turbulence." I still get a sinking feeling in my gut each time I remember the worst of these experiences. A red-eye flight in January out of Orange County airport had a stop in Las Vegas, about an hour's flying time away, before proceeding directly to New York. Because it was a night flight, I had hoped to sleep on the plane. Losing three hours on the West to East Coast junket, I was scheduled to arrive in New York at about the time I had to get ready to go in to work. Sleeping on the flight was what I needed to do most.

After departure from California, however, the pilot came on and announced that previous flights to Las Vegas had experienced severe turbulence and so he was dispensing with the in-flight beverage service on the first leg of the trip. He advised all attendants to strap themselves into their seats. I remember wondering what could be in store for us, and then the turbulence hit. Had I not been strapped in myself, I would have gone through the roof. We were bounced around uncontrollably for a half-hour by what seemed to me a hurricane. Every nanosecond was sheer torture, an agony that I can never forget. I pictured all the worst possibilities occurring—the wing coming off, an engine dropping off, the cabin breaking in two, the roof flying off, the pilot's windshield breaking with him getting sucked out of the plane, and on and on. It felt like the flight would never end, that we would be tossed about violently until we died, like those unfortunate children who suffer and die from Shaken Baby Syndrome. When it was over, and when I had successfully completed the journey to New York City, I thought of quitting my job there forever, so that I would never have to fly again. I was a wreck for several days, barely able to sleep even when I was away from work. Weeks went by, however, and soon I was back on the horse—or the plane, to be exact.

26

Bi-coastalism: Disorientation and Decompression

One fascinating aspect of air travel is that journeys are taken assuming that people are on their own before and after a flight, yet we often need lots of help on the ground. The assumption that we can manage by ourselves is not always correct. Being bi-coastal relieves some of these pressures because we are used to things on the ground in separate locations, but we are still occasionally inconvenienced by our surroundings. One problem is the strangeness of landing in a new airport, the shock of a strange, disorienting environment, such as a visit to a foreign country.

DISORIENTATION

The level of disorientation, of the bizarre, is unmatched in this form of space/ time compression. While it's always best to have someone meet you at a new airport, arriving at a foreign destination is especially disconcerting. This kind of shock is experienced in a somewhat milder form when traveling domestically to a city that you have never been to before. Trauma is the result of not possessing a *mental map* of the new territory. We disembark from the plane, but then are not sure where to go. We follow the crowd. We look for signs. We somehow manage to get ourselves and our baggage to ground transportation and the hotel. Only on the next visit are we better able to negotiate the exact same space with less stress. We now have the mental map from the previous journey. We disembark with less hesitation. We do not have to hold back to allow the crowd to show us the way. Once we are settled, actions become more automatic as we think ahead to our plans for the rest of the day. Being bi-coastal turns these arrivals and departures almost instinctual. The airport terminal frequented on a regular basis becomes much like our homes. We can find our way in the dark.

In the same sense, being bi-coastal means that we are assumed by others to be able to function when we land. Jetlag, however, is very inconveniencing. We are not always all right after a long plane trip. Air travelers require downtime. Eventually, the change in time zones catches up with you. I can recall occasions when I did my trip from California to New York, getting off the plane quickly, into a cab, into my apartment, changing my clothes, running back out to the elevator, going downstairs and to the bus stop, riding to work, teaching my classes, meeting with faculty, chit-chatting, and then coming back to my apartment at about 6:00 P.M., and collapsing on the bed, exhausted, and without taking off my clothes, sleeping straight through to the following morning. At these times, however, my unusual schedule was explained away without much thought, excused because of being bi-coastal.

DECOMPRESSION

Although the before and after aspects of flight are not part of the "official" discourse of traveling, pressure increases for on-the-ground facilities to address the needs of weary passengers. Some airports in Europe have specially equipped bathroom areas with showers, similar to facilities provided to long-distance drivers at American truck stops. Perhaps the most concerted effort to accommodate "after flight" needs is the availability of facilities installed at Narita International Airport's terminal outside of Tokyo. According to one account, "This bustling airport may hold a record number of people who haven't slept in 24 hours" (Lipton 1995, 54). To accommodate exhausted travelers, the terminal building offers "refresh rooms" that are quiet places to nap and unwind. Although it might sound strange, many seriously jetlagged and exhausted travelers might prefer to be left alone to decompress at an airport before assuming a schedule of activities when they land. More recently, hotels in the nearby area adjacent to the airport also have begun to offer a similar service. Now airlines like United have expanded the facilities available to passengers in the most expensive seats:

Full-fare First Class and Connoisseur passengers can relax and recharge in complimentary facilities that include fitness equipment, showers, light breakfast service, and business machines such as phone and fax. The new service takes place at hotels in Amsterdam, Brussels, London Heathrow, Madrid, Milan, Paris' Charles de Gaulle, Rome and Zurich. (Lipton 1995, 54)

If "refresh rooms" were available for bi-coastal travelers at the Los Angeles and New York airports, it seems evident that many people would take advantage of them. Refresh rooms make perfect sense at hubs where people change planes, and they would probably be used regularly in airports with considerable foreign travel, such as Kennedy International in New York. There might also be a market for facilities within terminals that are near major ski resort areas due to the frequent flying delays in the winter months.

Neither Narita airport in Japan nor United Airlines' special deals with cooperating hotels represents the first instance of locating refresh facilities adjacent to airports. An early pioneer of this type of service was Jay Pritzker, the founder of the Hyatt chain. In 1957, Pritzker, who already traveled frequently by air, discovered that his favorite hotel near the old Los Angeles airport was for sale. Buying it and retaining the name of its original owner, Hyatt, the entrepreneur Pritzker then wondered, "Why not put a hotel next to all the big airports so that a traveler need never worry about missing a plane, and would have somewhere to sleep at the end of a long journey? Many airports these days have a choice of hotels, but Mr. Pritzker was a pioneer" (*The Economist*, 1999b, 81).

As the convenience of hotel accommodations at airports became better known, the market grew. Airport hotels have branched out by offering conference facilities, exercise rooms, and first-rate restaurant dining.

While an increasing number of travelers need some facility to rest, staying at an airport hotel may not be the answer for everyone.

In March 1999, I had been visiting Greece and returned on a flight from Athens to the United States with a connection at Heathrow in England. I departed four days after the NATO bombing action in Kosovo began, although I had arrived in that area weeks before. Unexpectedly, the air corridors for commercial aviation had been shut down or restricted and my flight from Athens was delayed many hours. Needless to say, I missed my connection. I arrived so late at night that Heathrow—which doesn't operate on a 24-hour basis—had already closed. Without any plans, local currency, or even some knowledge of the surrounding area, I felt horribly lost. My only choice, it seemed to me, was to remain in the terminal, find a cozy place to curl up, and attempt to sleep, while hoping that I could make a connection out of England to the U.S. the next day. Exhausted beyond my limits, I found the prospect of being stranded at the airport quite unsettling and I could not imagine getting any rest that night.

By chance, I found an airline employee who informed me that there was a Hilton Hotel connected to the terminal. Armed with his directions, I found the walkway that led to the hotel. It was way past midnight when I arrived at what seemed like Oz—a gleaming glass-enclosed structure that appeared open. Within minutes I registered and was safely ensconced in a room. However, there is no real happy ending to this story. I had to be back at the airport at the crack of dawn to get a seat on the next available flight back home. This hotel room cost more than $200—and that was at a "special" promotional rate, according to the desk clerk. The listed price for this airport hotel was over $400 a night for an ordinary room. Because I fell asleep after 1:00 A.M., following my ordeal, and awoke to check out by 7:00 A.M. the next day, my stay cost me about $40 an hour! I did not need Oz or an ultra-fancy hotel that night, only a quiet place to sleep and relax.

Clearly, a more affordable solution to this traveler's dilemma is needed. Air terminals should not allow extravagantly expensive hotel chains a monopoly on providing convenient accommodations for passengers who simply need a comfortable place to sleep for a few hours. This is especially so for those cases when layovers are unanticipated and quite out of any single individual's control. Exploiting travelers under these conditions seems inhumane.

27

Living in the Air: How People Do It

With all the stress and trauma of frequent flying, it is justified to wonder why people do it. Being bi-coastal for me was a temporary situation. Some people make frequent flying a way of life—I suspect there is a kind of Darwinian force evolving that is producing a group of business people who are capable of surviving the rigors of constant trips. These are the executives on which corporations will most depend to conduct business around the world. Success in the 21st century working for global firms will come precisely to those who are immune from jetlag. One indication of this Darwinian selection process comes from the following report. It highlights a manager for a global business who "lives" on airplanes. Normally she spends "only one day every two weeks in the office."

A few months ago, she felt briefly proud that she had clocked up three "red-eye" flights in six days; then she ran into a colleague at a meeting . . . who was undergoing two such ordeals on successive nights. One recent Saturday night at Philadelphia airport, en route from her main home . . . she bumped into her opposite number at . . . a management consultancy, who was on her way to New Delhi. Five nights later the two knowledge officers met again, picking up their luggage at JFK. (*The Economist* 1999a)

We get a glimpse at the profile of this hardy breed of executive when the report adds that she has "a constitution immune to jetlag, two children who are grown up and two extremely efficient assistants, who she compares to Mission Control at NASA. . . . 'My place of work,' she says, 'is simply where I am'" (*The Economist* 1999a). According to this executive, there are many people at her management consulting firm who travel as much as she does. In the past, this lifestyle was reserved for secretaries of state, key diplomats, or the very top corporate executives. Now, the ability to exist under conditions of "constant travel," a more graphic term than frequent travel, has become a prerequisite for personal success in global business. In turn, a new type of everyday life associated with constant air travel has been created that seems to symbolize the global interconnections of people and business at the turn of the new century. An extreme case of de-territorialization, these executives carry their office with them. They use palm computers, laptops, fax machines, cell phones, and a host of credit cards to negotiate through and work in global space.

A common and key question that is asked rhetorically by some of the very best journalistic accounts of this new life in the air is whether it is really necessary to fly so frequently in business when we have such easy access to instant, electronic telecommunications (*New York Times* 1998; *The Economist* 1999a). As the account of the executive described above went on:

> Are these journeys really necessary? Ms. Knapp is, after all, a chief information officer. Surely one of the points of all the computer hardware . . . is to make big companies smaller. Company intranets are supposed to be ways to swap knowledge. Cheaper telecoms are meant to be killing distance. (*The Economist* 1999a)

According to one estimate, there has been an explosive growth of frequent business fliers, increasing by about 60 percent in the last 10 years (*The Economist* 1999a). Observers rightly wonder why more and more businesspeople need to travel regularly when executives have easy access to fax and Xerox machines, overnight couriers, e-mail and other Internet services, and satellite-assisted telecommunications. Clearly, these other modes of shrinking the space/time distances among the nodes of the global economy are extensively used. However, there is something else that is missing from the globalization equation: the role of personal contact. Electronic technology seems to serve business best by keeping executives in touch with their home office. Interactions with others who are less familiar to us in far-flung operations still require the personal touch. "As Ms Knapp points out, [her company] has nearly 150,000 people in 152 countries; a bossy e-mail from somebody you had never met could put you off them . . . you have to meet people first" (*The Economist* 1999a).

There are several reasons why frequent flying is still an important aspect of doing business, despite the availability of instant communications around the globe. While contemporary telecommunications technology works wonders in keeping two people in close contact even though they are separated by immense distances, it does *not* work well for more than two trying to do the same thing. Group discussions have their own emergent dynamics. Restricting a conversation on an important subject to a dyad (a two-person unit) may eventually aggregate to some consensus, but it cannot create the conditions for transcendence through the nurturing of emergent ideas and observations that come from an open-ended group discussion. Many institutions try to overcome this limitation through conference calls or teleconferencing. However, it is precisely here that the boundaries and shortcomings of the new technologies are reached. Better group discussions require the physical presence of participants.

Another important factor is the role of trust in business situations. In negotiations involving more than two people who do not know each other well, or who have never met, distrust is a factor in communication. Only personal contact seems to remedy this ailment. Strangers require face-to-face interaction to discuss big deals. Lack of trust has also plagued telephone conversations for decades. "The telephone was best used between persons who knew one another intimately and trusted one another fully" (Gottmann 1983, 27). In fact, typical e-mail chat rooms reveal empirically how electronic communications can so easily breakdown. "Flames" are common. People get easily offended. Some may respond to what they consider to be rudeness in the abrupt way messages are sent and received. Misunderstandings abound, despite our society's capability for real-time discussions via computers. For this very reason, the more foreign locations any business has and the more different cultures that are represented, the more it is necessary to connect personally and physically with company people.

Part 5

The Airline Business: Growing Concerns

28

The Emergence of Transactional Spaces

In the modern world, with its expanding and multiplying networks of relations, and a snowballing mass of bits of information produced and exchanged along these networks, the information services are fast becoming an essential component, indeed the foundation stone, of transactional decision-making.

Jean Gottmann, 1983

Frequent flying is a necessity in a global economy. The same need for personal contact in business that has created the frequent flier, however, has also reworked the airport itself. Today's terminals are important nodes in the new economic configuration not only because they facilitate flight but also because they facilitate *meetings*. Terminals are a new form of multifunctional, transactional space.

As mass suburbanization affected all central city areas in the 1970s, analysts were concerned about the flight of business from downtowns. Factories and other forms of manufacturing had already left the cities of the United States in a general trend known as "de-industrialization." As suburban populations increased, retailing soon followed. Giant malls began to dominate metropolitan regions. Central city department stores suffered and many closed down or moved to suburban malls. The once glamorous high-rise corporate towers that gave our largest cities their most famous icons were, by the 1980s, in danger of abandonment as well. The number of corporate headquarters in Manhattan, for example, was almost halved by business flight to adjacent areas like Connecticut or wholesale moves to the Sunbelt. During the 1980s it appeared that the downtown sections of some of our largest cities would lose their most precious function, office location.

Geographer Jean Gottmann argued against this impression. He claimed that business would always need an agglomerated command and control center where personal contacts could facilitate the exchange of information. This was so, he suggested, because of the very nature of the new transformations. Central to large-scale business today is the need for information processing. Requiring a host of different services, such as accounting, legal, computing, and secretarial skills, information processing had emerged as the key economic sector that enabled the far-flung success of global business. As Gottmann observed, "To put it briefly, the expanding activities in the cities have shifted from manufacturing work and distribution to transactional work and related services. . . . That means, in terms of buildings, a transfer of emphasis from industrial plants to offices" (1983, 12).

Gottmann's word for the new kind of work that was produced by the globalization of industry was *transactional* activities. These *quaternary services* are precisely the new kinds of businesses required by command and control centers for information processing. Gottmann believed that these types of jobs would be generated within the central city, and he was quite correct in making that assumption. He also suggested that the new kinds of office complexes, which he called "transaction spaces," would also come to characterize central city, downtown areas that had previously been decimated by de-industrialization.

> If we examine what has happened in cities, we see that suburban sprawl has not prevented but, on the contrary, in many cases, has been accompanied by the rise of skylines and the multiplication of all sorts of office buildings in central cities. . . . A city developing successfully as an active transactional center may very well lose much of its residential, i.e., nighttime population. . . . Such is the double growth that is often developing today. (Gottman 1983, 12)

Gottmann's vision of the future resonates with the growing need for information processing as the core of economic growth in today's society. The central districts of our largest cities that harbor command and control offices now have a rival transactional space. As we have seen, an increasing amount of business meeting activity takes place in and around airports. We have seen how the contemporary airport terminal has added on functions to become commercial mall space, warehousing space, the center of a manufacturing district, a site for business services, and even a place for gourmet dining or upscale shopping, along with fulfilling its primary transportation function.

Today we are witnessing the emergence of large terminals as transaction spaces that harbor an increasing array of business services and meeting and conference rooms. If the need for personal meetings fuels frequent business flying in the new global economy, despite the sophistication and ubiquitousness of modern telecommunications, then the new, multifunctional terminals are becoming the new transactional cities of the future. Airports like O'Hare, Heathrow, Denver, Dallas/ Fort Worth, and Frankfurt not only rival the central city in the generation of economic activity, they actually work in tandem with the traditional downtowns in grounding the regional economy. Today, airports are the new growth poles of contemporary business. They are also assuming the dominant role as transactional spaces in the global economy. In the future, it may very well be airport complexes—not central cities—where the business of society gets done.

Capitalism and the Path to Deregulation

If the Wright Brothers were alive, Wilbur would have to fire Orville to reduce costs.

Herb Kelleher, CEO of Southwest Airlines

Commercial aviation is intensely, vigorously, bitterly, savagely competitive.

Robert Crandall, CEO of American Airlines

Running an airline is like running an army, and competition for passengers is like fighting a war. Over the past several decades, especially since the deregulation of the 1970s, a bloody, no-prisoners struggle has characterized the business of air travel. Typical passengers see little evidence of the trench warfare, of the casualties, of the obsessive, head-to-head confrontations, yet the past is littered with the burned-out hulks of previous battles. The majestic symbol of American ingenuity and spunk that conquered the Pacific Ocean, Pan American Airways, is no more. Remember Eastern Airlines and its president, astronaut Frank Borman? One report has him back in the Midwest attending to his family's auto business (Petzinger 1995). Once a major airline, Eastern is now gone. So too are Braniff, People Express, and many others. They didn't just disappear over the course of time, like Hudson or Studebaker cars, they were massacred almost overnight by the forces unleashed after deregulation.

The business of air travel is everybody's business, especially the government's. Air transportation is the most privatized, capitalistic example of making money since Adam Smith observed the vagaries of pin manufacture, or more accurately, since Charles Darwin observed the struggle for survival as "nature red in tooth and claw." The public simply pays a price for tickets and gets a certain level of service. Only when the results of business battles affect scheduling and fares do we get to experience the echoes of some conflagration that was waged deep, deep in the bowels of corporate America. An airline gets taken over or goes into bankruptcy and flights are canceled. Ticket prices change and service is less convenient. Some places reap a harvest of new carriers; others are abandoned to a slow death by neglect. The public is affected, but has little say about the way the business is run, and the government has wanted things this way since the late 1970s.

The airline industry in the United States is a core form of free enterprise. It was the first major sector of the economy to be deregulated in the 1970s, and one of the first to downsize and to experience relentless mergers. Its recent history is characterized by contentious—sometimes even vicious—labor relations, by cutthroat fare wars, and by the tragic suicides of some of its top executives. Contrast this state of affairs with carriers in the rest of the world. Most are nationalized, meaning they enjoy hefty subsidies from their governments. Comparatively speaking, they have tranquil labor relations and a cushy operating environment. Once it was like that in this country as well.

Several authors have written eloquently about the history of commercial aviation in the United States (Davies 1972, Petzinger 1995). Briefly put, there are two main phases: the era of regulation until 1978, and the era of deregulation from that year to the present. The very first commercial flight occurred in 1914, for a reputed price of $5 that covered an 18-mile trip in Florida (Morris and Wilson 1995, 3). By the 1920s, with ranks swelled by aviators returning from World War I, many carriers appeared as small businesses throughout the country. For the most part, they earned money by flying airmail for the federal government or from the occasional thrill-seeking paying customer who went along for a joyride. Because it was out of the norm for ordinary people to travel by plane, mail contracts were the only reliable source of revenue. "By 1927 the Post Office Department had contracted out all airmail service to private carriers, and government regulation of the fledgling airline industry had begun" (Morris and Wilson 1995, 3).

During the Roaring Twenties, stories of daring pilots and their exploits filled the popular media, and the nation began its romance with flying. One of the reliable mail pilots was a Midwesterner, Charles Lindbergh. When he made the first solo Atlantic crossing, the entire world knew it had been changed forever, and perhaps humanity had also made its first true steps to the stars.

The success of Lindbergh's 1927 flight to Paris . . . sparked the Beatlemania of its time, except that it was much bigger. Major league baseball games came to a halt. Radio announcers sobbed. . . . The *New York Evening World* nominated the flight for "the greatest feat of a solitary man in the records of the human race." A new dance, called the *Lindy Hop*, was born. (Petzinger 1995, 4)

With a mail contract in place, carriers that allowed passengers to pay a fee and come along for the ride discovered pure gravy. As steady profits appeared, commercial aviation became a growth industry, but because its principal function was the transport of mail, it remained regulated by a division of the federal government, the U.S. Post Office. With the first breath of scandal, a price-fixing scheme launched by the four biggest carriers, the government stepped in to tighten its scrutiny even more in 1938 by establishing an independent commission, the Civil Aeronautics Board (CAB), that made the air carriers public utilities. For the next 40 years, the federal government regulated routes, fares, and profits. Each carrier had well-defined destinations and was told what to charge for passenger trips. Deviations from these arrangements had to be approved by the CAB, but few appeals were acted on favorably. In return, regular but nominal profits were guaranteed. Shielded from competition, the airlines prospered but typical fares were relatively expensive. Only the more affluent could afford to fly in the 1940s and 1950s.

According to Thomas Petzinger (1995, 8), by the 1950s there were four major national carriers that dominated the air lanes: United Airlines, formerly United Aircraft and Transport; Transcontinental and Western Air, renamed Trans World Airways; American Airways, renamed American Airlines; and Eastern Air Transport, renamed Eastern Airlines. United possessed the northern route from New York to California via Chicago, TWA the middle route through St. Louis, American the southern route via Dallas to California, and Eastern was given the north-south corridor along the East Coast. Many other "scrappy" regional carriers were also in operation at the time, such as Braniff in Texas, Delta out of Atlanta, and Varney Speed Lines, renamed Continental, located in the Northwest. In addition, a fifth major carrier, Pan American, operated exclusively overseas. It was Pan Am, in fact, that pioneered the 9,000-mile Pacific Ocean run in 1935, with the uniquely designed *China Clipper* flying boat.

> Second only to Coca-Cola in world wide recognition, the Pan Am trademark had become a fixture of popular culture, symbolizing the exotic. James Bond flew on Pan Am. . . . A spaceship bore the Pan Am trademark in *2001*. . . . Pan Am built the largest commercial office building in the world, a hulking structure defiantly set perpendicular to every other building in midtown Manhattan [that harbored for a time a famous heliport on its roof]. (Petzinger 1995, 17)

Beginning with the late 1950s, specific changes occurred that eventually culminated in a concerted call for abandoning the industry to unregulated, private enterprise. The first commercial jet airplanes, the Boeing 707s, were introduced in 1957, followed by improved aircraft that increased greatly the capacity of carriers to ferry passengers. In the 1970s, revolutionary change came again with the introduction of wide-bodied aircraft. The Boeing 747, McDonnell Douglas DC-10, and Lockheed L-1011 "would devastate the airline industry, bringing it as close to disaster as the government had ever permitted" (Petzinger 1995, 18). Potential passenger volume, or carrying capacity, had increased exponentially, yet there was only a steady demand for the relatively pricey seats. Some discounts were announced, such as "youth fares" and "family fares," but with limited ability to cut prices due to regulation, the carriers suffered from *over*capacity.

At about the same time, the federal government was under pressure to cut its bureaucracy. Usually associated with Republican Party ideology, the concept was actually brought to Washington by the newly elected president, Democrat Jimmy Carter, in 1976. By that time, the principal function of airlines was the transport of people, not mail. Many in and out of government viewed the Civil Aeronautics Board (and the legislation that created it in the 1930s) to be an anachronism. The initial idea of the Carter administration was not to rescind regulation, but to move incrementally to reduce government control in order to introduce competition among carriers that would improve routes, lower fares, and bring in more customers in order to make the business more profitable. It is hard to find a record of a single individual who anticipated, at the time, what the full effect of the new legislation would be, nor did the federal government understand what the unleashing of capitalist competition would do to air carriers that had operated for years as public utilities. In short, deregulation of the airline industry in April 1978 became the first great experiment of privatization experienced by the United States. According to Petzinger:

> The nostalgic persist in asking, "Was it of net social benefit or detriment?" The answer is neither. Deregulation was a massive exercise in the redistribution of wealth, a zero-sum game in which not billions but trillions of dollars in money, assets, time, convenience, service, and pure human toil shifted among many groups of people, from one economic sector to another. (1995, xx-xxi)

There is simply no clear way of telling whether deregulation has been good or bad, because its effects are uneven. Freewheeling capitalist competition created an immense transfer of wealth among people in the industry, as Petzinger observed. Restructuring also affected airlines in complex ways, making no single company a leader. According to Morris and Wilson, "Of all the carriers with annual revenues greater than $1 billion, American is the leader in revenue, but United leads in passenger miles and Delta in enplanements. These three measures create an ambiguous ranking because airlines differ in the types of routes they fly" (1995, 8).

Table 29.1 illustrates this complex structure. As the table shows, the performance of air carriers differs substantially. American, United, and Delta had approximately double the passenger miles of Southwest, America West, and USAir in 1993. American, United, and Delta averaged over $12 million in revenue while TWA, Southwest, and America West earned approximately $3 million or less. American and Delta averaged over 80 million enplanements; Continental, North-

Chapter 29

Table 29.1 Enplanements, Passenger Miles, Average Length of Haul, and Revenue by Major Carriers, 1993

Carrier	Enplanements (thousands)	Passenger Miles (millions)	Average Length of Haul (miles)	Revenue (millions of 1993 dollars)
American	82,536	97,062	1,176	14,737
United	69,672	100,991	1,450	14,354
Delta	84,813	82,863	977	12,376
Northwest	44,098	58,033	1,316	8,448
USAir	53,679	35,220	656	6,623
Continental	37,280	39,859	1,069	5,086
TWA	18,938	22,664	1,197	3,094
Southwest	37,517	16,716	446	2,067
America West	14,700	11,188	761	1,332

Source: Air Transport Association, 1994, *Air Transport*, Washington, D.C., 5; reprinted in Morris and Wilson (1995), 8.

west, and Southwest had half that amount, while TWA's and America West's enplanements were one-quarter the amount of the leaders.

Petzinger (1995, 290, 419) explains some of these differences by observing that today the airline industry has, in fact, become two industries. One caters to the convenience of passengers by flying just about everywhere and by maintaining an immense fleet of planes. These are the big carriers like American and United that make money on the long haul. Other carriers are niche marketers. They fill in the spaces with bargain fares, but they lack the large fleets of the others, so their schedules and connections are less convenient. Southwest, America West, and Vanguard make their money on short-haul flights between major cities. Their passengers most commonly seek bargain rates for single flights without connections.

Together, these two separate dimensions—long hauls with a change of planes by the major carriers and short hauls on bargain carriers—now characterize airline service in the United States. People can easily become confused and consequently inconvenienced by this structure. Used to the ease of flying on the major carriers, passengers may become upset by limited schedules offered for short-haul flights on bargain carriers. Conversely, those who patronize bargain carriers may balk at the high price of tickets for flights with the major carriers if they are convinced they are being ripped off. In short, one reason for the growing concerns about the airline industry in the United States is the incredibly confusing structure produced by deregulation and its ensuing competition among carriers.

30

Hubs, Spokes, and Deregulation

After deregulation, the major airlines focused traffic into selected "hubs" that served to concentrate passengers and then to propel them to their respective destinations on full aircraft. Connecting flights to lesser-traveled cities became "spokes." Before this *hub and spoke* system emerged, expensive and direct flights were more the norm. Someone wishing to travel from Indianapolis, Indiana, to New York City, for example, would take a direct flight operated by a carrier whose route was regulated by the Civil Aeronautics Board. After deregulation, there were fewer—if any—nonstop flights from the one city to the larger one, but there were many flights from the smaller city to an airline hub. The passenger would now fly *indirectly*, first from Indianapolis to Chicago or to Pittsburgh, for example, and then catch a flight to New York City. The hubs served to collect all passengers going to the same destination and flights were scheduled accordingly to maximize the number of passengers. A true hub has about 50 percent or more of its travelers passing through on connecting flights.

By eliminating the old restrictions on which carriers could fly where, deregulation gave airlines increased freedom and flexibility to restructure their networks into hub and spoke systems that feed travelers from all directions into a major airport (hub) from which they take connecting flights to their destinations. (Morris and Wilson 1995, 20)

American's hubs are at Chicago's O'Hare and Dallas/Fort Worth, United has hubs at O'Hare and Denver, Delta's are at Dallas/Fort Worth and Atlanta, USAir has a hub in Pittsburgh, and Northwest has two, in Detroit and Minneapolis.

One effect of this new structure is the convenience of catching flights to any destination in the United States. Because routes aren't direct, however, travel times have increased, including the time spent waiting in hubs for connecting flights. Deregulation has resulted in greater flight convenience but also an increase in total travel times for most passengers. When unexpected delays occur, stress escalates greatly. Hubs are now busy places where the majority of people wait for a change of plane. Small wonder that these airports have evolved into multi-functional sites offering mall shopping, a full array of business services, and diverse dining options. With passengers forced to spend time between planes, the hubs have become distinct places all their own. "At a typical hub, more than half the passengers boarding planes are in mid route rather than beginning a trip. In 1993, for example, 56% of passengers boarding at Chicago's O'Hare Airport were making connecting flights. Figures for Dallas-Fort Worth, Atlanta and Denver were 66%, 64% and 54% respectively" (Morris and Wilson 1995, 44).

As the numbers of passengers increase and more bodies are concentrated into hub terminals, there is additional pressure on the latter to expand its functions. This explains in part the recent growth of multipurpose airport centers.

Another important aspect of the new two-tiered structure concerns its effects on regional development. Airports that become hubs experience an explosive surge in the growth of businesses located in the adjacent area. Hub-level activity means more money for hotels, rental cars, air cargo, warehousing, business services, conference centers, and the like. Even more important, prospective companies are attracted to hub sites because of the abundance of nonstop flights that they provide. Hub status has been linked, for example, to the rapid growth of such places as Minneapolis, Phoenix, and Atlanta.

At the opposite end, in outlying spoke cities, flights tend to be expensive and inconvenient. Travelers have to change at other city hubs and these kinds of delays often amount to several hours tacked onto ordinary flights. When few airlines service a spoke city, the fares are outrageous even to destinations that are close by.

With the hub and spoke system in place, it was felt for decades that the best developmental strategy of any city was to vie for election to hub status even going so far as to give commercial carriers major incentives for locating or relocating at local facilities. Now, however, some different and more innovative thinking prevails. In cases where a single airline dominates a hub, the presence of frequent nonstop service is offset by comparatively higher overall fares due to the carrier's monopoly. Cities concerned with using airports in a general strategy of economic development understand that it is competition rather than the hub-spoke structure that counts the most.

> Fares from cities with a single dominant carrier have risen as much as 40 percent above those in nonhub markets. . . . Travelers in hub cities complain that service stinks because they can't vote with their feet. And loyalty hasn't always flowed both ways: eight years after Raleigh-Durham International Airport spent $120 million building a terminal for American Airlines, the carrier abandoned the hub. (Hale 1999)

While hub cities have made it clear that they do not seek to lose their status, spoke cities have successfully fought the deficit in service by increasing competition among carriers. The airport in Kansas City, Missouri, for example, boasts both expansive growth and comparatively low fares (Hale 1999). In addition to accommodating major carriers, the site is the home of upstart, bargain airline Vanguard, which has recently expanded its operations throughout most of the Midwest. Other spoke cities besieged by high fares, such as Buffalo, New York, have struck back by increasing competition using several bargain carriers, like Jet Blue, and have considerably lowered the costs of air travel for their local businesses and residents. While deregulation has distorted the costs of travel in many places because of the hub and spoke system, cities that understand the role of competition in keeping fares down have done much better in recent years. Success comes from understanding the two-tiered corporate structure of the deregulated industry. If a local airport is stunted in growth by the high fares and limited service of a major carrier, it can improve its situation directly by hosting one or two bargain carriers.

31

Discount Carriers

The "Southwest effect" has become a permanent revolution. Upstart, low-fare air carriers—most of them clones of Southwest Airlines—have sparked a revolution in the industry during the last three years, saving travelers more than $6.3 billion a year, according to government experts.

David Feld, 1996b

Southwest Airlines was the most profitable domestic carrier in 1993. As table 29.1 shows, however, its average haul length was 446 miles. Contrast this with United's average of 1,450 miles, the industry's leader. Southwest is a creature of deregulation. It is a bargain carrier that makes its money by connecting cities less favored by the national hub and spoke system with direct flights at prices that are only a fraction of what the larger airlines charge.

Southwest started as a local Texas airline in the 1970s. Governmental regulation affected carriers that crossed state lines. Southwest escaped regulation by flying completely within the state of Texas, serving people who needed to fly from, for example, Dallas to San Antonio, at cheap rates. After deregulation, it was allowed to expand to other areas of the country. At that time, its general counsel, a lawyer named Herbert Kelleher, who was originally from the New York area, took over as CEO. He is now a legend, having been glorified on the cover of *Time* magazine, and is routinely cited as one of America's best CEOs. The well-known story of Southwest after deregulation emphasizes that, under Kelleher, it stayed a discount airline offering low, unrestricted fares that operated in the shadow of the giants. Starting with only a few planes, all Boeing 737s, jets were kept flying back and forth between major cities of operation. To keep fares at their rock bottom, he instituted a revolutionary "10-minute turnaround" (Petzinger 1995, 290). Arriving planes were serviced *at the same time* that passengers were disembarking.

While the majority of people in the United States took advantage of the convenience of hub and spoke systems to travel anywhere on the same day with one-stop connections, many wanted the option of cheap fares. Southwest not only provided this service, first to travelers in Texas, Louisiana, and later California, but it became the model for all upstart, discount airlines that appeared in the wake of deregulation. As Thomas Petzinger (1995) argues, companies like Southwest have created a segmented industry structure. While the major carriers offer convenience and frequent connections for long-haul flights, the discount airlines offer "value" and cheap tickets to cities that have been overlooked in service by the major carriers. During the last two decades, many such discount companies have been started in the United States, but the phenomenon is becoming more frequent as an increasing number of people in places unable to find reasonable airfares from the major airlines condense into a ready market for low-cost carriers.

For example, in 1997, Kevin Stamper, the son of a Boeing executive, recognized that Northwest Airlines, the major carrier with a hub airport in Detroit, was creating a market of local, discontented travelers. He started a new airline, Pro Air, which had only four 737s in 1998, and offered discounted, unrestricted fares to Detroit's major connections in the Midwest and Northeast. The popularity of the new airline is typical of such Southwest-style upstarts:

> These days, the airport is filled with Detroiters who are defecting to Pro Air because of walk-up fares that are as much as 85% cheaper than Northwest's. For instance, an unreserved seat to Indianapolis, Ind., cost $578 round trip before Pro Air came to town with its deal of $138. . . . "We're on the edge of a revolution out here," boasts Stamper. . . . "All over the country, people are fed up with getting on planes and finding out that the person next to them paid one-tenth of what they paid." (Christian 1999)

Although Pro Air has done well in its fight against a corporate giant, even the most successful of the bargain carriers have had a rocky road to solvency. Vanguard Airlines, for example, a discount airline that flies out of two hubs, one in Kansas City and the other at Chicago's Midway Airport, has a colorful history. Its founder was Bob McAdoo, who had one of the most spectacular rises and falls of any executive while at the helm of People Express in the 1980s. The latter revolutionized low-cost flying only to fall victim to excessive expansion and competition from the majors. McAdoo's new effort began in December 1994 with two 737s that he flew out of Kansas City.

For the next two years Vanguard offered cut-rate fares to cities that were popular tourist destinations from the Midwest, such as Tampa, Orlando, and Las

Vegas. This passenger niche did not prove lucrative. Most of the people bought their tickets way in advance or used frequent flier miles to go on vacation. Vanguard didn't seem to attract the all-important walk-up fares from business. By 1997, after a disastrous public stock offering, McAdoo resigned and the airline faced bankruptcy. According to one report, at the time, "They'd lost $50 million in 18 months and never had a single monthly profit. There was no accountability, no cost controls, no strategic plan" (Forward 1999)

Vanguard's new CEO, Robert Spane, turned things around by targeting the cost-conscious business traveler, many of whom had to pay their own way but were often forced to take flights on short notice. As others have also noted, "Any start up needs to attract a base of business travelers and they are hard to pry away from the giant lines" (Perkins 1999). The airline also downsized its operations by focusing on a few destinations that would then be serviced with more frequent flights. Long-haul routes were completely abandoned. Finally, Spane also stripped each of the airline's 737s of several rows of seats, thereby increasing legroom by more than an inch. The airline has now experienced several years of profits and has expanded its operations out of Midway field in Chicago to several cities, including some in western New York.

Another interesting story concerns Northwest's competition. We have already noted the assault on its business from Pro Air out of Detroit. Now Northwest is being attacked at its home base in Minneapolis, Minnesota. As one report remarks, this is somewhat unusual.

> Most cities root unabashedly for their big hometown companies. But here—where Northwest Airlines has its headquarters, employs 21,000 and controls 80 percent of the airline seats out of the city—many people are rooting for Sun Country Airlines, a small, local charter airline that started flying regular schedules to a mere 15 destinations in June. (Zuckerman 1999)

Sun Country started in 1983 as a charter airline flying gamblers out of the Twin Cities to Las Vegas. It also served shoppers in the sparsely populated region of the upper Midwest who flew into Minneapolis International in order to visit the giant Mall of America, the United States's largest indoor shopping mall. Once it began its regularly schedule service, however, no matter how modest, Northwest took its competition seriously. Now it remains to be seen if Sun Country can stay in business.

The experience of discount airlines like Sun Country, or even People Express, is quite typical. Although there have been many bargain startups, few have survived. As one observer noted,

> Scores of new airlines have been started since the industry was deregulated in 1978, but only one, America West, has managed to enter the ranks of the majors. The rest have struggled to stay alive or have gone under, either as a result of mismanagement,

Table 31.1   Principal Airline Hubs and Their Carriers

1998 Airport	Primary Airline	Share of all Seats
Cincinnati	Delta	90.8%
Pittsburgh	USAir	87.6
Minneapolis–St. Paul	Northwest	82.0
Houston	Continental	79.3
Atlanta	Delta	77.9
Denver	United	72.4
Dallas/Ft. Worth	American	69.5

Source: Zuckerman C-1.

ruthless competition from the major airlines, or a combination of the two. Over the same two decades, the industry has consolidated into a cadre of giant corporations, each of which dominates one or more of the nation's major airports, where they are able to charge premium prices. (Zuckerman 1999, C-1)

Some examples of this near-monopolistic hold on hubs are shown in table 31.1.

According to a *Time* magazine report, the recently growing discontent of passengers is fueling a boom of new discount carriers and there are now "20 new airline companies that are applying to the Federal Aviation Administration and the Department of Transportation for certification" (1999). The report goes on to place this phenomenon in an industry context:

Certainly, discount airlines have taken to the skies before, only to be blown away like so many ducks by the megacarriers, which quickly matched their fares and added seats on competing routes. Yet the megacarriers are severely testing customer loyalty. Northwest, which controls about 62% of the passenger traffic out of Detroit, has a monopoly on local resentment due to high fares, a pilot's strike this summer and, most recently, January's snowstorm fiasco, in which, because of overcrowded gates, thousands of arriving travelers were trapped on the runway for up to eight hours without food or working toilets. (*Christian* 1999)

In places where major airlines' service is poor, like upstate New York and the heart of the Midwest, local business communities pine away for discount companies like Pro Air or Southwest, making the entire airline industry competitive but also unstable. At the same time, the record shows that, aside from Southwest, no domestic carrier turned a profit in 1993. Air carriers remain on the cusp of economic failure. Any shock can turn an ongoing concern into a bankrupt firm. Between 1990 and 1993, for example, American carriers experienced losses of $12.8 billion. Under deregulation the industry's future will still be marked by companies waxing and waning, with the customer caught in between.

At present (winter 2000), this state of affairs has turned more critical. Rapidly rising fuel prices are contributing to meltdown strains at the major carriers. Airlines raised leisure fares 20 percent and business fares 10 percent in 1999 due to their rapidly rising fuel costs. Southwest announced that these costs had increased for them by 48 percent in 1999 (Koenig 1999). The substantial increases in the cost for gas have yet to be addressed by the federal government, which can release reserves to ease the pressure. Consequently, airline passengers are facing new hikes for ticket prices as the fuel shortage continues. Unfortunately, the air companies that have been the worst hit by these comparatively new hard times are the discount carriers. Hence, their future remains questionable for all those who can find the bottom line and operate just above it.

32

Crazy Fares

I'm constantly asked by friends to tell them where they can get the cheapest ticket, or explain seemingly bizarre restrictions on their ticket, or how they were seated next to this guy who "paid three times what I did."
"Why Airlines Do What They Do," 1999

Airlines were free to set fares as they saw fit after deregulation. The outcome for most carriers is a crazy-quilt array of prices that differs greatly from passenger to passenger, depending on when and how they purchased their tickets. On the whole, according to the record, fares for long hauls have declined due to deregulation (Morris and Wilson 1995). If passengers can tolerate the longer travel times resulting from the two-step dance of connecting flights, they can wend their way through hubs and spokes to any city in the United States at a reasonable fare. Bargains exist for those people who purchase their tickets early. If travelers wait until close to the departure date, however, tickets can be very expensive. It is not uncommon for two people sitting next to each other to have spent a difference of double the lower amount for the same flight. Fares are also staggered in a confusing array of categories, each with its own set of regulations. While the government reduced limitations on travel through deregulation, air carriers have increased their own restrictions on the fares they offer. Some tickets must be purchased months in advance and are nonrefundable, others can be refunded after the payment of a penalty, and still others allow for transfers, layovers, and the like.

Long-haul trips have fares that are now lower after deregulation, making it possible for millions of people to fly without financial hardship. This democratization or mass marketing of air travel is in contrast with the days before deregulation when ticket prices were comparatively higher. At the same time, however, short-haul trips from smaller cities not regularly serviced by hubs have become astronomically expensive. Places like Cleveland and Nashville suffer economically because they do not have carriers offering cheap fares to surrounding cities. A trip from Buffalo, New York, to the state's capitol at Albany, some 250 miles away, costs more than a trip from Buffalo to London, England. Fares from cities in upstate New York, like Buffalo or Syracuse, to New York City can cost over $400 for a round trip. After deregulation,

> airline prices no longer bore the slightest relation to the cost of providing the service, which was why a 300-mile trip beginning and ending at a hub airport might cost three times that of a 1,000-mile trip *through* a hub airport. . . . The major airlines could only hope that when they had added together their $59 fares, their $1,200 fares, and everything in between, the sum exceeded the cost of having provided the service. (Petzinger 1995, 420)

Along with the effect on air carriers, the high cost of short-haul flights to and from marginalized cities made their economic growth more problematic and remains a serious problem today. In effect, the crazy fare structure has created uneven development. People in Los Angeles can fly for business comparatively cheaply to New York City, but business people living in Syracuse must pay exorbitant prices for the short trip to major cities such as New York and Chicago. The damage high airfares do to marginalized regions is well known and a cause of concern to planning and development groups. With deregulation in place, there is little that political influence can do to help alleviate the situation. There are critical business needs that aren't being met by the structure of deregulation, precisely the kinds of concerns that forced many countries to regulate and even nationalize their air industries in the first place.

33

When Lives Were Lost Due to Deregulation

A McDonnell Douglas MD-83 sits on the tarmac awaiting delivery to Alaska Airlines in November 1992. Just more than seven years later, this jetliner would be in pieces at the bottom of the Pacific Ocean.

<www.crashpages.com>, 2000

The American air travel industry has a glorious safety record despite the few crashes in recent years, yet the record today cannot erase the serious failures of some airlines during the decades following deregulation. Several recent air crashes in the United States, such as TWA flight 800 and Alaska flight 261, produced substantial controversy. We may never really know the cause of the TWA disaster, although there is considerable evidence that an empty center fuel tank was the source of the explosion that brought the plane down (Sanders 1997). Most of the worst incidents of tragic failure over the last few decades, however, involved discount carriers, valued for their niche marketing by marginalized cities across the nation.

Air Florida, for example, was a discount carrier that enjoyed immediate success in the early days following deregulation by plying the old Eastern Airlines route up and down the East Coast. On January 13, 1982, during snowy weather and icy conditions, an inexperienced cockpit crew screwed up fatally. Flying out of Washington National in D.C., they ignored the procedures for dealing with de-icing the wings. Ice on jet wings, a common occurrence in winter, decreases the plane's ability to generate lift. The plane took off in this condition but never attained cruising altitude. Instead it nose-dived shortly after departing the runway and plunged into the icy waters of the Potomac River, killing almost everyone aboard, including the crew. Pictures of the crash and the heroic effort of bystanders to rescue survivors shocked the nation. Air Florida never flew again.

More recently, another fatal crash served to place upstart discount carriers in a terrible light. In May 1996, a twin-engine DC-9, flight 592 belonging to ValuJet, a bargain carrier based in Atlanta, plunged into the Florida Everglades just after departing from Miami International Airport, killing everyone on board, including 105 passengers, its two pilots and three crew members. Equally appalling was the post-disaster report that confirmed most on board suffered a horrible death by poisonous black smoke and flames following the spread of the fire that brought the plane down. When all the facts were in, it became clear that the flight was doomed by careless operations. This sort of deliberate negligence represents the worst type of carrier operations appearing after deregulation (Langewiesche 1998, chapter 7). Unlike Air Florida, however, ValuJet was allowed to return to the skies as a carrier after a suspension and with "a renewed commitment to safety" (Langewiesche 1998, 193–196).

> Nonetheless, the ValuJet accident continues years later to raise a series of troubling questions—no longer about what happened but about why it happened and what is to keep similar accidents from happening again. As these questions lead into the complicated and human core of flight safety, they become increasingly difficult to answer. . . . It represents . . . a type of "system accident" which lies beyond the reach of conventional solution and which a small group of thinkers inspired by Yale sociologist Charles Perrow has been exploring elsewhere. . . . Perrow has coined the more loaded term "normal accident" for such disasters because he believes they are normal for our time. His point is that these accidents are science's illegitimate children, bastards born of the confusion that lies within the complex organizations with which we manage our dangerous technologies. (Langewiesche 1998, 193–196)

While the Air Florida crash was caused by the mistakes of an inexperienced cockpit crew, the ValuJet crash was a product of system errors that escaped controls, a failure of the checks and balances of the corporation that hired low-cost subcontractors and maintenance personnel. The outcome was a terrible fire in a compartment below the cockpit that spread poisonous smoke throughout the plane, killing everyone on board, while the jet went into an agonizing power dive and hit the ground with such force local residents thought they had experienced an earthquake.

As the post-crash investigation showed, however, the greatest failure was with the FAA. Despite the structure of deregulation, the federal government was still responsible for overseeing the operations and safety of the air travel industry. In the case of ValuJet, they simply failed to move quickly enough in countering its tendency to fall short of standards. According to Langewiesche (1998, 216), the ultimate responsibility for the crash lay with the FAA and its failure to ground the airline because of its poor safety record.

> Within days evidence emerged that certain inspectors at the FAA had been worried about ValuJet for years and had included their concerns in their reports. Their consensus was that the airline was expanding too fast . . . and that it had neither the procedures nor the people in place to maintain standards of safety. . . . By early 1996, concern had grown within the FAA about the airline's disproportionate number of infractions and its string of small bang-ups. (Langewiesche 1998, 216)

The ValuJet affair suggests that the operating environment of air travel is unstable for carriers caught in the ongoing pressures of competition and financial losses, and that the present structure itself—which ensures safety and which involves FAA oversight and air carrier standard operating procedures—may be seriously deficient. This is especially true for the oversight of upstart, discount airlines that cut corners ordinarily avoided by standard union contracts and operational understandings shared by trained personnel. However, there are still doubts of negligence in the case of Alaska Airlines' flight 261 as well (<www.crashpages.com> 2000). Consequently, the present hodgepodge of limited FAA involvement and deregulated businesses supplying air travel characterizing the domestic industry may require increased rationalization and increased oversight for both established and startup carriers alike.

34

Labor Costs and Contentious Employer–Employee Relations

Owners and stockholders of airlines live in a competitive world of cutthroat capitalism and so do their workers. Since the days of regulation, all aspects of labor were unionized from pilots to stewardesses to mechanics to baggage handlers. The vicious battles for survival unleashed by deregulation have played havoc with this social order. Yet contentious labor disputes were always characteristic of the airline industry. Flying can be a wonder of convenience. When workers rebel for whatever reason, however, basic air transportation is immediately affected everywhere in the country. During such times, the necessity of a freely functioning air carrier system and its status as a public good are keenly evident. Any type of job action can lead to the paralysis of the system and this, in turn, can cost businesses and people millions of dollars.

Consider what happened during the first two weeks of February 1999. A smoldering dispute between American Airlines and its pilots exploded into a full-fledged job action. The company had just bought out Reno Air, one of the small bargain air carriers out west, and absorbed its operations. Reno's pilots were flying for half of the wage that American's crews received. The latter perceived the merger as an incursion, through the back door, of a drastic wage cut for the entire company. Lacking support for a strike, however, the American pilots resorted to a job action. They began to call in sick by the hundreds. Off-duty pilots refused new assignments. When the effects of the refusal to work registered on the system, chaos occurred. According to American officials, 5,600 flights were canceled due to the job action, costing the company between $67 million and $90 million. On the first day of the sick-out, 1,170 flights were canceled; the next day, American dropped 1,102 flights. With these numbers, tens of thousands of people were affected and the national system went into overload with every major carrier inconvenienced.

A couple with air and hotel reservations for a vacation in the Bahamas as a much-anticipated respite from winter suddenly found themselves stuck at the airport staring blankly at the video terminal announcing the cancellation of their flight. Others who were equally disappointed milled around in the same state of bewilderment that slowly turned to anger. Business meetings were put off, vacations ruined, family events spoiled, job searches torpedoed, and so on, all because of the pilot slowdown, but the damage did not stop there. Other airlines tried to accommodate passengers on their flights, because corporations stick together in such times. Planes, already overbooked and crowded as a consequence of the ordinary life of air travel after deregulation, were now jammed to the limit. Fitting extra passengers into scheduled flights created delays and slowly dragged other systems down. In the end, the entire network of air carriers suffered. When one carrier goes down, others soon follow. If that is not a characteristic of a public utility, then what is?

Unions are a fact of life in the air transportation industry but both the corporate owners and the government hate them. In 1981 the overworked and underpaid air traffic controllers called a national strike. So essential were they to the operation of the industry, they thought, their walkout could not last more than a few days. Then, the unthinkable happened. Ronald Reagan, a vehement anti-labor president, fired all of them because they were government employees. Before their shocked eyes, scabs were brought in by the truckload, including air controllers from the military. Soon, a moderate national schedule of flights was back up and running. Eventually, a few former controllers were hired back, but a new labor force emerged that accepted conditions of lower pay and benefits.

There is a dangerous myth about this strike—that President Reagan was a victor. Reagan broke the back of the union, but this did not solve the labor problem of overworked and underpaid controllers, nor did it address the issue of an air control system that operates in this country with antiquated equipment, overseen by the hated FAA. "There is a new union now, the National Air Traffic Controllers Association, and it is growing as angry as the old one" (Langerwiesche 1998, 160). Like conditions in the 1980s when talk of a strike first boiled over, only now much worse, there are too many planes in the air, crowded air corridors funneling traffic into a few key destinations, and outdated equipment. Reagan did nothing to alleviate this situation except postpone the inevitable accounting, while

ruining the careers of highly trained professionals. Nor was the demise of the old
union cause for corporate defeat of its own worker associations. Not a single airline union went under in the air controller aftermath. According to the best analysis of some observers, the problem has always been and remains the FAA and
its system. As yet, no U.S. president has attempted to handle it (Langewiesche
1998).

In the current operating environment of almost microscopic profit margins and
heated competition, airlines have little room to maneuver in order to cut costs.
Decades of deregulation have resulted in an ongoing, contentious confrontation
between management and labor.

> To a degree unusual in business, the costs of running an airline are outside
> management's control. Fuel, for instance, accounts for roughly 20 percent of the
> cost of doing business. . . . Landing fees and airport rentals are another huge and
> mostly nonnegotiable expense. . . . Travel agency commissions became another huge
> item of expense. . . . That left only one big ticket item under management's control,
> and at most airlines it was the biggest of all: labor represented as much as 40 per-
> cent of the expense in running an airline. . . . When the starting gun of deregula-
> tion launched the race to cut costs, the fun was over . . . every airline came to feel
> the same pressure: cut costs in order to cut fares or say good-bye to a franchise that
> had taken decades to build. (Petzinger 1995, 154–55)

Several studies of the deregulation record have confirmed that the overall effect has been to reduce labor costs over the last two decades (Card 1989; Morris
and Wilson 1995, 13). But studies do not always mention that lower labor costs
have come at a price in bitter battles that have left a confrontational approach to
management/worker relations. Pilot actions, like the 1999 American Airlines sick-
out, leave embittered relations with the public as well. The conflictual labor relations characterizing the industry after deregulation sometimes became suicidal.
This was the case with the machinists' union and Eastern Airlines. Charles E.
Bryan of the International Association of Machinists and Aerospace Workers and
Col. Frank Borman, the CEO of Eastern Airlines, clashed head to head during
the 1980s. Eventually Bryan and his union won, but Eastern went bankrupt and
as a result many of its workers permanently lost their jobs and their retirement
benefits. Bryan was swiftly replaced as leader of the 13,000-member union but
the miscalculation cost everyone dearly (Petzinger 1995).

Worker/management relations in the airline industry are confusing because they
run the full spectrum of arrangements. But this very hodgepodge of agreements
makes relations contentious. After deregulation, for example, novice airlines were
allowed to start up and challenge the major carriers. Often the new companies
had *no* unions of any kind and new workers at the new carriers also had *no* seniority. Petzinger astutely observes that "at American the average employee had
nearly 12 years seniority" (1995, 129). Clearly this disparity was one of the key
unintended and negative effects of deregulation that haunt the industry to this day.

Another change was the introduction of a *split labor market*, a structural maneuver that characterizes many other industries caught in the era of downsizing. Splitting the wage scale does not bust a company's union, but it does weaken its bargaining power considerably and, at the same time, lowers labor costs, especially in the important area of the marginal cost of new labor. The company acquires the right, with the union's assent, to hire new employees at a pay scale that is lower than the existing one. Recent hires may also be offered, in some cases, a reduced benefits package as well. Longer-term unionized workers agree to these arrangements when they assess that their own bargaining power is weak and when they believe that they cannot win a strike that will raise their salaries. The result is a split labor profile. The older workers retain their more lucrative contracts and the newer employees do the same work for less pay. Overall the company saves money.

In the 1980s American Airlines introduced a version of split labor arrangements with the approval of their unions. The residue of resentment occasionally boils over in that company, as the recent pilots' job action shows. In the 1980s there was also a bitter strike of the pilots at United that was not settled to anyone's satisfaction and almost crippled the airline. This confrontation set in motion a series of events that culminated in another kind of accommodation. By the 1990s, having been unable to resolve its persistent conflict between management and labor and hemmed in as it was by losses, United became the first *employee profit-sharing* airline. Workers opted for a two-tiered split labor scale and management rewrote the structure of the company to allow ownership by the employees through stock options. Of all the arrangements at airlines, United probably solved the conflict base at the core of the entire industry, but the company still had problems with its pilots' union during July 2000.

In retrospect, it is United's profit-sharing structure that seems the most progressive and promising. Certainly the company seems able to avoid the kinds of debilitating strikes that occasionally afflict other air carriers. These strikes and job actions, however, reveal the dirty little secret of deregulation. Sixty years ago, airlines became publicly regulated utilities at a time when, under the Roosevelt administration, big government felt it could run critically needed businesses for the benefit of the public good. Deregulation pushed the carriers willy-nilly into a long journey in the opposite direction. Yet components are still saddled with government oversight, as in the case of the FAA's management of the nation's air controllers, a relationship that was made in hell, according to reports of some observers (Langewiesche 1998). At the same time, individual carriers have been left to their own devices to work out an accommodation with labor. As we have seen, these run the full gamut from nonunion market-driven wages to a split labor market to employee ownership. Under deregulation, however, none of these arrangements seems to be an overall solution for the persisting problems of marginal profits, minimal bargaining room for wage increases, and bitter feelings between workers and management. This completely arbitrary mix of arrangements, the direct legacy of the deregulation record, bursts forth in job actions and strikes, and the entire nation's air transport system suffers while passengers are treated to the nightmare of inconvenience that a failed system provides.

Whether the principals like it or not, the air travel industry *is* a public utility. Abandoning it to the bargained outcomes of deregulation, the way a pure capitalist theoretician might argue following the centuries-old vision of Adam Smith, has not led to a greater rationalization of this service. At the same time, the existing structure that has been produced by this confrontational competition does show that the nation requires a two-tiered system, one to service the long hauls and another to connect marginalized cities with their closest hub at a low price. At present, the existing arrangements can't satisfy both needs in order to become a truly functional air transport system. Because it remains prone to debilitating job actions derived from a base of contentious and sometimes bitter worker/management relations, the nation will continue to be held hostage to the negative effects of free enterprise. Governmental regulation must be a part of this industry because strikes and job actions paralyze the nation. Yet how do we structure the arrangements for a *quasi*-public utility?

We need a new system. We need to restructure air transportation to benefit from the lessons of the deregulation record. Profit making, profit sharing, fares, and wages all need to be rationalized, such as eliminating the crazy-quilt approach to ticket prices. Competition has shown us the bottom line and illuminated how an effective use of resources can be structured for the long haul. The system of hubs and spokes may not be the quickest way for us all to travel, but it is surely the most convenient for a nation that fields more journeys by air in any given year than there are people in the country—a remarkable 665 million passengers in 1998 according to Congressman Bud Shuster (R-Pa.). But long-haul service is only one aspect. Companies like Southwest, People Express, Pro Air, JetBlue, and others that have come and gone, clearly demonstrate the need for discount carriers, especially ones that service the short-haul connections. They also demonstrate that an increasing number of passengers do not mind "no frills" service. Complaining about airline food is one of the most frequently heard laments of our emergent millennial culture. It has become, perhaps, the most common aspect of our new *life in the air*. Following the astute advice of many critics like former flight attendant Diana Fairechild, why do people persist in wanting food service on planes? Why can't passengers simply bring whatever they like to eat on board and have the airlines dispense with dinner service altogether, replacing it with a beverage service and lower fares? Why can't we develop an air travel passenger culture that deals more directly with the boredom of flight? Why do we need food as a diversion?

More importantly, reexamining in a national dialogue our standard complaints about air travel, such as those about canceled flights or overcrowding, should serve as our guide for the next phase in the restructuring of the air transport system. Solutions should be searched for and implemented in the same quick way that there were tried during the past two decades of free fall under deregulation. Perhaps the present initiative in Congress involving the "Airline Passengers Bill of Rights" is one such national dialogue that will bear some fruit. Other, more cultural considerations, such as the preferred cognitive ways to approach air travel and problems like "air rage" and drinking, should also become the subject of a public debate. In short, we haven't seen rock bottom yet. Serious problems remain.

35

Complaints: Overcrowding, Overbooking, and Increasing Consumer Discontent

Annoyed by carry-on restrictions, disgruntled by ever-more-cramped quarters and enraged by being held on the tarmac for hours, air travelers are filing complaints against air carriers at the highest rate since 1991.

Thomas Goetz, 1998

The nation's commercial aviation network is descending into gridlock after the worst summer in history for delays and passenger frustration, aviation officials told Congress Thursday.

Buffalo News, October 15, 1999

Deregulation enjoys a mixed record, and the most obvious area where it can be measured is the growing discontent among passengers. Complaints about air travel have reached epidemic proportions since the late 1990s. One negative effect of the hub and spoke system, for example, is an increase in crowding. Planes are scheduled at hubs to take full advantage of feeder routes. As a result, passengers are jammed into flights that are almost always overbooked, if not simply full. In addition, because they are now free to configure their cabins, airlines have been cramming as many seats as they can into planes. With larger-capacity jets in service, the total crush of humanity on any given flight can be quite overwhelming.

As the number of passengers and the volume of daily flights across the United States have soared to unprecedented levels, the volume of complaints has assumed the dimensions of a major national issue. During the first half of 1999, "the number of passenger complaints filed with the U.S. Department of Transportation rose 79 percent over the number filed in a similar period" in 1998. "Complaints lodged against the 10 largest airlines increased by 55 percent" (Meyer 1999, A-1). American Airlines was the nation's leader in flight problems, sales problems, refunds, and customer service. Delta led the country in complaints about reservations and ticketing. United was first in complaints about high fares and baggage problems. In May 2000, statistics were worse. According to Zuckerman (2000), United led the nation in flights canceled (8.7 percent), followed by American (3.9 percent) and Alaska Airlines (3.6 percent). Two of the most common complaints that simply take the joy out of air travel are flight delays and bumping.

DELAYS, BUMPING, AND OTHER UNEXPECTED PROBLEMS OF FLIGHT

According to the Air Transport Association, in one period between April and August 1999, "more than 100,000 passengers a day endured delays averaging nearly 32 minutes" (*Buffalo News* 1999d, A-5). The spring and summer of 1999 were particularly bad. According to Reed and Keates,

> For passengers, airlines and airports, flight delays are making this the true season of discontent. The number of delays is up 44 percent on average in April and May, compared with a year earlier. It has been so bad that on a single day in May, Continental flights at Newark, NJ, were delayed a total of 31,000 passenger hours. . . . Any business traveler who isn't prepared for a four-hour delay these days is incredibly naïve. (1999)

During a congressional hearing in October 1999, aviation officials remarked that the uncontrollable delays were pushing the entire commercial airline network "into gridlock after the worst summer in history for delays and passenger frustration" (Reed and Keates 1999). They claim that the current record will only get worse unless the entire system is overhauled, something that the very logic of deregulation is against because that would mean the reintroduction of some form of governmental regulation. By the summer of 2000, this prediction proved accurate with cancellations and delays still increasing (Zuckerman 2000).

According to hearings on the subject, the single biggest contributing factor is the phenomenal increase in demand for air travel, especially during the summer. "We are under extreme pressure to squeeze more planes into an already congested airspace," said an official of the National Air Traffic Controllers Association. "Even in good weather, there's no way all the planes scheduled can take off on time. Airlines would rather have airplanes sit on the tarmac with no way to take off than lose money" (Reed and Keates 1999). Opposing the view of hard-pressed companies, airline officials blamed the federal government. In particular, they pointed to the hopelessly outdated equipment and structure of air traffic control. "If the federal government does not move quickly to fix its broken air traffic control system, future delays will even be worse," they said (Reed and Keates 1999).

Despite the debate over the causes of delays, the statistics show a problem in every commercial airport across the country, especially the busiest ones. During the summer of 1999, O'Hare in Chicago experienced an 86 percent increase in delays from the previous year, Detroit suffered a 160 percent increase and the figure for Minneapolis–St. Paul jumped 127 percent, while the figures for Las Vegas and Dallas/Fort Worth were 168 percent and 131 percent, respectively (Reed and Keates 1999).

Due to the unprecedented volume of passengers and the gridlock nature of the present system, airlines also overbook their flights as a regular practice to guarantee they will be full. The consequence is that an increasing number of passengers find their airplanes inconveniently overcrowded and often experience delays due to being bumped from their scheduled flights. As one observer remarked, "Airline passengers buy their tickets with the expectation they're assured seats on the flights they want, but, more and more airlines are 'bumping' them because of overbooking. . . . Delta Airlines led the way with 8,144 passengers knocked off their expected flight—nearly as many as the other nine major carriers combined" (Johnson 1999a, A-8).

According to the airlines, overbooking and bumping actually aid passengers because the practice keeps flights full and airfares down. They claim that as many as 10 to 15 percent of ticketed passengers never show up for regularly scheduled flights (Johnson 1999a, A-8). Aside from the unexpected delay that bumping causes, there is a great inconvenience when a passenger is involuntarily bumped. Most of the time, airlines try to deal with the situation by bribing passengers with dollar incentives to give up their seats. When there are no volunteers, however, the flight continues without the latecomers, despite their confirmed tickets. In the latter case, the Department of Transportation has set guidelines for involuntary bumping compensation:

> If the passenger is placed on another flight and arrives within an hour of his original arrival time, there is no compensation required. If he arrives between one and two hours late, the airline must pay a penalty equal to the cost of his ticket, up to a maximum of $200. If he arrives more than two hours late, the penalty is double the price of the ticket, up to a maximum of $400. (Johnson 1999a, A-1)

DEALING WITH THE PROBLEM OF INCREASING DISCONTENT

There is little debate over the observation that the recent phenomenal increase in the number of passengers has thrown our air transportation system into a deepening crisis of inadequate infrastructure. Heightening these concerns is the realization that, unless checked, the present conditions will only get worse in the future.

> The Federal Aviation Administration says that by 2012, another 8 million takeoffs and landings will be added to the 27 million expected this year. The number of pas-

sengers will rise from an already staggering 680 million to 1 billion in that time frame. . . . Unless we see significant expansion—and unless it starts right now—one third of the 100 largest airports will have more than 20,000 hours of delay a year, costing fliers $4.5 billion annually. (Borcover 1999, G-2)

The winter of 1999, however, may mark a new turning point in the affairs of the air transportation industry. Negative feelings, nagging concerns, and some outright system failures now have accumulated to a level that has sparked a new call to reexamine the industry by the public sector. Recall this incident: On January 3, 1999, a snowstorm shut down the Northwest Airlines hub at Detroit. Eyewitness accounts estimate that there were over 10,000 travelers crammed into the facility for over 24 hours. But what of the people left on the planes? Newspaper reports indicate "more than 4,500 travelers were stranded . . . for up to 8½ hours aboard 34 Northwest planes unable to take off or reach passenger gates during a storm that dumped 10.6 inches of snow on the area" (*Buffalo News* n.d.).

The brief report goes on to say that Northwest, after apologizing for the breakdown, has gone on to focus "improvements in 15 problem areas." The public does not yet know what those "problem areas" are, but the number 15 indicates that our air transport system is presently operating with numerous hidden problems at a level the public might find intolerable and unacceptable. The debacle at Detroit in January's snowstorm suggests it is the tip of an iceberg that responsible people at both corporations and the federal government prefer not to face. The public, having seen the story of the *Titanic*, knows full well what happens when icebergs are ignored.

According to figures published in the *Wall Street Journal* (Goetz 1999), complaints by passengers have been rising steadily since 1995, after some years of declining. Between 1997 and 1998, complaints per 100,000 passengers increased by 26 percent. "'Tensions are running high,' says [the] president of the Air Travelers Association, a consumer group in Washington. 'You're being squashed into tighter planes without a lot of service'" (Goetz 1999, B-1).

As the *Wall Street Journal* states, "The bulk of last year's complaints focused on late flights, cancellations and 'customer service.' Eight of the nation's 10 largest carriers experienced complaint increases last year. . . . According to Department of Transportation figures, complaints about flight delays and cancellations jumped 35% last year, while complaints about frequent-flier programs were up 8%" (Goetz 1999, B-1).

In 1999 the stream of passenger complaints reached critical mass. The public intervened and Congress held hearings on the matter, in part because they travel frequently by air and had experienced the same kinds of discomforts as had their constituents. As one report noted, "Frustrated airline passengers have allies in the Congress. There are 435 House [members] and 50 Senators who do a lot of traveling" (*Buffalo News* 1999b, B-1). The report also mentioned that some congressmen even suggested publicly that a form of regulation should be reinstated.

Senators Ron Wyden (D-Oreg.) and John McCain (R-Ariz.) introduced a bill aimed at guaranteeing more passenger rights. Following suit five days later, Representative Bud Shuster (R-Pa.), the powerful chairman of the House Transportation Committee, introduced "passenger rights" legislation of his own (*Buffalo News* 1999b, A-8). The Senate's version, the Airline Passengers Fairness Act, "would require airlines to do everything from refunding tickets within 48 hours of purchase to telling passengers the real reason for a flight delay or cancellation" (Goetz 1999). The House's version, which responds more directly to the January experience in Detroit, also requires airlines to compensate passengers delayed within the planes. Shuster recommends "airlines that held passengers for two hours or more would have to repay them twice the value of their ticket. Passengers held for three hours or more would receive three times the value of their ticket, with the same trend holding true for passengers held four hours or more" (*Buffalo News* 1999b, A-8).

Other provisions of the proposed legislation include providing consumers full access to all fares for that carrier, notifying each passenger whether flights are overbooked, delivering a passenger's mishandled luggage within 24 hours after arrival, and refunding the full purchase price of a ticket if a refund is requested within 48 hours (Borcover 1999, G-2).

Congress's proposed new bill of rights may do little to address the looming iceberg before us, but at least people will have someplace to go to express their complaints, until some real changes are made. One place that collects complaints is the Aviation Consumer Protection Division of the U.S. Department of Transportation, located at 400 7th Street, S.W., Washington, D.C. 20590 (phone: 202-366-2220).

Happily, congressional pressure has already borne some fruit. During the tail end of 1999, major commercial airlines announced voluntary measures to improve passenger service before a government crackdown becomes fact. "Facing a congressional crackdown, carriers pledged in September to be more forthright with their customers all the way through their travel experience . . . they announced 12 point plans that would take effect December 15th" (Johnson 1999b, A-12).

Among the pledges are items that mirror provisions of proposed legislation including: responding promptly to complaints; "making every reasonable effort to provide food, water, restroom facilities, and access to medical treatment in the event of long, on-aircraft delays" (Johnson 1999b, A-12); and better handling of lost baggage, including an increase in airline liability to $2,500 from the present $1,250 for each bag. Airlines pledged to inform passengers more regularly and with better information than in the past whenever there are flight delays and to inform customers of the lowest possible fares or inform them of cheaper travel options whenever they call for reservations. In short, although there has yet to be a consumer revolution against commercial airlines, both congressional pressure and the rising tide of complaints have forced the major carriers to make changes on their own. How successful the new policy will be in the future still remains to be seen. To date, results are not optimistic.

Just-in-time computerized management, hub and spoke scheduling, explosive demand, and slow expansion of facilities persist as the condition of air travel. Under these arrangements, air passengers must continue to expect planes brimming to the excess with humanity, unexpected delays, cancellations, deathly boring waits, on-plane physical discomforts, bad food, poor air, and unanticipated events that wreck the most important personal plans. What passengers will not have to face in the future are declines in the overall safety of flying with domestic carriers.

The public fight for a passenger bill of rights is still bogged down in Congress (as of July 2000). During the last half of 1999, however, airlines have tried to make some accommodation to the growing army of frustrated passengers by announcing their own 8- or 10- or 12-point plans for improvement of service. Some of these very public pronouncements may already have brought relief to travelers, such as the announcement to remove the sardine can seating on select flights, but it is difficult to do much with an industry that always presses each company's back against a hard wall of crushing competition.

In May 2000, I traveled to Athens, Greece, from Buffalo, New York. I booked myself on American Airlines because I am a frequent flier of that airline. I chose to fly the transatlantic portion of my journey out of Kennedy, connecting to Olympic Airlines at Heathrow. This particular itinerary put me on a rather tight schedule. The Buffalo–Niagara Falls International Airport is serviced by American to Kennedy with Saab-built propeller planes. When the weather gets rough, these flights are frequently canceled or delayed. Before leaving the house, I called the airline and was told that my flight would leave on time. Twenty minutes later, at the check-in counter (Buffalo has quick access to the airport), I was informed that my flight was canceled due to thunderstorms upstate. Luckily I had followed recommendations and arrived for check-in two hours before my scheduled departure. American was able to reroute me to O'Hare, where I could catch a nonstop flight to Heathrow that would get me there in time to make my connecting flight to Athens on the other airline. Had I cut my air terminal arrival time closer, I would have blown all chances of completing the journey when expected—an event too costly for me to bear—and I would never have flown American again.

So, on this particular trip, I flew one and one half hours in the exact opposite direction of my destination, waited another two hours for a connecting flight, then flew one hour back across my earlier route, over my house and starting point again, before starting on a trajectory to England. Two months later, having forgotten completely about the insanity of this experience, I received a very nice letter from American Airlines apologizing for the inconvenience of the canceled flight that day in May. They explained the unforeseen problems with weather and the like, without, of course, going into the issue of why they persist in running the Buffalo-to-Kennedy connection using prop planes. They also offered me extra credit miles for my frequent flier account as a token of their gratitude and asked that I remain their customer. The letter said, "As a valued customer, your patronage is very important to us and we wish to make amends for this experience. The mileage bonus is our way of saying we are sorry for the inconvenience, and thanks for bearing with us."

Frankly, there would have been no way any airline could have possibly compensated me for having missed an international flight. In this case, I was glad to get the letter, because it did signify that, after the events of 1999, the airlines were trying harder to recognize the pain of customer air travel. Prior to this year, they would not have apologized in this manner at all, nor are they even now obligated by law to do so.

It is difficult to judge how much things have improved for the massive number of passengers carried by the system today since the voluntary adoption of changes last June 1999. According to a report released one year later, however:

> Consumer complaints to the Department of Transportation have almost doubled. Virtually every independent measure of customer satisfaction has declined. Lines at airports seem longer, and many travelers say the airlines are not living up to at least some promises. . . . The unfortunate truth is that flying on an airplane today, while the safest way to travel long distances, is as unpleasant for many passengers as it has ever been. (Leonhardt 2000, 13)

In the midst of the greatest expansionary boom in the thousand-year history of capitalism, we may be reaching the limits of unregulated free enterprise. At least this seems true of the airline industry. For the moment (July 2000), neither the carriers nor the Congress have any encouraging words for consumers, despite the unprecedented success of the industry itself in servicing close to 700 million people a year. Can Congress save the American air passenger with legislation? The answer lies in our future and in the future of deregulation.

36

The Future of Deregulation

America has never been able to evolve a stable mix of public and private means between the extremes of unbridled capitalism and yoked government intervention. We have never come into our own as a civic culture like continental Western European countries. Neither so-called free enterprise nor intrusive federal regulation seems to work here. Is there a third way that might? Over the decades, industries have tried many different third ways, but none has succeeded for the country as a whole. We leave the 20th century still tinkering, still trying to bolt down forever the great engine of growth that is our economy. Increasingly, however, we are aware of the limitations of both our imagination and our intellectual tools in bending to that task.

The airline industry illustrates this national dilemma well. Running at the very edge of profit margins, requiring huge debt service, the scene of disastrous labor relations, beset by multimillion dollar mergers, by hostile takeovers, by corporate raiders, by downsizing, by split labor markets, and by the engineering of minute amounts of food, fuel, time, and space in order to extract the last cent from its operations, air travel epitomizes the way computer-assisted giant corporations work. Even so, this massive system remains unstable. Change is always a prospect. Changes come that are disturbing, unnerving, and ultimately inconvenient to all the people and businesses that rely on air transportation, who have to calculate the costs of spending time and money on air travel as part of their very being.

At the same time, the industry performs a miracle. Domestically, it moves over half a billion people in the air to their destinations every year. It does so safely and at a reasonable price. Flying in the air, mobilizing more than the entire population of the country up into the air and back down to the ground without as much as a single travel-related fatality in 1998 was an unprecedented feat of industrial society. Our present record of domestic air safety is the single most impressive accomplishment of our culture.

Perhaps, then, the air industry demonstrates that there will never be a single solution, or more accurately, a mode of operating, that can combine public and private elements in a stable system. Perhaps, too, the domestic air transportation industry represents the best argument we have for the case of "muddling through." Not choosing either free enterprise or governmental regulation, we simply go with the flow, making adjustments in our daily lives and business operations according to what the airline industry is experiencing each day and what the market will bear. Maybe the record of the airline industry in the 20th century means for people in the 21st that it is more important to let forces find their own way with a minimum of regulation than it is to have industries that can be stable and consistently turn a profit. Muddling through—nothing more than an empirical reality that masks the successes and failures of the entire air transport system, sometimes paid for heavily in lives—may just be the only answer, the much sought after third way, to the theoretical and intellectual questions we have always asked of our economic system.

Air carriers provide us with an unprecedented level of transportation service, despite the complaints, but we remain terribly uncomfortable because we suspect that the current system is reaching its limits. Still worse, we know from experience how easily the well-oiled machine, the thousands of intermeshing airline trips that crisscross the nation every day, virtually every hour, can come crashing down all at once, because of some single system failure, and lay paralyzed with personal and business plans left in smoking ruins.

The year 1999 may well have ushered in a period of more intense governmental scrutiny of air carriers. In response, airlines seem willing to do what they can to make improvements, perhaps out of fear that Congress will reinstate regulation. Exactly how all the current muddling through will play itself out when the federal government's oversight activities clash with the private sector's resistance to regulation remains to be seen, especially because the level of complaints about present service continues to rise. Already some in Congress who are friendly to the airline industry have stated their opposition to the newly proposed passengers rights legislation, suggesting that it is simply a "recipe for higher fares." As in the past, however, muddling through means no plans but much attention to the forces most powerful at the moment. At present, these seem to be emerging from the consumer side. If travel continues to become inconvenient to more people, a change in the public/private mix of American aviation seems inevitable.

Part 6

Epilogue: The Most Important Thing

37

Flying and the Future

The play *Jet Lag* is a conceptual piece conceived by the architects Elizabeth Diller and Ricardo Scofidio in collaboration with the Builders Association, a performance group. It ran briefly during January 2000 in Manhattan.

> In part two of the play, we watch an older woman and her grandson as they fly endlessly back and forth across the Atlantic. Perhaps the two are searching for the lost sailor (the woman's son, the boy's father), or trying to escape from him. In reality, the two are spellbound by the jet-age ethos of travel, the ethereal anonymity of airports, the routine of flight protocols, the pseudo-drama of in-flight movies. (Muschamp 2000)

This play defines behavior in the air as a form of everyday life where the context for commenting on interaction comes from sharing the environment of the jet cabin and the air space that is the subject of this book.

> The grandmother spouts platitudes of correct passenger behavior, as if she were a walking handbook for human cattle in a jet-age stockyard. . . . The multimedia setting, which shifts from passenger compartments to airport waiting lounges to

escalators to people movers to video surveillance images of them, puts a twist on the familiar period-dating question, "What time is this place?" In airports, we're more likely to wonder, what place is this time? . . . *Jet Lag* sends the dystopian message that we are all rudderless across the techno-environment we have made. (Muschamp 2000, sec. 2, 37)

Jet Lag may very well be the first attempt in art to give expression to the recent awakening that our lives in air space constitute an increasingly larger share of our time alive. Its dystopian take on this fact comes from contemplating an extreme form of de-territorialization brought on by endless air travel. Were we sentenced to crisscross the globe on an eternal and futile quest, all sense of space and time would be obliterated in an infinite present without home, friends, or work.

Frequent fliers, the most de-territorialized of the human species today, may indeed spend an increasing amount of time in the air, but most do so for business purposes. They remain grounded by work, by career obligations, and by their attachments to others. In a sense, these road warriors are only the 21st century incarnation of the last one's traveling salesmen, now perhaps with as many women as men. *Jet Lag*'s conceptualization of life in the air, its motivations for frequent flying aside, seems close to the mark. We are at the mercy of the airport architects' abilities to create a sense of place within the global space of air travel. We are equally at the mercy of airline companies when it comes to creating the kinds of experiences that might make our flights not only less stressful, but also more harmonious with our daily needs for physical, spiritual, social, and career fulfillment. Taken to an extreme, without such cares by those individuals and companies that have the power to shape and manage air space so that it fulfills a larger vision of *humanizing* air travel, flight can be a frightening immersion in space/time disorientation, de-territorialization, and minimal, alienated human contact. People make the difference. By expressing our needs as consumers and enlightened public leaders, we can transform our travel options from a dissonant, alien experience to a more harmonious one. Corporate owners of airlines caught in bitter competition and inviolable bottom lines are critical to this equation, in the way that several companies have already increased basic legroom for weary travelers who are fed up with sardine-can crowding. In the end, we as a society will have to deal with our lives in the air in much the same way as we already deal with those lives on the ground—through effective environmental planning, psychological counseling, architectural design, political vision, and smart corporate management.

THE MOST IMPORTANT THING

Several years ago I flew from Los Angeles, where I was living, to Rio de Janeiro in Brazil. The plane I took left LAX in the afternoon. I had a window seat and as evening settled in, the sky went pitch black. Looking out I tried to see land-marks as we made our way across the expanse of South America. We came upon a city all lit up at night. I asked the flight attendant what it was. "Bogotá," she said. Then I realized that we were about to enter the air space of the Amazon Basin. *Let's just see how vast this thing is*, I thought, and settled in to watch.

Soon, the earth below us was dark. A vast blackness spread from horizon to horizon. The color of ground was darker than the darkness of the night sky, which by that time was punctuated by the light of stars. Soon the moon rose, making everything appear like ghostly shadows in its pale, white light. Still I could see nothing except the great landmass of the rain forest.

Time passed and I dozed off. Hours went by. Out the window there was still nothing. It was a Nothing of the highest order, much like the emptiness I experi-enced flying over the ocean. After a time, on an ocean flight, when there are still no signs of land, the sea below takes on monumental proportions. The space of the airplane interior begins to shrink in comparison. Suddenly it seems that we are of no significance, a little plane with its frail cargo of little lives. Ocean flight was like an encounter with eternity. There were echoes of the *Ancient Mariner* in the great vastness below.

Flying over the Amazon Basin was like that. At 35,000 feet, I saw the curva-ture of the earth as moonlight cast just enough illumination to separate the im-mense dark sky from the vast land mass. I lost track of time after a short nap. It seemed to me that we were still flying over nothing but rain forest for four hours. *Could that be possible?* I wondered. *At 500+ miles an hour, that makes over 2,000 miles!* Chills captured my body and I shivered all over. I knew it was the encounter with the Amazon that provoked that response and I looked around to see if any-one else had been watching. From seven miles high, I lost myself in the immense scale of things, like contemplating the night sky full of stars or the ocean.

One March I was flying from Los Angeles, where I lived, to Chicago. Back home it was already hot and I had been to the Orange County beaches several times. As we descended, I saw the checkerboard quilt of farms, stretching for hundreds of miles, blanketing the Midwest. Despite what Californians thought, places like Kansas, the Dakotas, Minnesota, and Wisconsin were still America's breadbasket. Every square was outlined by roads. I noticed the snow still on the ground, typical for that time of the year. Poised in the air like that, miles above the earth, I was reminded of the seasons and the cyclical changes of the planet, something foreign to Southern Californians. Sitting at the window with minutes to go before touchdown, I couldn't help but contemplate both farming for a liv-ing and the weather, a much-needed corrective to life in Los Angeles.

On another trip I was flying to Los Angeles from New York. It was afternoon when we hit the Rocky Mountains. I was in a 747 about 35,000 feet high with a window seat. Crossing over the peaks, I saw the sun reflecting off the ice and snow of the western slope. All the rest was dark brown above the tree line with the green of trees further down. The peaks were so sharp, their edges accentuated by the high contrast light. Soon we were past the great mountains heading southwest. The land changed appropriately to an earth tone brown, with many different shades. The pilot interrupted my reverie with an announcement that we would be flying over the Grand Canyon and I watched out the window expectantly. I saw several winding rivers and deep gorges in the terrain. Dusk changed the colors again to darker, more muted tones with still higher contrasts. Then the great gorge of the Grand Canyon appeared. Although I had visited it several times as a tourist by car, this was the first time I actually "saw" the canyon. It was enormous, with a silver string of river at its bottom. The setting sun played against the red, tan, brown, chestnut, and bronze earth. What a magnificent sight!

On another flight to the West Coast, we were cruising eight miles high. There was a cloud cover obscuring the earth but everything above was clear. The sun hung on the horizon, flaming out before it appeared on the other side of the world, turning the high clouds red and pink. A jet stream above us stood out like a chalk mark on a deep blue blackboard. The pillowy clouds formed a soft underbelly for the approaching night. Our jet chased the fading sun, flying into that red-bronze colored light.

Airplanes give you a God's eye view. It wasn't only the Grand Canyon that I saw for the first time because I viewed it from the air. On many occasions when taking a flight into New York, we buzzed the city in order to make a landing at LaGuardia. If you fly into Kennedy or Newark, you can't get that experience, because the glide path is over the vast suburban hinterland. The plane pirouetted on its downward glide path, down over the tops of the giant buildings, before flying over Queens and the airport runway approach. I lived in Manhattan for many years, but I never saw the city like that. Neither Los Angeles nor Chicago from the air could compare with the sight; no other American city was in New York's league—except two: Las Vegas and San Francisco. Las Vegas is also something from the air, but you have to get real close. It's not New York. You get a glimpse of something special, especially at night, just before landing, seconds before landing, but it's not the same thrill as banking over Manhattan. San Francisco is special once you leave the East. Its unique appeal has something to do with the varied terrain and geographical features rather than the comparatively unimpressive corporate buildings of the skyline. Only if you circle before you land do you get the good view. The undistinguished city of South San Francisco and the coastline fall away as you approach the rust-red of the Golden Gate Bridge with Mount Tamalpais in the background and then, as the plane swoops and banks, you see the green of the bay with the city on the right and all the houses on the hills. What a thrill!

Writing this book has convinced me that it is the heavens that may be humankind's destiny, not the deep sea or even our earth. Marilyn Vos Savant is a newspaper columnist. She bills herself as the smartest person on the planet, she possesses the highest recorded IQ, and she answers letters from readers in the

Sunday papers. She knows *everything*. On Sunday, February 28, 1999, she answered this letter in the *Parade Magazine* supplement.

Question: "What is your favorite poem?"

Answer: "It is called 'High Flight,' composed by Pilot Officer John Gillespie Magee, Jr., while flying 30,000 feet over England. Soon after, in 1941, he was killed at age 19 while serving with the Royal Canadian Air Force:

> *Oh, I have slipped the surly bonds of Earth*
> *And danced the skies on laughter-silvered wings;*
> *Sunward I've climbed, and joined the tumbling mirth*
> *Of sun-split clouds—and done a hundred things*
> *You have not dreamed of—wheeled and soared and swung*
> *High in the sunlit silence. Hov'ring there.*
> *I've chased the shouting wind along, and flung*
> *My eager craft through footless halls of air.*
> *Up, up the long, delirious, burning blue*
> *I've topped the windswept heights with easy grace*
> *Where never lark, or even eagle flew.*
> *And, while with silent, lifting mind I've trod*
> *The high untrespassed sanctity of space,*
> *Put out my hand, and touched the face of God.*

References

ABC Nightly News, 6 July 2000.

airmall.com. 2000. The "No Rip-Off Guarantee." <www.airmall.com>, [accessed 6 July].

Airplane Etiquette. 2000. <www.airportcitycodes.com/aaa>, [accessed 29 August].

Alesii, Brenda. 1995. Air Travelers Find That Killing Time Can Be a Terminal Challenge. *Buffalo News*, 12 November, sec. F.

Alexander, Brian. 1998. Is There a Doctor on the Plane? *New York Times Magazine*, 8 March, 40–42.

Amsterdam Airport Website. 2000. <www.schiphol.nl>, [accessed 22 July].

Anderberg, Ken. 1988. Nurturing Airport Growth. *American City and County*, July, 56–62.

Appadurai, A. 1996. *Modernity at Large*. Minneapolis: Univ. of Minnesota Press.

Architectural Review. 1991. Eastern Promise. 189, no. 1131 (May), 83–90.

Associated Press. 2000. Union "Day of Action" Seeks Crackdown on Air Rage. *Buffalo News*, 6 July, sec. A.

Ayers, Andrew. 2000. Pan Am Flight 103. <www.crashpages.com/reports>, [accessed 6 July].

Barry, Dave. 1999. *Buffalo News*, 28 February, sec. E.

Barthes, Roland. 1973. Semiology and Urbanism. In *VIA: Structures Implicit and Explicit*. Philadelphia: University of Pennsylvania Press, 155–58.

————. 1986. Semiology and the Urban. Quoted in *The City and the Sign,* edited by M. Gottdiener and A. Lagopoulos. New York: Columbia University Press.

Belden, Tom. 1999. Airlines Face Rising Level of Complaints from Frustrated Passengers, Lawmakers. *Buffalo News,* 14 March, sec. A.

Berman, Shelly. 1986. *Up in the Air.* Los Angeles: Price/Stern/Sloan.

Best, A. 1991. Taking Flight. *Architectural Review* 189, no. 1131 (May), 58–61.

Bittman, Mark. 2000. Indigestible Flying Objects. *New York Times,* 25 June, sec. 5.

Bonfatti, John. 1999. Congressmen Offer Tales of Their Own Costly Flights. *Buffalo News*, 21 September, sec. B.

Borcover, Alfred. 1999. There's No Relief in Sight for Air Travel Complaints. *Buffalo News*, 26 December, sec. G.

Boyne, Walter. 1999. By 2015 There'll Be a Major Airline Crash Every Week. *Buffalo News*, 7 November, sec. H.

Bruegmann, R. 1988. High Flight. *Inland Architect* (September/October).

Budget Traveller's Guide to Sleeping in Airports. 2000. <www3.simpatico.ca/donna.mcsherry/airports.htm>, [accessed 29 August].

Buffalo News. 1999a. Woman Held after Attack on Flight to New Zealand. 17 January, sec. A.

————. 1999b. Bill Aims to Make Airlines Shape Up. 10 February, sec. A.

————. 1999c. How Did It Happen? 20 July, sec. A.

————. 1999d. Aviation Industry Officials Call for Overhaul of the System. 15 October, sec. A.

————. 1999e. Data Shows Possibility of Struggle in Cockpit. 13 November, sec. A.

————. n.d. Northwest Admits Errors in Storm.

Card, David. 1989. Deregulation and Labor Earnings in the Airline Industry. Princeton University Industrial Relations Section Working Paper #247, January.

Castells, M. 1996. *The Rise of the Network Society.* Newton, Mass.: Blackwell.

Christian, Nicole. 1999. Motor City Air Raid. *Time,* 22 February, 40.

Clarke, Caroline. 1994. No More Fear: There Is Help for Fearful Fliers. *Black Enterprise* 24, no. 7 (February).

Cohen, S., and L. Taylor. 1992. *Escape Attempts.* New York: Routledge.

Colors. 1995. No. 11 (June–August).

Copeland, Douglas. 1994. Rem Koolhaus, Post-Nationalist Architect. *New York Times*, 11 September, 45.

Crewdson, J. n.d. Critically Ill Passengers on Two Flights Saved by Airline's Pioneering Efforts. Reprinted in *Buffalo News*, sec. A.

Dallas/Fort Worth International Airport. 2000. <www.dfwairport.com>, [accessed 6 July].

Davey, Peter. 1991. Airports Come of Age. *Architectural Review* 189, no. 1131 (May), 34–57.

Davies, R. E. G. 1972. *Airlines of the United States since 1914.* London: Putnam.

The Economist. 1999a. On a Wing and a Hotel Room. 9 January, 64.

————. 1999b. Jay Pritzker. 30 January, 81.

Eisenberg, D. 1998. Acting Up in the Air. *Time,* 21 December, 40.

Elkus, Barry, and M. Tieger. n.d. *Fearful Flyers Resource Guide.* Argonaut Entertainment.

Fairechild, Diana. 1992. *JetSmart.* Berkeley, Calif.: Celestial Arts Publishing.

Fehr, Stephen. 1995. More than Just Pie in the Sky. *Washington Post*, 22 August, sec. B.

Feld, David. 1995. Skies Are Friendly, but Airports Are Jammed. *Insight on the News* 11, no. 14, 39.

———. 1996a. When Rudeness Arises out of the Clear Blue. *Insight on the News* 12, no. 21 (June 3), 42.

———. 1996b Cheap Ticket, Will Travel. *Insight on the News* 12, no. 21 (June 3), 42.

Flinn, D. 1962. Transient Psychotic Reactions during Travel. *American Journal of Psychiatry* 119, 173–74.

Forward, David. 1999. Vanguard's Rocky Road. *Zoom* (Vanguard's in-flight magazine), August, 13–15.

Goetz, Thomas. 1999. Fear of Flying: It's Actually Getting Safer. *Wall Street Journal*, 9 July, sec. W.

———. 1998. Furious at Airlines, Travelers File Flurry of Complaints. *Wall Street Journal*, n.d., sec. B.

Gottdiener, M. 1997. *The Theming of America*. Boulder, Colo.: Westview Press.

Gottdiener, M., and N. Komninos. 1989. *Capitalist Development and Crisis Theory*. London: Macmillan.

Gottdiener, M., and A. Lagopoulos. 1986. *The City and the Sign: An Introduction to Urban Semiotics*. New York: Columbia University Press.

Gottmann, Jean. 1983. *The Coming of the Transactional City*. University of Maryland Institute for Urban Studies Pamphlet #2.

Hale, Sarah. 1999. Kansas City Thrives Despite Not Boasting a Major Airline Hub. *Wall Street Journal*, 2 July.

Handy, Edward. 1998. Landing. *American Way* (in-flight magazine of American Airlines), 92–96.

Hanson, Gayle. 1997. In-Flight Air Recycling Fouls Friendly Skies. *Insight on the News* 13, no. 6, 18.

Hart, W. 1985. *The Airport Passenger Terminal*. New York: J. Wiley and Sons.

Harvey, David. 1988. *The Condition of Postmodernism*. Oxford: Blackwell.

Holloway, Lynette. 1995. Airport Homeless: A Long, Pleasant Layover. *New York Times*, 3 February, sec. B.

Hopper, Kim. 1991. Homeless at the Airport. *Urban Anthropologist* 20, 155–75.

Hunt, Al. 1999. Fear of Flying . . . But Our Flier Doesn't Care. *Wall Street Journal*, 9 July, sec. W.

Hutcheson, Ron. Aviation Industry Officials Call for Overhaul of the System. *Buffalo News*, 15 October, sec. A.

Iyer, Pico. 1998. The New Business Class. *New York Times Magazine*, 8 March, 37–38.

Johnson, Glen. 1999a. Air Travelers Grounded by Flight Bumping. *Buffalo News*, 12 May, sec. A.

———. 1999b. Airline's New Policy to Improve Service for Passengers to Take Effect. *Buffalo News*, 15 December, sec. A.

———. 1999c. Airlines Aim to Treat Passengers Better. *Buffalo News*, n.d.

Kasarda, J. 1991. An Industrial/Aviation Complex for the Future. *Urban Land*, August, 16–20.

Kluger, Jeffrey. 1999. Should He Have Flown? <www.timemagazine.com>, [accessed 26 July].

Koenig, David. 1999. Airlines Hike Business Fares; Leisure Rates May Be Next. *Buffalo News*, 14 December, sec. D.

Konigsberg, Eric. 1998. The Cheating Kind. *New York Times Magazine*, 8 March, 64.

Kraft, S. 1997. Man Stranded Six Years at Airport. *Buffalo News*, 20 May, sec. A.

Kramer, Farrell. 1998. Support Is Growing for Smoke Hoods in Aircraft. *Buffalo News*, 13 December, sec. A.

Langewiesche, N. 1998. *Inside the Sky*. New York: Pantheon Books.

Lash, Scott, and John Urry. 1994. *Economies of Space and Time*. London: Sage.

Leonhardt, David. 2000. Promises in the Sky. *New York Times*, 25 June, sec. 5.

Levin, Alan, and Blake Morrison. 2000. A Potentially Fatal Delay at Many Airports. *USA Today*, 24 January, sec. A.

Lichfield, Nathanial. 1977. Airports as Employment Generators. *Built Environment Quarterly*, 3 September, 192–195.

Lipton, Sheree. 1995. Nirvana in Narita: Meditations on a Layover. *Hemispheres* (in-flight magazine of United Airlines), August, 53–54.

Maher, William. 1991. Retailing at Airports Lifts Off. *Urban Land* 50, no. 5 (May), 18–20.

Marin, Rick. 1999. When Flying Tourist Meant Going in Style. *New York Times*, 28 March, travel section.

McCarthy, Scott. 1999. Feeling Confined? You May Be Flying in One of Boeing's New 737s. *Wall Street Journal*, 2 August, sec. 1.

Meyer, Brian. 1999. Unfriendly Skies: Air Passenger Complaints Soar. *Buffalo News*, 9 September, sec A.

Miller, W., and V. Zarcone. 1968. Psychiatric Disorders at an International Airport. *Archives of Environmental Health*, 17.

Morris, S., and C. Wilson. 1995. *The Evolution of the Airlines Industry*. Washington D.C.: Brookings Institution.

Morse, Jodie. 1999. Death on Autopilot. *Time* 154, 8 November, 19.

Moseley, Ray. 1999. Iranian Exile to Leave Paris Airport after 11 Years. *Buffalo News*, 21 September, A-6.

Murdoch, Guy. 1994. Air Safety. *Consumers Research Magazine* 77, no. 8 (August).

Muschamp, Herbert. 2000. Exploring Space and Time, Here and Now. *New York Times*, 6 February, sec. 2.

National Public Radio. 1997. Bicoastal Commuting Gives Birth to Bizarre Dreams. "All Things Considered," 11 March.

Okun, Janice. 1996. At the Airport a Dining Experience Takes Wing. *Buffalo News*, 17 April, sec. D.

Pearson, C. 1998. Hong Kong's New Airport. *Architectural Record*, November, 92–103.

Perkins, Ed. 1999. Airline Coach Seats: A Needless Squeeze. *Buffalo News*, 28 November, sec. G.

Petzinger, Thomas. 1995. *Hard Landing*. New York: Random House.

Piore, M., and C. Sabel. 1984. *The Second Industrial Divide*. New York: Basic Books.

Plane Spotting. 1999. <www.geocities.com/Cape_Canaveral/1273/airnicks.html, [accessed 9 May 2000].

PRNewswire. 1997. 25 November.

Pynchon, Thomas. 1973. *Gravity's Rainbow*. New York: Bantam Edition.

Rayner, R. 1998. Nowhere, U.S.A. *New York Times Magazine*, 8 March, 41–46, 89.

Reed, D., and N. Keates. 1999. Fliers Fume as Air Delays Become a Way of Life. *Wall Street Journal*, 2 August, sec. B.

Relph, Edward. 1976. *Place and Placelessness.* Harmondsworth, Middlesex: Viking Penguin.

Ring, Ray. 1995. The West Sings the Denver Blues. *High Country News* 27, no. 1.

Ritzer, George. 1992. *McDonaldization.* Newbury Park, Calif.: Pine Forge Press.

Salvaggio, Salvino. 1999. Letter to author.

Sanders, James. 1997. *The Downing of TWA Flight 800.* New York: Zebra Books.

Savona, John. 1992. The Airport Terminal. Master's thesis, School of Architecture, University at Buffalo, Buffalo, N.Y.

Shapiro, S. 1982. A Study of Psychiatric Syndromes Manifested at an International Airport. *Comprehensive Psychiatry.*

Sudjic, Deyan. 1992. *The One-Hundred-Mile City.* Orlando, Fla.: Harcourt Brace.

Tedeschi, Bob. 2000. Web Helps Deal with Delays. *New York Times,* 25 June, sec. 5.

USA Today. 1996. Airlines Go High Tech to Cut Security Waits. 20 August, sec. B, p. 1.

Visitor's Guide to Denver International Airport. 1996. Denver: Denver International Airport.

Vos Savant, Marilyn. 1999. *Parade,* 28 February.

Wade, Betsy. 2000. Coping with Canceled Flights. *New York Times,* 25 June, sec. 5.

———. 1995. Privatizing Airports: Cities' Successes and Giuliani's Plan. *New York Times,* 3 January, sec. B.

Wald, Mathew. 2000. Getting There: A Reality Check. *New York Times,* 25 June sec. 5.

Wallace, W., et. al. 1995. Managing In-flight Emergencies. *British Medical Journal* 311, no. 7001 (August), 374.

Wallis, D. 1998. What Do They Really Want up There? *New York Times Magazine,* 8 March, 76.

Wayne, Leslie. 1995. Road Warriors—Mega Travelers. *New York Times,* 14 May, sec. 3.

Weller, M. P. I., and P. Jauhar. 1987. Wandering at Heathrow Airport by the Mentally Unwell. *Medicine, Science, and the Law* 17, 453–56.

Why Airlines Do What They Do. 1999. <www.cowtown.net/users/whyairdo>, [accessed May 2000].

Windsor, Natalie. 1993. *How to Fly.* Silver Springs, Md.: Corkscrew Press.

Woodyard, Chris. 1995. The Need for Medical Care in the Air. *Buffalo News,* 12 November, sec. D.

www.crashpages.com, [accessed 6 July 2000]

Young, E., and G. Caveney. 1992. *Shopping in Space.* New York: Atlantic Monthly Press.

Zaldivar, Ricardo. 2000. FAA, Airlines, Workers Agree on a Plan to Improve Safety, Head Off Accidents. *Buffalo News,* 15 January, sec. A.

Zoroya, Greg. 1999. Passengers Behaving Badly. *USA Today,* 19 November, sec. D.

Zuckerman, Lawrence. 1999. Firing on Fortress Northwest. *New York Times,* 25 August, sec. C.

———. 2000. Rising Tide of Passengers Fumes over Delays at Nation's Airports. *New York Times,* 26 July, sec. A.

Index